Lecture Notes in Computer Science 1364

Edited by G. Goos, J. Hartmanis and J. van Leeuwen

Springer
Berlin
Heidelberg
New York
Barcelona
Budapest
Hong Kong
London
Milan
Paris
Santa Clara
Singapore
Tokyo

Wolfram Conen   Gustaf Neumann (Eds.)

Coordination Technology
for Collaborative Applications

Organizations, Processes, and Agents

 Springer

Series Editors

Gerhard Goos, Karlsruhe University, Germany
Juris Hartmanis, Cornell University, NY, USA
Jan van Leeuwen, Utrecht University, The Netherlands

Volume Editors

Wolfram Conen
Gustaf Neumann
University of Essen, Information Systems and SoftwareTechniques
D-45117 Essen, Germany
E-mail: (conen/neumann)@wi-inf.uni-essen.de

Cataloging-in-Publication data applied for

Die Deutsche Bibliothek - CIP-Einheitsaufnahme

Coordination technology for collaborative applications :
organizations, processes, and agents / Wolfram Conen ; Gustaf
Neumann (ed.). - Berlin ; Heidelberg ; New York ; Barcelona ;
Budapest ; Hong Kong ; London ; Milan ; Paris ; Santa Clara ;
Singapore ; Tokyo : Springer, 1998
    (Lecture notes in computer science ; Vol. 1364)
    ISBN 3-540-64170-X

CR Subject Classification (1991): H.4-5, C.2, I.2, J.1, J.4

ISSN 0302-9743
ISBN 3-540-64170-X Springer-Verlag Berlin Heidelberg New York

© Springer-Verlag Berlin Heidelberg 1998
Printed in Germany

Typesetting: Camera-ready by author
SPIN 10631829   06/3142 – 5 4 3 2 1 0   Printed on acid-free paper

Preface

In June 1996, we co-organized the WETICE'96 workshop *"Web Infrastructure for Collaborative Applications"*. The need to intensify the inter-disciplinary exchange of ideas, concepts, and results related to collaborative applications became obvious as we tried to formulate a consolidated workshop report. Motivated by these experiences we organized the ASIAN'96[1] post-conference workshop *"Coordination Technology for Collaborative Applications"*. Again, people with an interesting mix of opinions and perspectives contributed to the workshop. At the end of this workshop several encouraging and fruitful discussions between the participants emerged. However, we still had the feeling that a more general framework was needed to unify the viewpoints and to obtain a deeper understanding of this area. We hope that this book is a small contribution to this ambitious goal.

We selected the best contributions to the ASIAN'96 workshop and complemented them with invited position papers. The outcome is a collection of papers focusing either on the technical background, the organizational perspective, or the application context. These viewpoints should enable a stimulating and interesting discourse and we hope that reading this book will extend the perspectives on coordination technology and its use for collaboration.

We hope that you enjoy reading the book as much as we enjoyed editing it.

If you have questions, comments, or remarks, don't hesitate to contact the editors.

October 1997   Wolfram Conen, Gustaf Neumann

---

[1] The workshop "Coordination Technology for Collaborative Applications" was held as part of the ASIAN'96, the Second Asian Computer Science Conference in Singapore, December 2-5, 1996. The conference was organized by the Department of Information Systems & Computer Science, National University of Singapore. The workshop was organized by Wolfram Conen (University of Essen, Germany), Gustaf Neumann (University of Essen, Germany), and Peter Bernus (Griffith University, Australia).

Acknowledgements

We would like to thank Joxan Jaffar and Roland Yap for the excellent organization of the ASIAN'96 conference, and for giving us the opportunity to organize the workshop that led to this book. Many thanks to Peter Bernus for his help in preparing and organizing the workshop. The workshop would not have been possible without the contributors that submitted papers and the participants that encouraged us with their discussions to proceed towards this book. Finally we would like to express our special thanks to Alfred Hofmann and the Springer-Verlag for giving us the opportunity to work on this book.

Table of Contents

Collaborative Work

Technological Considerations

A Perspective on Technology-Assisted Collaboration

Wolfram Conen and Gustaf Neumann

Information Systems and Software Techniques
University of Essen
Essen, Germany
email: {conen,neumann}@wi-inf.uni-essen.de

1 Collaboration and Information Systems

The traditional view of information systems is primarily data oriented within the scope of a single enterprise. Typically, the maxim of an information system development project is to develop an enterprise-wide conceptual model based on the main business processes and to implement it in a more or less centralized database system.

We think that it is time to question this traditional view since it does not reflect the current needs and trends. Firstly, the traditional view is too narrow in scope. With the acceptance of Internet technology and the resulting range of cooperation chances the scope of an information system must be extended beyond the firewall of the single enterprise.

Secondly, and even more important, the strong data orientation of the traditional view should be replaced by a human orientation: the main purpose of an information system should be to enable efficient and effective collaboration between individuals and groups. This should be valid for collaboration within the enterprise and for collaboration with external partners. The information system should not freeze the current state but should offer individuals access to the information assets of the enterprise and allow them to be reused in creative ways. The information system should become more of a communication and coordination system that eases and fosters collaboration. The huge acceptance of Web technology even in its current, immature state is evidence that this human collaboration centered view is gaining a lot of momentum.

Coordination technology is one of the basic building blocks required to enable collaboration. This book concentrates on the relationship between coordination technology and business and application requirements. The book tries to identify general elements of a coordinative infrastructure allowing the construction of collaborative applications.

2 A Road Map for this Book

Keeping this in mind, we arranged the papers into five groups, namely *Organizational Coordination*, *Agent-Based Coordination*, *Workflow and Coordination*, *Collaborative Work*, and *Technological Considerations*.

Certainly, this arrangement is not free from overlap and could have been done in several different ways. However, it does reflect the diversity of perspectives that we regard as important in the context of this book, coordination technology for collaborative applications.

2.1   Organizational Coordination

The papers in this group focus on the relationship between organizational aspects and collaborative techniques. Two papers (Schiefloe et al. and Fernandez et al.) directly relate organizatorial issues to technology, while Bernus et al. emphasize the importance of a method based analysis of the relations between organization and decision structures, which in turn may offer an instrument to improve the creation and maintenance of goals and values that Schiefloe et al. consider important. Fernandez et al. describe an architectural framework for implementing such instruments in an applicational context.

The first paper of this group, "Coordination in Knowledge-Intensive Organizations"[1] by *Schiefloe* and *Syvertsen*, emphasizes the importance of social and human aspects of coordination for the success of knowledge-intensive networked organizations. Coordination is seen as the key instrument for handling dynamic complexity in an emerging knowledge economy. The role of coordination is considered on both, the inter- and intra-organizational level. Methods and techniques for creating and maintaining values and goals are identified as a primary target for future development efforts.

The paper "Co-ordination of Management Activities – Mapping Organizational Structure to the Decision Structure"[2] by *Bernus* and *Uppington* examines the interrelation between organization and decision structures. The analysis is based on the GRAI Grid and enables the design of organizations that take into account the individual as well as organizational objectives of the individual organizational actor thus leading to a better management structure.

In their paper "A Cooperative Approach to Distributed Applications Engineering"[3], *Fernandez* and *Wijegunaratne* model an enterprise as a collection of cooperating distributed application domains and derive a federated architecture to support enterprise-wide distributed computing and to minimize the architectural mismatch between software architecture and organizational reality.

2.2   Agent-Based Coordination

The second group presents foundational as well as applicational aspects of agent-supported or agent-based coordination technologies. The first paper of this group concentrates on the low-level coordination of computational agents and thus contributes to the foundations of multi-agent system design. The second paper presents an innovative application of an agent which helps to coordinate human

---

[1] Invited paper.

[2] Workshop paper.

[3] Workshop paper.

argumentation in a discussion. The third paper analyses the role of computational agents for the support of collaborative work and discusses general aspects relevant for this broad area of applications.

In "Towards Logic Programming Based Coordination in Virtual Worlds"[4], *Tarau, Dahl* and *De Bosschere* propose a unified framework for coordination in multi-user virtual worlds. Based upon experiences with LogiMOO, a BinProlog and Linda based programmable and sharable virtual world, the framework emphasizes an 'object based' approach. Their experiments with agent coding in LogiMOO and Java show the practicality of the constructs for real life programming.

The paper "Enhancement of Creative Aspects of a Daily Conversation with a Topic Development Agent"[5] by *Nishimoto, Sumi,* and *Mase* concentrates on two aspects of collaboration that are difficult to handle: free conversation and creativity. The paper proposes an agent that is adaptable to daily conversations and that is able to enhance creative aspects of the conversation by supporting the introduction of new topics into the conversation. The agent enters daily conversation as an equal participant in order to keep the conversation lively. The experimental results suggest that this agent can provide timely information that introduces new topics, and that it has the ability to effectively coordinate creative aspects of conversations without imposing any special restrictions. Both the underlying technological design considerations and the experimental results are described in the paper.

Keith S. Decker focuses in the paper "Coordinating Human and Computer Agents"[6] on the development of support tools for distributed, cooperative work by groups of human and computational agents. This work is motivated by the observation that task-related decisions are often hard to make because of coordination problems. These problems are due to the complex interrelations between tasks and are influenced by many sources of uncertainty. Decker discusses the design of a set of distributed autonomous computer programs ("agents") that assists people in coordinating their activities. Several ongoing implementations are presented and relevant research tasks/questions are identified.

2.3   Workflow and Coordination

The coordination of actors within workflows and processes is an important application area for coordination technologies. The papers focus on technological and theoretical foundations, discuss a specific application and the shortcomings of today's solutions, and point out opportunities for further development.

The first paper offers a technical solution for flexible implementations of coordination policies in workflow systems. The second paper proposes a mathematical model to support modeling and understanding of groupware requirements. The third paper describes the BPR-driven development of a specific workflow

---

[4] Workshop paper.
[5] Workshop paper
[6] Invited paper.

application and discusses the shortcomings of the approach used. The fourth paper gives a general perspective on coordination technology and assesses the usability of coordination technologies in a process/workflow context.

In "Coordination in Workflow Management Systems – A Rule-Based Approach"[7] *Kappel, Rausch-Schott,* and *Retschitzegger* identify coordination as "a key requirement of software systems where different parts have to be adjusted in order to reach a common goal." Along the example of workflow management systems (WFMS), they present concepts that allow for the flexible implementation of coordination policies. These concepts are based on the Event/Condition/Action (ECA) rules used in active object-oriented database systems. Frequent changes in the business environment lead to the need for flexible mechanisms to adjust coordination policies. By encapsulating coordination policies within ECA rules, general knowledge can be represented independently from specific business processes. The paper identifies various coordination policies related to the three main application areas of ECA rules, namely *activity ordering, agent selection,* and *worklist management.* Finally, the role of transactions in workflows is briefly discussed.

The paper "A Framework and Mathematical Model for Collaboration Technology"[8] by *Clarence A. Ellis* presents a functional framework for groupware. The paper introduces a mathematical model for groupware architecture (Team Automata), gives examples on how it can be used to understand and analyze collaboration technologies and defines the terms "cooperation" and "collaboration" within this context. The analysis of real time shared applications serves as an example for the applicability of the framework. The summary relates the possibilities of the framework to the needs of integrating technical, social, and organizational concerns to produce truly beneficial groupware system. Finally, the general limits of the framework as well as an area for future work are identified.

In "Practical Experiences and Requirements on Workflow"[9] *Kim* and *Paik* describe their experiences originating from the implementation of a workflow-based business process automation system. Limits of the current automation technology are identified and directions for improvements are suggested. The authors clearly point out the importance of linking the modeling of business processes with the implementation of workflows. The identified main topics are: dynamic change and exceptions, transactional workflows, and merge of build and run time.

In "Coordination Science: Challenges and Directions"[10] *Mark Klein* reviews some of the major weaknesses with current coordination technology and suggests several technical directions for addressing these weaknesses. Departing from the identification of the need for coordination technology, current coordination technologies are discussed and their weaknesses are pointed out. Among the proposed concepts for solving some of the mentioned problems are the integration of co-

---

[7] Invited paper.
[8] Invited paper.
[9] Workshop paper.
[10] Invited paper.

ordination technologies, the improvement of process representations, and the exploitation of product and software design technologies.

2.4 Collaborative Work

General support of collaborative work is the common topic of the papers in the third group. In many instances collaborative work is necessary in situations where unpredictable work pattern make it difficult to deploy standard workflow management systems. The first paper discusses the problem of re-integrating the results of autonomous work mostly in the context of decoupled databases. The second paper analyzes the role and the support of group and workspace awareness for collaborative work. The last paper of this group proposes a generic meta-database model to ease collaboration across database boundaries. All papers briefly refer to existing or planned applications of the concepts presented.

In "Supporting Autonomous Work and Reintegration in Collaborative Systems"[11], *Berger, Schill*, and *Völksen* focus on the reintegration of autonomously performed work in collaborative systems. Their goal is to provide an infrastructure for flexible and unrestricted decoupled work using primarily database applications which have to be consolidated from time to time. The requirements for efficient and flexible reintegration are discussed and existing reintegration mechanisms are compared with respect to these requirements. The paper presents MARC, a generic Merge and Resolve Conflicts component which provides history based automatic conflict detection and semi-automatic resolution based on object nets. MARC is implemented as an extension to the groupware system CoNus.

Schlichter, Koch, and *Bürger* emphasize in "Workspace Awareness for Distributed Teams"[12] the role of awareness for successful cooperation of distributed teams. The paper first presents a human-level view of distributed problem solving. The coordination perspective leads to the identification of group and workspace awareness as key elements for a successful support of cooperation within distributed human teams. Related topics are discussed in detail and an application of the concepts and their implementation in the area of support for distributed collaborative writing is presented.

Finally, the paper "GeM and WeBUSE: Towards a WWW-Database Interface"[13] by *Sivadas* and *Fernandez* describes a generic meta-database model to enable efficient browsing of structured databases by remote users in the World Wide Web environment. To overcome the problems of unknown database schemata, and the related difficulties of semantic and syntactic interpretation of schemata, the generic meta-data model GeM is proposed. To enable the elicitation of maximum information about the available schemata, the Web-based uniform schema browsing environment (WeBUSE) is presented. This is a suite of tools which enable remote users to browse augmented database schemata using conventional Web browsers.

---

[11] Workshop paper.
[12] Invited paper.
[13] Workshop paper.

2.5   Technological Considerations

An important element of the basic tiers for the implementation of collaborative applications is the low-level coordination of objects. The first paper contrasts message passing and shared memory approaches, and argues that the latter is superior because it avoids the asymmetry of message passing client/server systems. The second paper analyses two different implementations related to a typical client/server situation, the transmission of video/audio streams. The third paper presents a distributed object management system allowing the handling of client/server and peer-to-peer applications.

In their paper "Post-Client/Server Coordination Tools"[14], *Kühn* and *Nozicka* identify advanced coordination support as a prerequisite to the exploitation of new application possibilities, like collaboration and cooperation. They argue that the use of distributed shared memory is conceptually superior to traditional, message passing based approaches. CoKe (Coordination Kernel) is a middleware layer that follows the latter paradigm and particularly eases the development of fault-tolerant, distributed applications. The paper discusses the requirements of distributed applications, contrasts the above mentioned approaches (especially CoKe vs. CORBA), and presents the underlying concepts of CoKe in detail. Finally, application scenarios are given and the role of cooperative data structures for easing implementation is pointed out.

The paper "An Experimental Delay Analysis for Local Audio Video Streams for Desktop Collaborations"[15] by *Kim, Lee, Kang, Han,* and *Jung* presents an experimental analysis of a low-level component of collaborative applications, namely of audio/video streams. It compares the effect of the use of push and pull approaches on the local delay of continuously inflowing streams of encoded data. The experiments demonstrate that the push model outperforms the pull model.

Lee, Park, Yoon, Kim, and *Shin* present the distributed object management system DOMS in "Supporting both Client/Server and Peer-to-Peer Models in a Framework of a Distributed Object Management System"[16]. DOMS supports both client/server and peer-to-peer models. The DOMS is based on the C++ object model and offers concurrency and persistence as extensions. The paper discusses access control issues and application interrelations, and presents a structure for the propagation of updates. Additional topics such as distributed object management, concurrency control, and group communication are briefly addressed and a review of the current status of their work is given.

3   Future Work

This book is one step in the discussions necessary to fully understand the relations between coordination technologies and collaboration requirements. We will

---

[14] Invited paper.
[15] Workshop paper.
[16] Workshop paper.

continue this discussion at the WETICE'98[17] with the workshop "Web-based Infrastructures for Collaborative Enterprises: Ready for a Second Generation?". If you are interested in the results of this workshop, please contact us.

---

[17] The WETICE is an annual, international forum for state-of-the-art research in enabling technologies for collaboration. The WETICE'98 will take place in Stanford between the 17th and 19th of June, 1998. Further information can be found at http://www.cerc.edu/WETICE/.

Coordination in Knowledge-Intensive Organizations

Per Morten Schiefloe and Tor G Syvertsen

PAKT – Program on Applied Coordination Technology,
Norwegian University of Science and Technology,
Trondheim, Norway

Abstract. The emerging knowledge economy is not only changing existing industries and companies, it is also creating entirely new business opportunities which are purely knowledge based. The global, digital information network known as the Internet, enables information products to be duplicated and distributed at virtually no cost, and almost at the speed of light.

The rapid production and dissemination of new knowledge creates turmoil for most organizations, and establishes a dynamic business environment where communication and coordination become more important than ever. The traditional mechanisms for coordination are not sufficient, simply because they are too cumbersome and require too much attention.

The digital network removes many of the constraints imposed by physical communication media, and hereby creates opportunities for new organizational forms that may be capable to cope with the dynamic complexity of the knowledge societies.

1 The Knowledge Economy

The economy of the industrialized countries is changing, rapidly and dramatically. Obvious signs are problems in traditional industries, low growth rates, fiscal deficits and rising unemployment. Popular as well as political understanding often interprets this as a cyclic problem, expecting that the reappearance of prosperity and new jobs is just a question of time. An alternative and more firmly grounded hypotheses is that we are witnessing signs of a dramatic shift in the fundamental structure of the economy of the modern world.

This shift is exhibited not only by the growing content of knowledge in ordinary industrial products. It is also manifested by the spectacular growth in the "pure" knowledge sector in the economy, where information and knowledge is the primary basis for business development, illustrated by companies like Microsoft and Netscape.

The knowledge economy is becoming a reality, based on a shift from capital and energy to competence and information as the main economic driving force, as observed by Peter Drucker almost 30 years ago [5]:

"But knowledge has already become the primaryindustry, the industry that supplies to the economy the essential and central resource of production."

The industrial production will continue to expand in absolute terms, but the relative importance is declining. The basic strategic factors are no longer natural resources or low-skilled labour, but knowledge [16].

Knowledge differs from other resources in being *immaterial*, which means that the creation, distribution and use of this resource do not necessarily obey the physical laws that applies to physical matter. The principles for organization of knowledge-creating work may differ significantly from the traditional organization of physical work, including redundancy, task variation, and multidisciplinary teams [10, 3].

2   Dynamic Complexity

The amount and diversity of knowledge involved in production processes is increasing. Even standard commodities (like nuts and bolts) and standard services (like hair-cutting) have embedded a lot of knowledge about customer needs, marketing, production technologies, supplier delivery, environmental issues, etc. In order to maintain an updated knowledge-based process, continuous information supplies are required, hence the production chain has to be accompanied by an information chain in order to stay competitive.

At the same time, social changes and technological development appear to be accelerating so that the durability of current knowledge may be extremely short, may be only a few months or years within many specialist fields (such as computing and other leading-edge technologies). Well-established business strategies, markets, or products five years ago, may be obsolete today. A situation familiar for the haute-coiture business is now shaking almost any competitive business: banking, insurance, leisure, travel, publishing, media, education, and so on.

Dynamic complexity is the rapid change of a large amount of knowledge embedded in knowledge-intensive products or processes. The situation is characterized by a turbulent environment, and a variety of options and combinations to react upon the changing demands from outside the organization.

3   Digital Configurations

The Internet explosion has in few years literally created a world wide web of digital information. Ubiquitous computing is becoming a reality, making the statement *"information at your fingertips"* more than a slogan.

Digital information is represented as a string of (binary) digits, constituting a logical sequence which we denote a *digital configuration*. A digital configuration may contain any type of information, being it text, pictures, sound, video, animations.

Digital configurations are immaterial, and they may be created, copied, distributed and accessed at marginal cost when the information infrastructure (i.e. the Internet) is in place. The medium for creating digital configurations is computer software, for instance a word processor. The medium for distribution is the digital network (which substitutes physical media like the CD-ROM). The medium for accessing the digital configuration is again computer software, for instance a document viewer or a web browser.

The computer is a universal information processing machine, hence any kind of process (i.e. software) may be applied to create or to access the digital configurations. Since no physical distribution medium is involved, a communication process may deliberately be initiated either by the producer or by the user of the information, according to specific needs.

By monitoring the flow of information, the dominant communication patterns may be revealed, primary sources and sinks will be easy to discover, and instant adjustment to information needs may be performed. Embedding a remuneration system based on *use of* (as opposite to *production of*) information might automatically create an efficient market-based system for the creation of useful information (for the principle of *superdistribution*, see [4]).

The digital, networked communication media bring individuals freedom to communicate over geographic distances and across organizational boundaries, but also brings organizations a freedom to develop knowledge work processes in any fashion one might imagine.

4   The Need for Coordination

Any organized activity consists of two basic processes, the division of activities between participating actors and the coordination of the resulting sub-activities in such a way that the goals of the organization are fulfilled, as effectively as possible. Methods and mechanisms for coordination are recurrent themes in the literature on organizations. A prominent example is Mintzberg's well-known description of five basic coordinating mechanisms; mutual adjustment, simple structure, standardization of work processes, standardization of work outputs, and standardization of worker skills [13]. According to Mintzberg, the structuring of organizations, that is the way they are constructed and kept together, is a direct consequence of the coordinating mechanisms chosen. Complex organizations have traditionally relied on some kind of bureaucratic coordination, more or less centralized, depending on the level of professional expertise involved.

The phenomenon of coordination is somehow intuitively meaningful. Participating in a well-run scientific conference, passing smoothly through a busy airport or witnessing a top-performing soccer team, we may notice how well coordinated the actions between different actors or team-members seem to be. The foremost criterion for highly coordinated organizations is, somewhat paradoxical, that the coordination itself is almost invisible. Coordination as a theme is usually placed on the agenda when it is failing, with poor performance, ineffective time consumption and pressing needs for compensatory mechanisms as results. "Invisible" coordination does not, however, mean that coordination does not exist or is not taken seriously. Quite the contrary, efficient coordination of complex activities is usually a result of conscious strategic choices and thorough efforts in planning and training, making coordination a built-in attribute of organizational behavior. The term "organic coordination" can be used as a denominator for this kind of automatic functioning.

A comprehensive list of different definitions of coordination will rapidly fill up several pages. Frances et. al. [6] say that coordination *"implies the bringing into a relationship otherwise disparate activities or events"*, and by doing this *"something can be achieved which otherwise would not be."* Malone & Crowston [11] suggest a broad and uncomplicated version, defining coordination simply as *"the act of working together."* Coordination theory is correspondingly defined as *"a body of principles about how activities can be coordinated, that is, about how actors can work together."* Malone & Crowston at the same time underline that the concept "coordination theory" must not be understood as a coherent and consistent body of theory, and that theories, concepts and results from many different fields can contribute to the development of such a theory. Among the fields to be recognized are sociology, economics, linguistics, law and computer science.

Looking more closely into the concept, we can identify three main components of organizational coordination; goals, actors, and activities. According to traditional approaches these components can be addressed independently or in a mechanical fashion. Looked upon in a coordination perspective, however, the components are related through a set of interdependencies. Dependencies (like all relationships) are not physical entities, but logical constructions. The relations are, nevertheless, determining how the processes are developing over time.

Goals are something to be achieved as a result of organized efforts. Economical and technical reasoning often takes the organizational goals for granted, be it profits, growth or other kinds of well-known and agreed-upon achievements. Empirical studies in complex organizations have demonstrated that this assumption more often than not is a dubious one. Formulation and selection of specific, operationalized goals is regularly a question of internal struggles, contesting interests and different perceptions of reality. March & Olsen, in their well-known "garbage-can" theory, even suggests that coincidence may play an important role [12].

Activities are the actions necessary to perform the different sub-tasks of the goal. Actors may be individuals or social systems, within as well as outside of the organization, whose efforts have to be combined in order to reach the goals.

Actors and activities are linked by interdependencies. According to Malone & Crowston a more narrow definition based on this decomposition may be formulated as follows: *"Coordination is the act of managing interdependencies between activities."* Compared to a more traditional way of looking at organizational activities, focus is shifted from the components to the relationships between them. This represents a more fundamental change than may be apparent at a first glance; the dynamics of a system are determined primarily by the relationships between the components, not by the components themselves.

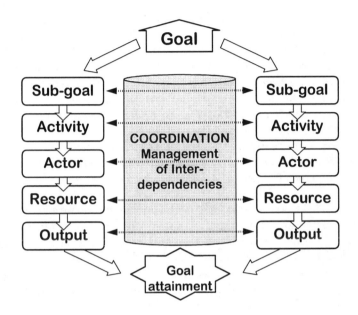

Fig. 1. Coordination Model

5   Levels and Dimensions

Complex organizations have to perform coordination on different levels. Coordination between organizations are dealt with at the *inter-organizational level.* The importance of handling challenges at this level is rapidly growing, as the value-chains are getting more integrated. Outsourcing, just-in-time, networking, strategic alliances and virtual organizations are catchwords for contemporary trends, which are rapidly changing the global, economic scene.

A complex organization is also faced with problems concerning *intra-organizational* coordination. Coordination on system-level concerns the relations within the internal value-chains, as well as the relations between material-handling, information-/knowledge handling and the necessary supporting processes. Increasing demands concerning cost-effectiveness, speed, quality and ability to adjust to rapidly changing environments are making this part of organizational activities more and more important. Important tools for improved coordination on this level are different methods for enterprise modeling [20].

Coordination on sub-system level deals with the relations between internally dependent parts of the organization, typically between departments. An example from the offshore petroleum industry can illustrate several aspects of entirely new ways of organizing work based on new organizational principles and digital coordination technology [8]:

> *"Norne is a new oil production ship being put into operations by Statoil (the state oil company of Norway) in mid 1997. The new installation is different from former permanent concrete and steel constructed giants that up to now mainly have inhabited the Norwegian Continental Shelf. Norne has a very lean organisation, about 1/3 compared to its older counterparts. Still, it is the same functions (production of oil), and these must be more efficient in Norne. The Norne onshore support organisation is placed in Northern Norway, Harstad. In addition, Norne needs technical support from centralised Statoil units in Stavanger, Trondheim and Bergen (500-1100 km away), and external vendor support on production and maintenance from both inside and outside of Norway."*

The Norne field organization has developed an enterprise model as a backbone and interface for its information system. Here the work processes (155 in number) are identified and described in the form of interactive, graphic flow charts, in which a description of work assignments is linked up to production philosophy, requirements and procedures, etc., functions for reporting, access to supplier information, E-mail and video conferences for communication with experts. The technical infrastructure is based upon Lotus Notes 4.0, combined with intranet and Internet, which gives great flexibility at a reasonable cost. Norne will produce over 200,000 barrels of oil per day with an extremely slender organization and extreme requirements are imposed in terms of cost effectiveness and flexibility. The basis for achieving this is the skills amongst employees and an overall understanding of what they are engaged in. In order to avoid sub-optimalisation, it is crucial that those who carry out the work should have a holistic insight into how the operation works. Shared mental models can be effectively developed by the personnel being involved with their skills and insight in the modelling process and not simply taking delivery of a ready-chewed result. If the organization is to be capable of being changed over time, it is also necessary that those who are familiar with the work processes and who use the information system should be able to play an active part in the improvement work.

The lowest level in the coordination hierarchy deals with coordination between individuals. In knowledge-intensive organizations this will often be between experts or professionals. Typical for many of the tasks to be performed, is that they are subject to interpretation, both regarding content, operationalization, means and methods. The need for common understanding, effective communication and agreed-upon decision processes is obvious. The steps towards coordinated efforts may be sketched as in Figure 2. From this figure one can also get a visual impression of what happens if the coordinating processes fail, namely that a proportion of the participants' efforts strays off in different directions, making little contribution to common goals.

It should be observed that the upper part of the figure is related to goal definition and interpretation. These activities are not part of the coordination efforts in the traditional sense. In traditional project management, for instance, an assumption is that a project has a "clearly stated goal". In most cases, this assumption simply does not hold. As well-known from research literature, conflicting interests and priorities are an inherent part of the daily life in most complex organizations. The analytical consequence is that organizations must be analyzed and interpreted also as political arenas where various actors may have conflicting goals. A proper goal definition process must sort out not only different perceptions of reality, but also bring out in the open differing interests. Such a process may reduce the need for coordination in the execution phase in two ways: first by harmonizing the actors' interpretation, next by establishing procedures for handling conflicting interests. Teamwork methods and systematic planning tools like the Quality Function Deployment have proved to be very useful for this purpose [1].

Fig. 2. Coordination Process

The basic coordination processes can also be described in terms of three different dimensions, which separates between vertical, horizontal and time-dependent coordination. The vertical coordination regards strategic choices, resource allocation, regulatory mechanisms and decision structures within the organization, to a large extent corresponding to well-known management processes.

The horizontal dimension sheds light on the need for concurrent coordination between actors and activities, whereas the time-dependent coordination has to do with experience transfer and organizational learning.

6   Preconditions for Coordination

The working conditions for any organization can be roughly classified by two dimensions, well-known from the literature on organizational theory, namely the complexity of the tasks to be performed and the rate of change in the organization's environment. Main factors defining the degree of complexity have to do with the size of the operation, the technologies used, the knowledge content necessary to perform the different tasks, as well as with the level and variation in the professional expertise employed. Important change factors have to do with markets, political and economic factors, as well as with technological and scientific developments. Combining the two dimensions, we get the following picture :

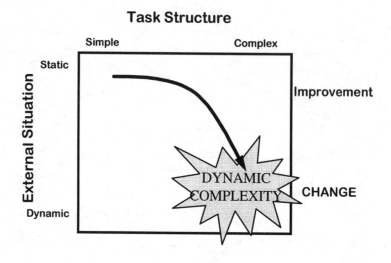

Fig. 3. Dynamic Complexity

Following the developmental logic presented earlier, we can conclude that a growing proportion of knowledge intensive organizations have to face the challenges of the lower right-hand corner, dealing at the same time with increasing complexity and accelerating change. We can characterize such a situation as a field of dynamic complexity.

In this corner, simply improving the existing organization will in most situations not be sufficient to prosper. Profound changes may be required, and if the situation becomes permanent, the organization will face the challenge of permanent change. Since most organizations are constructed for stability; this means that basis for organizational understanding may have to be turned around. From a coordination perspective, the field of dynamic complexity can not be managed by applying the traditional principles for organizing and coordinating.

7   Mechanisms for Coordination

Strategies for coordination can in principle be of two different kinds, characterized by the terms constitutive and concurrent. *Constitutive coordination* is based on some kind of centralized management or planning, the main elements of which can be described as a series of steps : decomposition of goals, operationalization of goals into specified activities, assigning activities and responsibilities to actors, establishing procedures for handling activities and merging part results into wholes. All these elements are well-known ingredients of bureaucracy, and traditionally such hierarchical methods have been first choice for obtaining coordination. Mintzberg [13] distinguishes between two kinds of bureaucratic coordination. The classic model is called *machine bureaucracy*. The main emphasis here is on behavior formalization, vertical and horizontal job specialization, functional grouping and centralization of power. With increasing complexity focus is shifted towards standardization of skills, with a corresponding vertical and horizontal decentralization. This leads to a structural configuration sometimes called *professional bureaucracy*, typical for organizations like universities and hospitals, performing advanced activities in complex, but relatively stable environments. Well-known for observers, organizations of this kind can obtain high professional qualities but are usually not very effective when it comes to handling shifting working conditions. The combination of decentralized responsibilities and strong professional interests also make such organizations extremely difficult to manage.

Coordination by hierarchical and bureaucratic means may generally be classified as *procedural*. The main governing principle is adherence to formal authority, expressed through some kind of *formal structure*. Within this paradigm efforts to improve coordination usually implies some kind of structural change.

Basic preconditions for effective use of procedural approaches are that both tasks and means for solving these are known in advance, so that the necessary procedures can be developed, determining responsibilities as well as how specific jobs shall be performed, alternatively what kinds of professional expertise which are needed. From this follows logically that procedural mechanisms are not well suited for handling dynamic situations.

Challenges presented by situations of dynamic flexibility must be dealt with by some kind of *concurrent coordination*. Successful concurrent mechanisms must have qualities making it possible to take care of tasks and solve problems which are either not known on before-hand, or are of such a complexity that it is impossible to develop proper procedures or to assign responsibilities to a predefined group of actors. Typical for such coordination mechanisms are that focus is shifted from procedures and expertise to relations and involvement. Basic ingredients are dissemination of values and goals and methods for developing shared constructions of reality, accompanied by delegation of responsibilities and decision-making, as well as the removal of unnecessary structural barriers.

Two different kinds of mechanisms can be observed in complex organizations trying to deal with such problems. One of the strategies often adopted has to do with the exploitation of the "guiding hand" of the free market, which, according to classical economic theory, takes care of the coordination almost "automatically". The pursuit of self-interest by maximizing actors will lead to the best possible outcome, not just for themselves but for the system as a whole. The exploitation of market mechanisms for coordinating activities within an organization can be witnessed in the establishment of so-called "internal markets", the attempt of which is to mirror some of the features of natural markets in the internal functioning of the organization. Without going into a detailed discussion of such strategies, one can readily state that both positive and negative effects flourish. Cost consciousness and effective transaction mechanisms on the one hand may rapidly be outweighed by sub-optimization and new bureaucratic procedures on the other. It is also difficult for established organizations to face some of the consequences, i.e. layoff off colleagues, if the internal markets are really taken seriously. The critical factors for obtaining coordination by market mechanisms are the introduction of and adherence to economic principles as guidelines for handling interdependencies. Strategies for improving coordination usually implies measures for obtaining more efficient transactions, with availability of information as a key factor.

The other main strategy for obtaining coordination in complex and changing environments consists in exploiting the strength and flexibility characteristic of many kinds of informal structures, grounded in personal relations based on trust and cooperation. This may be called a network approach. Nohria [14] claims that *"all organizations are in important respects social networks and need to be addressed and analyzed as such."* The organizational network approach, focusing on the development, maintenance and use of direct and indirect personal relations and acquaintances, resembles what Mintzberg classifies as "mutual adjustment." Observations of such informal structures in knowledge-intensive organizations reveals beyond doubt their potential as communication channels and arenas for cooperation and knowledge sharing and development. Recent research and theoretical developments within the field are rapidly adding to the knowledge reservoir of sociology in general, as well as contributing to our understanding of modern organizations [21, 17, 14, 22]. Networks, understood like this, as social phenomena, must not, however, be confused with the corresponding term prevalent in modern economic literature, which deals mainly with different kinds of formal alliances between organizations. Basic to coordination by networks is the development and handling of interpersonal relations. Network based coordination is effective when interpersonal processes of communication, cooperation and exchange flow efficiently. A fundamental precondition for establishing this is availability of competence.

In addition to the constitutive and concurrent mechanisms, Mintzberg also describes a mechanism called simple structure, where coordination is taken care of by direct supervision. In practice this means that all important decisions are centralized in the hands of one or a few persons. As should be rather obvious, this kind of mechanism is only suited for rather small and surveyable operations.

Mapping the different coordination mechanisms along the two basic dimensions classifying an organization's working environment, we get the following picture :

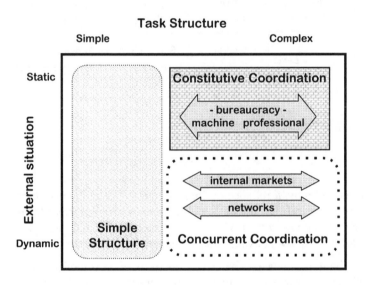

Fig. 4. Modes of Coordination

8   Coordination Focus : Management of Interdependencies

Different coordination mechanisms are not only suited for different organizational working conditions, there is also a correspondence between mechanisms, basic preconditions and coordination levels. Figure 5 illustrates this.

Choosing a strategy for coordination within a work process means selecting a specific combination of level, mechanism and coordination focus as basic. This choice in turn influences the possible use of other mechanisms. Focusing on structure, authority and performance control on one hand, has implications for the possibilities to exploit market mechanisms and informal relations on the

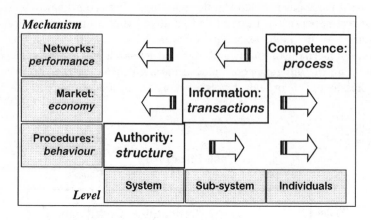

Fig. 5. Coordination Focus

other. Correspondingly, a reliance on informal networks as means for communication and cooperation can not be combined with a strong formal bureaucracy. A system of internal markets also has consequences for formal structures as well as for the development and availability of interpersonal relations.

It should be noted, however, that various parts of an organization may have tasks of different characteristics, hence a combination of coordination principles will be applied. Repetitive activities may be structured according to procedures, and highly automated, thereby leaving attention to important issues, changes, and new developments.

9   Coordination Technology

Coordination technologies are methods and tools for improving coordination. The interconnections sketched above can also be used as a basis for discussing the use of such technologies. Basic for this discussion must be coordination mode, principles of coordination and planning horizon, as illustrated in the following table:

Coordination Mode	Constitutive	Concurrent	
Principle	Professional bureaucracy	Internal markets	Networks
Planning horizon	**Long**	Medium	Short
Technology intent	Centralized overview and control	Information exchange	Distributed overview and cooperative action
Technology use	Predefined and pre-programmed	Pre-programmed	Instant and flexible
Freedom to act	No	Yes	Yes
Possible actions	Few	Few	Many

The planning horizon indicates how well the coordination principle applies to dynamic (i.e. changing) business environments. The professional bureaucracy requires a high degree of stability in order to be efficient over time, while the network has a potential to be far more flexible.

The intent of coordination technologies addresses issues that must be in place in order to make the corresponding coordination principle work. Certain technologies may give support to a particular coordination principle better than others, but this is mainly a question of how technologies are used. Email, for instance, is well suited for instant and flexible communication between actors in a network. Email may, however, also be used as a technique for centralized and bureaucratic distribution of information. The same goes for a system like Lotus Notes, which may be organized as anything from open and egalitarian to highly structured and hierarchical.

Pre-programmed use of coordination technology means that the intended use has been embedded (programmed) in the information system. Predefined means that possible actions also have been determined in advance, and to some extent embedded in the information system, as typical found in legacy systems.

The freedom to act and the number of possible actions are probably the most distinctive feature of the informal network compared to the other two coordination principles. In the extreme bureaucratic case, human actors are regarded as no more than operators that in any situation act according to predefined procedures. Humans are reduced to wheels in the machinery, needed primarily to alleviate imperfections of the information system.

It seems obvious that the field of dynamic flexibility (as depicted in Figure 3) can not be managed by relying on constitutive coordination with predefined and pre-programmed use of coordination technology. A more feasible approach is to develop a networking organization, employing networked, instant and flexible technologies for communication and coordination.

Within this paradigm individual actors are the masters, having a high degree of freedom to act, and with several possible (and self-defined) actions in any given situation.

The networked and networking organization requires coordination technologies that supports the members in performing together:

- Planning the work and keeping track of the state of affairs
- Collecting, creating, analyzing and presenting information
- Combining or linking individual contributions into higher level results
- Monitoring changes in the environment
- Communicating with peers, subordinates and supervisors

Many existing systems (e.g. for accounting, project management, etc) will of course continue to be useful, depending on how they are applied.

The architecture and design principles of the internet and the world wide web seem to be a conceptually perfect match between coordination needs and coordination technology for the networking organization. The web can be regarded as a distributed medium for creation, distribution and accessing digital configurations. In a communication perspective, the web is receiver-oriented in the sense that the technology is completely pull-based. Anyone who needs information has to actively fetch it from where it might be found. A passive actor will not receive a single bit of information.

It seems obvious that technology is a necessary, but not sufficient prerequisite in order to create a networking organization. There are at least three other factors that need to be in place: competent people, common goals and shared values:

- Paradoxically, less organization and less formal coordination will require more competence in organizing and coordinating distributed throughout the organization. Acquiring competence is no more just hiring people, because the educational systems tend to produce one-eyed specialists. As a consequence, additional training becomes crucial, to provide skills in team-working, holistic thinking, and business understanding.
- Common goals may be difficult to achieve, but when in place many of the traditional needs for coordination will disappear. Several methods and techniques are available for goal-setting processes, see ,for instance, Bicknell [1].
- Shared values and beliefs may be even more difficult to achieve than goals. Values and beliefs are purely mental constructs, that act as strong guidelines in chosing options and making decisions.

The technological aspects of coordination are still difficult and require expertise in physical and logical aspects of digital information networks. The social and human aspects are, however, even more important because they create the foundation and playground for organic coordination in knowledge-intensive networking organizations. Methods and techniques for creating and maintaining values and goals are still in their infancy, and need further development combined with support from digital technologies.

References

1. Bicknell, Barbara A, and Kris D Bicknell (1995) The Road Map to Repeatable Success. Using QFD to Implement Change, CRC Press, Boca Raton
2. Boeing (1996), 777 Computing Design Facts, http://www.boeing.com/bckhtml/Boe777comp.html

3. Choo, Chun Wei (1997) The Knowing Organization: How Organizations Use Information To Construct Meaning, Create Knowledge, and Make Decisions. To be published by Oxford University Press, also http://128.100.159.139/FIS/KO/KO.html
4. Cox, Brad (1996) Superdistribution: Objects as Property on the Electronic Frontier, New York, Addison Wesley
5. Drucker, Peter F (1969) The Age of Discontinuity, London, Heinemann
6. Frances, J., Levacic, R., Mitchell, J, Thompson G. (1991) "Introduction", in Thompson, G, Frances, J., Levacic, R, Mitchell, J (eds.) Markets, Hierarchies & Networks. The Coordination of Social Life. London, Sage
7. Goldberg, Carey (1997) Cyberspace Still No Substitute for Face-to-Face Meetings, The New York Times, February 25
8. Hepsø, Vidar (1997), The Social Construction and Visualisation of a New Norwegian Offshore Installation, Proceedings of the ECSCW97, Kluwer Academic Press
9. Negroponte, Nicholas (1995) Being Digital, New York, Alfred A Knopf (selected bits on http://www.obs-europa.de/obs/english/books/nn/bdcont.htm)
10. Nonaka, Ikujiro and Hirotaka Takeuchi (1995) The Knowledge-Creating Company: How Japanese Companies Create the Dynamics of Innovation, New York, Oxford University Press
11. Malone, Thomas W., Kevin Crowston (1992) Toward an Interdisciplinary Theory of Coordination, Centre for Coordination Science, Massachusetts Institute of Technology
12. March, James G., Johan P. Olsen (eds.) Ambiguity and Choice in Organization. Oslo, Universitetsforlaget, (1976)
13. Mintzberg, Henry (1979) The Structuring of Organizations. Englewood Cliffs, Prentice-Hall
14. Nohria, Nithin, Robert G. Eccles (eds.) (1992) Networks and Organizations. Boston, Harvard Business School Press
15. Sabbagh, Karl (1996) Twenty-First Century Jet. The Making and Marketing of the Boeing 777, New York, Scribner
16. Schwartz, Peter (1993). Post-capitalist, A conversation with Peter Drucker. Wired, 1(3), 80-83.
17. Scott, John (1991) Social Network Analysis. A Handbook. London, Sage
18. Singh, Kamar J. (1992) Concurrent Engineering Pilot Project at GE Aircraft Engines - Concurrent Engineering in Review, Volum 4-92
19. Thompson, Grahame et.al. (eds.) (1991) Markets, Hierarchies and Networks. The Coordination of Social Life. London, Sage
20. Totland, Terje (1997) Enterprise modeling as a means to support human sensemaking and communication in organizations, doctoral thesis, department of computer and information science (IDI), Norwegian University of Science and Technology (NTNU), Trondheim, Norway. In preparation
21. Wellman, Barry, S.D. Berkowitz (eds.) 1988. Social structures : a network approach. Cambridge. Cambridge University Press
22. Wasserman, Stanley, Katherine Faust (1994) Social Network Analysis. Cambridge. Cambridge University Press

Co-ordination of Management Activities - Mapping Organisational Structure to the Decision Structure

Peter Bernus and Gregory Uppington

School of Computing and Information Technology,
Griffith University Nathan (Brisbane),
Queensland 4111, Australia

Abstract. The GRAI Grid is used for the presentation of co-ordination in a virtual enterprise. A set of examples are presented which show how the organisational structure and decisional structure interrelate, making it possible to evaluate the two structures in conjunction. The technique can be used to design organisations which take into account the individual as well as organisational objectives of the individual organisational actor thus leading to a better management structure.

1 Introduction

Production management, and on a more general level, enterprise management is a function carried out by management personnel. Management personnel includes organisational players from the CEO down to the foreman on the shop-floor. Doumeingts [2, 3] model the enterprise as consisting of a production system and a decision system, interconnected by the management information system. The decision system is then modelled according to the time horizons for which decisions are taken and according to the types of decisions that need to be made. Once the decision model of an enterprise is created [1] there are two questions to be answered:

1. Is the decision structure adequate for co-ordinating all activities of the enterprise to achieve the overall enterprise objectives?
2. Is the management organisation which implements the decisional structure adequate?

This article aims at demonstrating the interplay between the two structures. This is an important consideration, because a perfect decision structure can still be working below its expected performance, if the organisational implementation does not take into account the following two factors: (a) the individual organisational player's objectives, and (b) the decisional objectives which the organisational player is supposed to achieve in the role played in the decisional structure. In Section 2 we present the GRAI Grid modelling language [2] which will be used for modelling the decisional structure of the enterprise. In Section 3 we present how organisational structure can be mapped to the decisional structure. Section 4 presents the particular problem of decision structure in the co-ordination of virtual enterprise (4.1) and the problems of mapping organisations to the decisional structure (4.2).

2   Decisional Modelling Using the GRAI-Grid

2.1   The Natural Hierarchy of Decisions

Any management decision that needs to be taken is made with reference to a horizon of time. This is the span of time at which the decision maker is looking ahead and expects the decision to be valid for. For example, a strategic decision is intended for a longer horizon, say 2-5 years, while a tactical decision may plan ahead for a horizon of one to four months. Because of the changing nature of the environment decisions which have been made for a given horizon, have to be re-considered. This is either because an event occurs that invalidates (or is likely to invalidate) the assumptions underlying the decision made for the given horizon, or at planned periodic intervals to adjust decisions based on the new information which became available since the last time decision was made. The length of this period is typically two to three times shorter then the horizon for which the decision has been made.

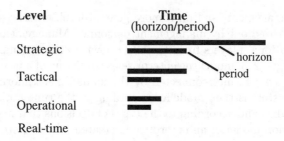

Fig. 1. The Natural Hierarchy of Decisions

Those decision functions which have a shorter horizon are provided control by management decisions taken for the longer horizons in order for the entire enterprise to act in a co-ordinated manner to achieve higher level objectives (i.e. objectives of longer horizon). The horizon of the lower level decision function is the same, or shorter than the period of the higher level decision function (see Fig.1). The real-time level does not have an overall horizon or period; the frequency and speed of intervention (control) functions is individually determined by the needs of the controlled process-component. This hierarchy of horizons (periods) defines a natural hierarchy of decision functions. It is customary to define strategic, tactical, operational and real-time levels, although in practice more levels are often practical - according to periods and horizons which have a special meaning in the given business domain (e.g seasons in agriculture).

2.2 The Three Major Categories of Decisional Function

The primary aim of any enterprise management should be that the operations of the enterprise (i.e. all service- and production functions) are carried out in line with the current enterprise mission. We can consider the enterprise's service and production functions as a transformation (see Fig.2), in which the input (information and material) is transformed into output (information and material) by the application of human and machine resources. (Note that in service enterprise the transformation is often applied to the customer, i.e. the customer is both input and output of the service process, and the customer undergoes a transformation while the service is consumed.) The functions of management can be categorised on the basis of this model, distinguishing

- Product management (section 2.2.1)
- Resource management (section 2.2.2)
- Co-ordination / planning (section 2.2.3)

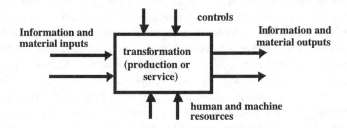

Fig. 2. Service and production as a transformation process

Product Management The aim of product management functions is to make sure that information and material inputs are available for the service and production (transformation) process

- When and where needed
- Accessible to the resources of the enterprise
- In the quality and quantity needed

Also, product management is to make sure that information and material outputs as produced by the service and production (transformation) process of the enterprise become available

- When and where needed (i.e. reach the customer)
- Accessible to the resources of the enterprise (no additional resources are needed to reach the customer)
- In the quality and quantity needed

Resource Management The aim of resource management is to make sure that human and machine resources are available for carrying out the service and production (transformation) process.

- Resources must be available when and where needed
- Resources must be available in the quality and quantity needed
- Resources must be reachable by the operational and real time resource management functions

Operational and real-time level resource management is responsible for giving operational / real-time control to the resources to achieve the necessary transformation. Thus process control is the lowest level resource management function in the natural hierarchy of decision functions. Informally: product management takes care of the inputs and outputs, and resource management takes care of the resources and the controls for the transformation process (Fig. 2).

Co-ordination and Planning Product management and resource management functions alone are incapable of providing the necessary controls for the enterprise. This is because the product-related and resource-related objectives are mutually constraining, with many possible courses of action available to satisfy these constraints. There are usually many possible solutions to harmonise the product-related and resource-related objectives and to balance these two in an optimal manner, and the way this balance is achieved depends on the overall objectives of the enterprise. For example, if the overriding objective is to provide some service or product then the resource management task should follow suit to make sure that the necessary resources are available. If, on the other hand, resource constraints are given precedence then product-related objectives must be adjusted accordingly. Co-ordination and planning is therefore the third type of management task, which covers those management tasks which co-ordinate among product and resource management. This co-ordination is necessary on all levels of the decisional hierarchy. On the strategic level this type of management function decides on the general direction of the company, e.g. whether to keep the existing resources and use them in the best possible way, or to use every possible product / market opportunity and make sure the resources are available for being able to meet the demand. On the lower levels this management function plans or schedules the production and service activities balancing product requirements and resource requirements. There is no operational / real-time level activity in co-ordination and planning; on the operational level direct control is exercised through allocating resources to tasks and giving them the necessary controls to execute these tasks.

Figure 3 shows the three types of management function repeated on the strategic, tactical and operational / real-time levels. In real situations there are more levels then three, depending on the horizons and periods for which the given enterprise needs separate, meaningful management tasks.

Horizon/Period	1. Manage Products	2. Coordinate/Plan	3. Manage Resources
strategic			
tactical			
operational			
real-time			

Fig. 3. The three types of management function

2.3   The Decision Centre Model

Definition: For each type of management task and each horizon it is possible to define a so-called Decision Centre (DC). A decision centre makes its decisions on the basis of its Decisional Framework, which is handed to it by some other DC (see Fig. 4).

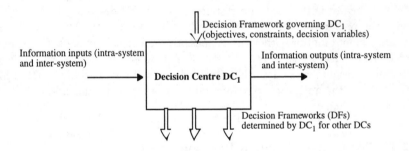

Fig. 4. The Decision Centre model

Definition: A Decisional Framework (DF) is defined as the collection of the following elements (DO, DV, DConstr):

- Objectives - Decisional Objectives (DO) (management objectives) are the aims that the DC is supposed to achieve.
- Decision variables (DV) a) for all but the operational management/control level the DVs are the means through which the DC is allowed to manipulate other DCs below it; b) for the operational control level management/control the DVs are the means through which to manipulate/control the service / production process;
- Decisional constraints - Decisional constraints describe the limitations under which the DC is allowed to manipulate DVs to achieve the objectives. This includes the amount or quality, or timing of resource usage both for the DC's own use and the resources that the DC is allowed to make available for DCs which the DC manages / controls. Definition: Management of DC by another

DC - A DC1 manages / controls DC2 if DC2 receives its DF from DC1. DCs exchange information within the enterprise and external to it, i.e. with
- Other DCs anywhere in the DC hierarchy;
- The management information system (MIS) which aggregates operational or other lower level information such that it becomes usable for the given DC's level of decisions
- The environment (customers, other enterprises, government agencies, professional bodies, individuals of influence etc.). Definition: resources of DC - A DC has resources that make it possible to carry out the decisional task to achieve the objective of the DC. These resources include:
- Human resource: including the decision maker and its helpers (e.g. administrative helpers)
- Machine resource: including all the hardware and software resources utilised by the human resource to carry out its decision making task (hardware and software here extends to both information processing hardware / software, such as copying machines, computers, word processors, as well as other machine resources, including those for communication, and transport)
- Monetary resources (funds) that support the decision making task. It is to be specifically noted that the resources of the DC are not to be confused with the resources managed by the DC (provided that the DC is a resource management function -otherwise it does not even dispose over other resources than those needed to carry out its own management task). These latter managed resources are described in the decisional variables of the DC which the DC has the authority to manipulate (and thereby to allocate, distribute, or control them).

2.4   The Co-ordination of Decision Centres

Information Links of DCs In addition to the DF provided to a DC by another DC above or on the same level of the decision hierarchy DCs obtain information from
- the management information system;
- from other DCs (via information links);
- from the management information system (MIS) that collects, aggregates and presents information about the operation (service and production);
- from the external environment, (via information links); Similarly, a DC provides information output, which includes the DFs determined by the DC for another DC, and information to
- other DCs (on either level of the decision hierarchy);
- the MIS;
- the outside environment.

The Control of DCs Functions of DCs are either period- or event driven (or both). Period-driven functions are executed regularly, according to the horizon and period of the decision function. Event-driven functions of a DC are triggered by externally or internally generated events. The source of internal events may be directly in the operation, (the event being generated through the mechanism of the MIS), or in other DCs. At any moment in time the current content of a DF codifies the agreement between the controlling and controlled DC. The DF may remain unchanged over a longer period of time as long as the agreement is extended beyond its original period. The controlling DC may change the DF of the controlled DC. The form of conversation between them may take various forms, depending on wether the two DCs are implemented by the same agent or by two separate agents. In the first case a 'private conversation' develops the acceptance of the new DF, in the second case an overt conversation takes place between the two agents, with the aim of achieving an agreement. The DFs of resource management and product management are not independent (they are mutually constrained) and as earlier described, there exists a separate type of decision function (co-ordination / planning) to satisfy these constraints. Co-ordination and planning type decision functions therefore:

- obtain information, via information links, from the DCs to be co-ordinated (such as initial - intended - product plans and present resource plans);
- investigate the constraints and the possibilities to satisfy these, so as to achieve the objectives as determined by the co-ordinating DC's own DF;
- determine mutually consistent Dfs for the DCs to be co-ordinated.

Note, that because of the possible information links the DCs so co-ordinated the DF may only have to determine the rules of constraint satisfaction (e.g. precedence rules) and delegate the details of the actual constraint satisfaction to a conversation between the co-ordinated product- and resource management DCs. (This form of co-ordination allows management with much less intervention then explicit constraint satisfaction by the co-ordinating DC.) DCs have two type of co-ordination link: non-hierarchical and hierarchical (see Fig.5) A non-hierarchical link assumes a conversation that does not involve the changing of DFs of either DC, hierarchical co-ordination links involve on DC imposing a DF on the other, but based on information links for conversation (e.g. negotiation).

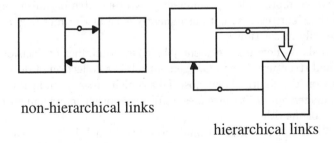

non-hierarchical links

hierarchical links

Fig. 5. Co-ordination links

2.5   The Aim of Co-ordination of Management Functions

Individual members of the enterprise behave as agents, in the sense of AI planning agent, i.e. they have a set of objectives (including 'personal objectives' and 'imposed objectives') and as planning agents are able to plan their activities (or an outside observer can describe them as if they were planning their activities), as well as are able to change the plans if activities appear not to progress toward the objectives believed at any one time. The principal aim of production management is to achieve that the enterprise behave as an agent, in order to achieve the objectives of the whole enterprise. Since the activities of the enterprise are composed of activities of its individual agents (organisational players) the production management system must co-ordinate the decisional objectives within the enterprise (i.e. to achieve a mutually consistent set of objectives on all levels of decision). Also production management must co-ordinate the objectives of the individual agents (i.e. personal objectives) with the organisation's decisional objectives - although personal objectives are not under the co-ordination / control of the management system, they can not be ignored.

2.6   The Decision Centre as an Organisational Role

DCs are functionally defined, and various ways exist to assign management personnel to DCs. Therefore a DC is, from the point of view of organisational design [6, 4]), is a management role to be assigned to an organisational entity, or actor / agent - such as an individual, committee, or board.

3   Mapping Organisational Structure to Decisional Structure

Any management entity justifies its existence in the organisation through the decisional roles it is playing. Furthermore, only those organisational roles are necessary which determine at least one DF, or which provide direct operational control (this latter can be through of as a special case of DFs). Traditionally DCs are covered more-or-less permanently by designated organisational entities - although these entities may not permanently exist at all times (e.g. a committee is available only at set times).

Figure 6 shows how management jobs cover a number of decisional roles in the decisional structure. Each management job is a collection of decisional roles. The arrows on the figure show those DFs which cross boundaries of jobs, i.e. where a management entity provides a DF for another management entity (one is the 'boss' of the other).

Figure 7 shows the organisational structure (which is in this case hierarchical) that corresponds to the decisional structure in Fig. 6. The organisational hierarchy is determined by the decisional links (DFs) crossing boundaries of organisational entities. As examples demonstrate in section 4 the same decision structure can be satisfied by extremely different organisational forms. Neither

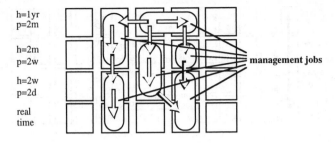

Fig. 6. A management job consist of the decisional centres (roles) assigned to the manager

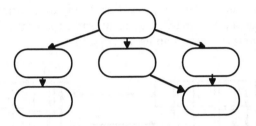

Fig. 7. Organisational structure abstracted from Fig. 6

the decision structure nor the organisational structure alone can ensure good management of the enterprise, therefore we set out demonstrating how the two can be considered in conjunction.

4   Forms of Organisation and Corresponding Co-ordination Problems

Co-ordination possibilities and problems stem from either decisional structure inadequacies (section 4.1) or from problematic mapping of organisation to the decisional structure (section 4.2).

4.1   Co-ordination of Decisional Systems

We present decisional structure problems on the level of a value chain (i.e. co-ordination of multiple or virtual enterprises). We do not treat in the present article the more local problem of decisional structure within the enterprise. Fig. 8 shows the traditional value chain, where two enterprises interact on the operational level. Clearly, the 'virtual enterprise' that is supposed to implement the value chain of the product supported by these two enterprises, does not exist, since there is not decisional mechanism to create the strategic or tactical level decisions, either for the product or for the resources.

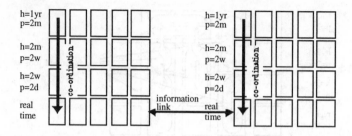

Fig. 8. Un-coordinated value chain (operational co-ordination only)

An integrated value chain supposes that there are information links on all levels of the decisional hierarchy. This arrangement is necessary to ensure that the integrated enterprise act as an agent (Fig. 9).

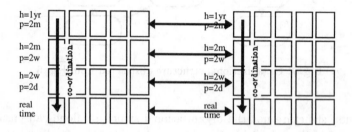

Fig. 9. Integrated value chain (information links on all levels of decision)

One form of the integrated value chain is the consortium. The consortium form limits co-ordination to a defined domain of action and acts as an agent appearing as a virtual enterprise in its defined domain. (Fig. 10). The reader may notice that this kind of analysis would allow the development of a detailed typology of virtual enterprise.

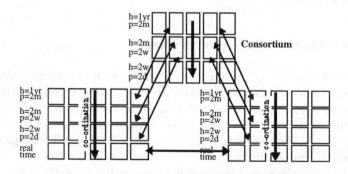

Fig. 10. Consortium with limited co-ordination

4.2   Mapping of Organisations

We shall demonstrate through examples various forms of organisations. In particular we are interested in identifying rules of organisational design to make the best use of the designed decisional structure. Fig. 11 shows a characteristic flat hierarchy, where three managers have distributed among themselves all higher level management, except operational (real time) control. DFs indicated in this figure suggest that co-ordination is achieved from the top (there are no hierarchical control links between the three areas of management). This is acceptable as long as the DFs leave enough freedom for the lower levels to engage in non-hierarchical co-ordinating conversations via their information links.

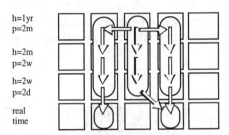

h=1yr
p=2m

h=2m
p=2w

h=2w
p=2d

real
time

Fig. 11. Flat hierarchy

Fig. 12 shows a strong decentralised hierarchy, with too many management layers in the organisation.

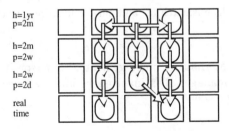

h=1yr
p=2m

h=2m
p=2w

h=2w
p=2d

real
time

Fig. 12. Strong decentralised hierarchy

Fig. 13 shows a case where conflict is created through the way in which organisational roles are assigned to organisational actors. Manager A in 'one hat' dictates to manager B while in 'another hat' A obeys B.

Fig. 14 shows 'narrow' management, strategic level management should be lateral and not compartmentalised into too many small functional areas. This figure also demonstrates the case of skill mismatch; managers are allocated tasks on both strategic and operational levels. For many organisations this is not

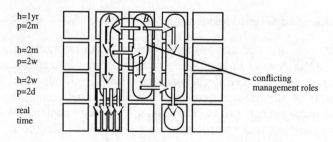

Fig. 13. Conflicting management roles A and B

appropriate, because of the mismatch of skills needed for operational control and strategic management. However, for the professional organisation' [4, 5], strategy making may involve the operational level personnel, in which case there is no skills mismatch.

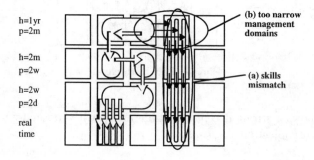

Fig. 14. Skills mismatch (a) and narrow management domain (b)

Fig. 15 shows 'paternalistic' management; the person in job A is not given enough autonomy; manager B is involved in low level decisions which would better be made by person A.

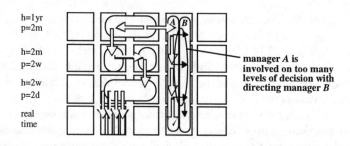

Fig. 15. Paternalistic Management

In this section we have given an introduction to the analysis of organisational properties that organisational mapping is able to identify in the management of the enterprise.

5   Conclusion

We presented a brief overviuew of the GRAI Grid modelling language to model the decision system of an enterprise. We demonstrated the use of multiple grids for the co-ordination of a virtual enterprise and showed that the same decision structure can be implemeneted by different organisational structures. The mapping of organisation to decision structure allowed us to identify typical organisational problems in the enterprise.

References

1. Bernus, P.; Nemes, L.; Williams,T.J. (1996) "Architectures for Enterprise Integration", Chapman and Hall, London.
2. Doumeingts, G. (1985), "How to Decentralise decisions in production management", Computers in Industry, 6 (6) pp 501-514
3. Doumeingts, G.; B.Vallespir,D.; Darracar, M.; Roboam (1987), "Design methodology for advanced manufacturing systems", Computers in Industry, 9(4) pp271-296
4. Mintzberg, H. (1993), "Structure in fives : designing effective organizations" Prentice Hall, London 1993
5. Mintzberg, H. (1994), "The rise and fall of strategic planning", The Free Press, London
6. Mintzberg, H. (1989) "Mintzberg on management: inside our strange world of organizations", Free Press, London

A Cooperative Approach to Distributed Applications Engineering

George Fernandez[1] and Inji Wijegunaratne[2]

[1] Department of Computer Science,
Royal Melbourne Institute of Technology,
Melbourne, Australia
[2] Logica Pty Ltd,
Melbourne, Australia

Abstract. A central problem that researchers and industry analysts are facing is how existing distributed computing technology can be used to derive the most benefits for organisations. There is no consensus as to what constitutes a good distributed application architecture, and there seems to be a lack of understanding of how the different components of a distributed application should appropriately use the communication infrastructure to interact with one another while cooperating to achieve a common goal. Although the model of processing and transactional interactions has served well the traditional applications and database arenas, we contend here that other interaction models should be contemplated when considering a distributed application architecture. In this paper we analyse the nature of communication middleware with respect to the strength of interaction induced by different modes of distributed communication. We model an enterprise as a collection of cooperating distributed application domains, deriving a federated architecture *in context* to support enterprise-wide distributed computing, where tightly and loosely integrated groups of applications, as well as legacy applications, can co-exist and interoperate. This approach intends to minimise the architectural mismatch between the software architecture and organisational reality. The proposed architecture has been successfully applied in Australian industry as a framework for distributed computing.

1 Introduction

In this paper, our central concern is how to develop enterprise-wide distributed applications to support and enhance existing operations, enabling businesses to seize new opportunities. From both technical and organisational political perspectives, it is unrealistic for an enterprise to produce or impose a single global system meeting all of its requirements [10]: typically there are several foci of organisational power [7, 2]; user groups who value their autonomy [8]; possibly geographic distribution of organisational activities; and a variety of already existing systems with their own process, data models and implementation platforms. On the contrary, use of the technology should reflect and support the way the enterprise operates: we take the view that an enterprise-wide system should be based on the cooperation of loosely coupled components, and that naturally-tightly-integrated local domains should be established and allowed to operate with as much autonomy as possible. The system thus becomes the software counterpart of the enterprise, its architecture *in context* [3] reflecting physical and organisational boundaries, enabling the federal model of information exchange proposed by Davenport *et al* [2]. Although there has been considerable interest in the incorporation of distribution issues into development methodologies, so far the majority of research effort has been focused on the extension of current analysis and design techniques to address distributions concerns [9, 12, 6]. These efforts concentrate on the provision of a distributed model of interacting objects, transactions or processes, without including in the analysis a model of the infrastructure that mediates in the interactions. We approach research in distributed applications primarily from the standpoint of distribution: what are the distinctive problems and oportunities of distributing data and processes, and what are the consequences of the different types of interactions in distributed systems for their development, maintenance and enhancement. To date, we have extended Yourdon and Constantine's work on coupling [16] to a distributed environment to form a basis for the development and comparison of application architectures [13, 14].

2   Enterprise Information Technology

2.1   Change Initiatives

In our experience, the information technology structure of an enterprise is the result of management reaction to successive tactical needs. When there is a perceived need for change, an individual assessment is made and a response is implemented. New technology is then brought in, without too much regard for the impact that the new system should have on the rest of the organisation. As a result, even if the new system satisfies the requirements, its benefits are limited to the scope of the department or unit driving the implementation. Several problems can be pointed out with this approach:

- the changes are led by the particular technology of choice, instead of the consideration of how the technology should be used to derive the most benefits for the whole organisation
- the newly introduced system increases the complexity of the information infrastructure because there is no architectural consideration when decisions are made
- there is no integration of the new system with the rest of the enterprise, and when there is, it is via the establishment of point-to-point connections with other individual systems
- the resulting information technology infrastructure typically becomes expensive to maintain and enhance

Alternatively, a decision can be made to implement a very large, monolithic system to cover the new requirements and a number of existing ones. These systems are typically of high complexity, and consequently very expensive and failure prone. There are many reports of these catastrophic failures in the literature, describing the waste of effort and money for little or no result [17]. Often, these projects are abandoned once management become convinced of their impracticability.

Distributed computing was supposed to resolve all these issues. Here there was a chance to integrate what was previously incompatible, divide complex closely-coupled structures and facilitate inter-organisation interaction through carefully planned incremental development. But many industry analysts report otherwise: the cost of distributed computing can be much higher than traditional systems. Distributed systems can be easier to implement and quicker to deliver but, if poorly designed, they can also be very complex, messy to administer, and as unresponsive to change needs as the *status quo*. Our contention is that good design is the key: what is required is an architectural approach, one that leverages the distinctive features of distribution and and makes sure that there is an *effective* use of the technology.

2.2   The Politics of Enterprise Information

Part of the difficulties with the development of distributed applications can be attributed to the lack of consideration for the human structure and functioning of the enterprise by system designers. Generally organisations are comprised of business units or cost centres, under the control of a manager of some status within the enterprise. Due to their differences in leadership, culture, language and goals, these groups are reluctant to share their information since that may lead to outsiders taking unwanted advantage. In this sense, information is treated as currency within the organisation, and it would be naive to expect the owners to give it away. The idea of unfettered cooperation among groups that enjoy their independence, and sometimes even compete with each other, to achieve a common goal is idealistic in the extreme [2].

These units are usually supported by computer systems, running autonomously or semi-autonomously, to help them perform their tasks. Local system administrators have control over the information they manage, and their attitude can reflect the parochialism of the users. Distributed computing technology, if used appropriately, offers the potential to address this type of issues. The implementation of a distributed system incorporating these local components has necessarily a negative impact on their performance, so there should be a determined effort to reduce as much as possible the coupling among components. We take the view that the aim of an enterprise-wide federated architecture should be to enhance data accessibility while minimising disruption to existing component systems. This can be achieved better if users perceive that they keep as much as possible their autonomy, with the global system supporting the right of access to relevant remote data. One such approach is described here.

3   Coupling, Software Dependency, and Middleware

3.1   Middleware

Communication middleware is the infrastructure that enables geographically distributed application components to interact with each other [11]. For the purpose of this paper we primarily classified middleware as SQL-based products, RPC (Remote Procedure Call) products, Distributed Transaction Processing (DTP) monitors, Object Request Brokers and Message Oriented Middleware (MOM).

3.2   Coupling

Coupling was introduced by Yourdon and Constantine [16] in the context of centralised applications as the strength of interconnection between two software modules. When providing guidelines in object-oriented systems, Booch [1] also includes coupling and cohesion as fundamental criteria for the construction of good quality classes and objects. The thrust of these authors' work is that, for software to be easier to understand correct and maintain, a system should be partitioned so that individual software modules are as cohesive as possible while the coupling between modules is as loose as possible. Since current middleware infrastructures enables executing modules to communicate over a network mimicking local interaction, the notion of coupling can be naturally extended to a distributed environment, although with a somewhat more complex connotation. We posit that:

- different degrees of coupling can exist in a distributed system;
- different degrees of coupling are required to satisfy different software dependency needs;
- different types of middleware have different degrees of default coupling associated with them. That is, the properties of a given type of middleware impose by default a certain degree of coupling between application components using that middleware.

3.3   Types of Coupling

The degree of coupling between application components in a distributed application system can be determined by the following criteria:

- Knowledge Coupling: the extent of the knowledge that one component needs to have of another.
- Interface Coupling: the complexity of a component's interface.
- Availability Coupling: the need for *sychronicity*, that is the need for a component to available at the time of effecting a service to another component.

In terms of the three coupling criteria above, this translates to a certain degree of coupling that the middleware imposes on the application; that is, the type of middleware fixes the degree of certain dimensions of coupling. In general, the coupling that a particular distributed application exhibits is a combination of the natural coupling introduced by the middleware, and that introduced by the designer. Our analysis of coupling shows that the greatest extent of coupling is associated with DTP middleware. SQL stored procedures induce the next highest degree of coupling, followed by RPCs and Object Brokers (with dynamic invocation involving a lesser degree of coupling than static invocation). Message Oriented Middleware requires the lowest level of coupling.

Systems with low levels of coupling are easier to implement and maintain [16]. Consequently, when there is a chance, a systems' designer should try to minimise the overall coupling present in the system. This can be done in several ways:

- reducing as much as possible point–to–point connections between components
- adopting a middleware technology appropriate to the interaction taking place
- when coordination is required, using as much as possible the facilities provided by the infrastructure rather than at the application level

3.4 Types of Software Dependency

There are two types of software dependency: Processing dependency occurs when an application component needs, for its own processing, some remote work to be performed. There are two categories: a. Simple Processing Dependency: Application component A cannot progress or complete its processing until another application component B performs some work. b. Distributed Transactional Dependency: A distributed transactional dependency occurs where application component A needs, for its own processing, some work to be performed remotely by other application components in a given order, in an 'all or nothing fashion'. Informational dependency: occurs where there is no expectation of processing associated with a message. That is, as a consequence of some event within its jurisdiction, application component A needs to convey some information to one or more remote components.

3.5 Implementing Software Dependencies

Certain types of middleware are compatible with the types of dependencies that exist in the application system. The level of compatibility is a function of the coupling characteristics of the dependencies and the coupling characteristics of the middleware.

- Simple processing dependency: (non-TP) RPC or RPC-like capability is a suitable implementation candidate.
- Distributed transactional dependency: a distributed transaction processing monitor is needed.
- Informational dependency: asynchronous messaging is the ideal candidate.

Accordingly, where there are dependencies between two or more entities or processes, a decision on transactional vs non- transactional dependency hinges upon the degree of business tolerance to transient inconsistencies. A transient inconsistency can be tolerated under two circumstances:

- an inquiry, processing, or update that entrenches or exacerbates the inconsistency cannot occur in the critical period, or
- the consequences of such an action during transient inconsistency are relatively unimportant.

In our experience, designers often do not adequately exploit opportunities to implement non-transactional interactions. Although processing and transactional interactions are the common paradigms in the area of mainframe applications and databases, message based cooperation has been very successful in areas such as operating systems. The costs of additional coupling introduced when implementing a non-transactional dependency as a transactional interaction in terms of performance, increased complexity and difficulty of maintenance, although significant, are often overlooked. Messaging can be naturally used to implement a certain class of business interactions; one such model is articulated in Section 3 below.

3.6   Software Dependencies and Systems Design

In designing a distributed application system, it is necessary to: (a) identify the dependencies between modules and associated coupling; (b) minimise the discretionary component of coupling; and (c) select the appropriate communication middleware

4   A Federated Architecture

4.1   Application Architecture

In this Section, we develop a particular federated application architecture style for distributed applications.

- The federation consists of several relatively autonomous cooperating domains. Their inter-domain coupling should be as low as possible.
- Each domain contains a single application or related group of applications: a cluster of applications and supporting technology.
- Domains, though largely autonomous, cooperate in order to preserve the integrity of the federation. A domain has responsibilities and obligations to the federation is defined by a contract, which defines the domain interface to the rest federation.

In this architectural form, domains are partitioned such that only information dependencies exist between domains. This partitioning limits the runtime responsibilities of the domain to the federation to maintaining the inter-domain information dependencies. In implementing informational dependencies we have shown [14] that domains need not have responsibility for addressing or acknowledgement, since both can be suitably handled by MOM without loss of integrity. Thus, a domain only "tips over the wall" into a "federal highway" information of more than local significance generated within, and picks up from inter-domain traffic any information of interest. Conceptually, one or more software modules are required at the logical boundary of a domain playing a gatekeeper role to implement the domain's contract to the federation:

- trapping events of global significance within the domain and messages intended for inter-domain travel, and ensuring that these messages are correctly prepared and placed for routing by the inter- domain middleware;
- from inter-domain traffic, selecting those messages relevant to this domain, and passing them on to the appropriate application component within the domain; and
- under abnormal conditions such as recovery from failure, behaving in a pre-specified manner that is understood by the federation.

Since inter-domain dependencies are limited to information dependencies, message-oriented middleware (MOM) is best suited for inter-domain communication. Within a domain application components may exhibit transaction, processing, or information dependencies. Within this federated form, each domain can consist of applications with their own autonomous data and process models such as two-tier or three tier client/server [15], or legacy applications. Data and processes within each domain can grow or change autonomously so long as the inter-domain information dependencies are preserved according to the contract.

4.2 Federated Architecture and Organisational Structure

We propose that the federation be the software counterpart of the enterprise. In partitioning the domains within the enterprise, there are three competing candidates:

- Organisational boundaries:
  (a) boundaries of organisational units such as departments, divisions, etc;
  (b) boundaries of organisational functions [4] or processes [5];
- Physical boundaries: physical locations or sites where the enterprise is located.
- Boundaries of the existing application architecture.

In addition to supporting structure and process, this architecture supports a range of organisational behaviours as well. Davenport et al [2] propose federalism, a model where potentially competing or non-cooperating parties are brought together to cooperate by negotiation, as the preferred archetype in most circumstances. The proposed federated architecture is well placed to support this type of behaviour: the exclusion of processing and transaction dependencies from inter-domain interactions mean that a process belonging to another domain does not exert control (as in locking records during a distributed transaction) over local processes or resources. This represents the extension into the organisational domain of Yourdon and Constantine's [16] dictum of the scope of effect not exceeding the scope of control. Furthermore, the external interface to the domain, provided by the gatekeeper software is confined to the information placed in and read from the inter-domain MOM. Apart from this window into it, a domain is made opaque to other domains. Hence, the nature and extent of the domain's dealings with the federation can be negotiated, and the internal workings of the domain are exposed to the federation to only the extent that the organisational owners of the domain are comfortable. The outcome of the negotiation is the contract, which determines the domain's runtime behaviour vis-a-vis the enterprise. This federated architecture attempts to minimise the "architectural mismatch" between the software architecture and organisational reality. (We extend the term "architectural mismatch", originally proposed by Garlan *et al* [3] to describe assumptions in the technical domain that conflict with reality, into the organisational domain).

4.3 Benefits

This architectural form has the following advantages:

- Inter-domain dependencies, being only informational dependencies, require far looser coupling than others types of dependency, especially in the dimensions of application and infrastructure knowledge. Therefore, as the enterprise-wide system grows, this architectural form imposes much less administrative and maintenance overhead when compared with other types of dependency between domains, and therefore it is easier to operate and maintain.
- The architecture is scalable to enterprises encompassing several remote sites, in different locations or even different countries. The architecture may be extended to accommodate a group of companies or a multinational with country-based subsidiaries, and also to cover interactions of two or more enterprises who agree to cooperate along certain well-defined lines.
- Inter-domain communication, being message based, can be flexibly implemented over a wide variety of, probable heterogeneous, technologies such as LANs, WANs, Intranets, Web-based technologies, etc.
- There is the greatest possible autonomy within a domain, so that a domain is free to change and grow without the constraints placed by tighter coupling/dependency with other domains.
- The domains discharge their wider responsibilities by "throwing over the wall" required information, so that the work within a domain is insulated from conditions existing outside the domain.
- Legacy applications can be integrated relatively easily into this framework, to have a whole or part of a domain consisting of legacy applications. Limiting inter-domain dependencies to informational dependencies means that

the scope of effect of legacy applications can be contained within a domain. Furthermore, in general, message-oriented middleware offers the easiest connectivity to legacy applications.

- With informational dependencies/MOMs, synchronicity of sender and receiver does not matter. Therefore, messages can be sent as the events occur, or as consolidated information at designated times. Messages can be read as they arrive, or at convenient designated times. This provides a great deal of flexibility of the timing/scheduling of inter-domain communications.

- A great deal of congruence is possible between the architecture on the one hand and the organisational structure, as well as the politics of organisational behaviour on the other. Given that the development of enterprise-wide distributed applications would involve the bringing together of disparate parties at all stages of the software life-cycle, this is the preferred paradigm. The concept of domains embodies the idea of independent organisational units brought together by cooperation, rather than imposition or confrontation.

References

1. Booch G. *Object-Oriented Design with Applications*   2nd Edition, Benjamin-Cummings, California, 1991.
2. Davenport T. H., Eccles R. G., Prusak L.. *Information Politics* Sloan Management Review, Fall 1992
3. Garlan D., Allen R., Ockerbloom J. *Architectural Mismatch: Why Reuse Is So Hard* IEEE Software, Nov 1995, pp 17-26
4. Gerloff, E. A. *Organisational Theory and Design* A Strategic Approach to Management, McGraw-Hill, 1985.
5. Hammer, M. & Champy, J. *Reengineering the Corporation*. Harper Business, Harper-Collins Publishers, New York.
6. Henderson-Sellers B., Edwards, J.M. *BOOKTWO of Object-Oriented Knowledge: The Working Object* Prentice-Hall, Sydney, 1994.
7. Kling, R. *Social Analysis of Computing* Computing Surveys, Vol 12 p 60-110, 1980.
8. Land, F. Detjejaruwat, N. and Smith, C. *Factors Affecting Social Control: The Reasons and Values* Systems, Objectives, Solutions, Elsevier Science Publishers, 1983
9. Low G.C., Rasmussen G., and Henderson-Sellers B. *Incorporation of Distributed Computing Concerns into Object- Oriented Methodologies* . Journal of Object-Oriented Programming 9 (3), pg 12-20, 1996.
10. Norrie M, Schaad W., Scheck H-J, Wunderli, M. *Exploiting Multidatabase Technology for CIM* ETZ Institute Technical Report No 219, Zurich, July 1994
11. Orfali, R. Harkey, D. and Edwards, J. *Essential Client/Server Guide* Van Nostrand Reinhold, 1994.
12. Shatz, S.M. *Development of Distributed Software: Concepts and Tools* Macmillan, New York, 1993.
13. Wijegunaratne, I. K., and Fernandez, G. Coupling and Dependency: the Key to Distributed Applications Engineering, submitted for publication to IEEE Software, 1996.

14. Wijegunaratne, I. K., Fernandez, G.: *A Federated Application Architecture for the Enterprise*, submitted to the Joint International Conference On Open Distributed Processing (ICODP) And Distributed Platforms (ICDP), Toronto, Canada, May 27-30, 1997
15. Wijegunaratne, I. K. *The Structure and Behaviour of Distributed Client/Server ApplicationsA Three-tier Application Architecture* to appear on the Australian Computer Journal.
16. Yourdon, E., Constantine, L.: *Structured Design*, Prentice-Hall, 1979.
17. Land F., Lequense P., Wijegunaratne I.: *Effective Systems: Overcoming the Obstacles*, Journal of Information Technology, Vol 4 (2), June 1990

Towards Logic Programming Based Coordination in Virtual Worlds

Paul Tarau[1], Veronica Dahl[2] and Koen De Bosschere[3]

[1] Université de Moncton
Département d'Informatique
Moncton, N.B. Canada E1A 3E9,
tarau@info.umoncton.ca
[2] Logic and Functional Programming Group
Department of Computing Sciences
Simon Fraser University
Burnaby, B.C. Canada V5A 1S6
veronica@cs.sfu.ca
[3] Vakgroep Elektronica en Informatiesystemen,
Universiteit Gent
St.-Pietersnieuwstraat 41
B-9000 Gent, Belgium
kdb@elis.rug.ac.be

Abstract. We propose a unified framework for coordination in multi-user Virtual Worlds, based on our experience with LogiMOO, a BinProlog+Linda based programmable shared Virtual World. LogiMOO adopts unification for pattern retrieval while using exclusively deterministic operations, unlike most Prolog based Linda systems. Moving beyond the Linda framework LogiMOO is based on, we describe a coordination logic for agent programming based on ideas from (affine) linear logic and Java's synchronized object system as well as a set of new primitives describing uniformly Linda operation, database updates and hypothetical assumptions.

The main novelty is that our constructs emphasize an 'object based' approach, with synchronization information built in 'container objects' and allowing more flexible wait/notify negotiations between consumer/producer agent components, as well as inheritance and agent component reuse.

Our experiments with agent coding in LogiMOO and Java and interaction with external visual and logic components, show the practicality of our constructs for real life programming.

Keywords: coordination languages, blackboard-based logic programming, distributed programming, groupware, virtual worlds, Internet applications

1 Introduction

MUDs and MOOs (Multi User Domains - Object Oriented) have started with virtual presence and interaction. Their direct descendents, Virtual Worlds are a strong unifying metaphor for various forms of net-walk, net-chat and Internet-based virtual presence in general. They start where usual HTML shows its limitations: they do have state and require some form of virtual presence. "Being there" is the first step towards full virtualization of concrete ontologies, from entertainment and games to schools and businesses.

Some fairly large-scale projects (Intel's Moondo [12], Sony's Cyber Passage [16], Black Sun's CyberGate [2], Worlds Inc.'s AlphaWorld [24]) converge all towards a common interaction metaphor: an avatar represents each participant in a multi-user virtual world. Information exchange reuses our basic intuitions with almost instant *learnability* for free.

The sophistication of their interaction metaphor, with VRML landscapes and realistic 'avatars' moving in shared multi-user virtual spaces, will require soon high-level agent programming tools, once the initial fascination with 'looking' human is translated into automation of complex behavior. Towards this end, high-level coordination and deductive reasoning abilities are among the most important additions to various virtual world modeling languages. This paper proposes such a "coordination logic" which comes out from our experiments in programming agents for the LogiMOO Virtual World as well as some agent programming techniques in high-level distributed programming framework.

2   LogiMOO: A multi-paradigm virtual world

LogiMOO [8, 23, 18] is a BinProlog-based Virtual World running under Netscape or Internet Explorer for distributed group-work over the Internet and user-crafted virtual places, virtual objects and agents.

LogiMOO is implemented on top of a multi-threaded blackboard-based logic programming system (Multi-BinProlog 5.25) [19] featuring Linda-style coordination[1]. Virtual blackboards [9] allow efficient mirroring of remote sites over TCP/IP links while Solaris 2.x threads ensure high-performance local client-server dynamics.

Embedding in Netscape (Fig. 1) allows advanced VRML or HTML frame-based navigation and multi-media support, while LogiMOO handles virtual presence and acts as a very high-level universal object broker.

The LogiMOO kernel behaves as any other MOO while offering a choice between interactive Prolog syntax and a Controlled English parser allowing people unfamiliar with Prolog to get along with the basic activities of the MOO: place and object creation, moving from one place to the other, giving/selling virtual objects, talking ('whisper' and 'say'). At login time, a main interactive shell and background notifier (for messages and events targeted to the user) are created. Netscape 3.0 is used to implement CGI-based BinProlog *remote toplevel* interacting with a remote LogiMOO server (Fig. 2). Objects in LogiMOO are represented as hyper-links (URLs) towards their owners' home pages where their

---

[1] An important difference between Multi-BinProlog and predecessors like [4] is direct use of Linda operations, instead of a guard notation.

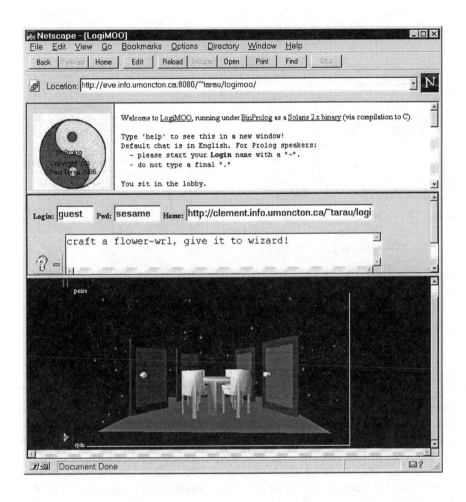

Fig. 1. LogiMOO as a Netscape application

'native' representation actually resides in various formats (HTML, VRML, GIF, JPEG etc.).

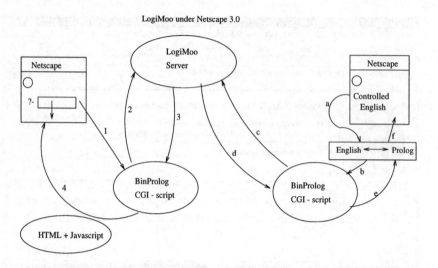

Fig. 2. LogiMOO on the Web

2.1   LogiMOO's Linda operations

Linda [7] based frameworks like Multi-BinProlog [9] offer a wide variety of *blocking* and *non-blocking* as well as *non-deterministic* blackboard operations (backtracking through alternative answers). For reasons of embeddability in multiparadigm environments and semantic simplicity we have decided to drop nondeterminism and return to a subset close to the original Linda operators (combined with unification), and a simple client-server architecture (although LogiMOO's design is now rapidly evolving towards a 'web of interconnected worlds').

```
out(X): puts X on the server
in(X):  waits until it can take an object matching X from the server
all(X,Xs): reads the list Xs matching X currently on the server
run(Goal): starts a thread executing Goal
halt: stops current thread
```

The presence of the all/2 collector compensates for the lack of nondeterministic operations. Note that the only blocking operation is in/1. Notice that blocking rd/1 is easily emulated in terms of in/1 and out/1, while non-blocking rd/1 is emulated with all/2.

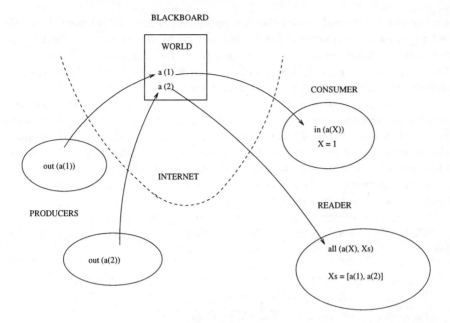

Fig. 3. Basic Linda operations

3   A Coordination Logic for Agents

To be able to put together complex agent scripts it is convenient to see agents as
sets of synchronized behaviors ('scripts') each performing a 'component' action
(this is quite close to the usual way to do event-driven visual programming). To
go beyond simple agent programming and to be able to reuse agent components
through inheritance mechanisms, a further step, beyond the Linda coordination
protocol is needed. The basic ingredients are:

- Linda [7] + unification
- a variant of *linear logic* [10] with good computational properties [13], *affine*
  logic
- an emphasis on distributing the produce/consume and wait/notify 'negotiation' in 'code' as well as in the 'data'

Our proposed 'coordination logic' has this objective in mind. Moreover, we will
show that a natural concept of 'mobile agent' emerges as agents 'go' (as in
any MOO) from one place to another. Our coordination logic will be described
informally as set of primitive operations.

We have two classes of objects, *components* and *containers*. Every container
is also a component (as usual in windowing classes of OO languages). Note that
a container is, in general, a dynamic entity, corresponding to a set of terms on
a blackboard, matching an object through unification. In particular, a fixed set
of components associated to a given key qualifies as a container.

Objects can be either *clonable, unique* or *empty* (the null object). Clonable objects allow *arbitrary* uses through *copying*, unique objects are usable only *once*. Attempts to clone or use an *empty* object generates an *exception*.

Components inherit such properties from the containers they belong to, although, as usual, overriding can be used if necessary.

A component can be *moved* from one container to another. An *agent* is a set of *behaviors* describing such operations, as well as the usual code for logical inferences and arithmetics. Each behavior is usually attached to its own thread, although thread sharing mechanisms can be used on some machines for actual implementations. An agent *'located'* in a container is called an *avatar*.

Agents performing actions on objects can either *fail, succeed, wait* (to succeed) or *warn* about an *error* or *exception*.

The exact behavior of an agent in a `move(Object,From,To)` transaction is negotiated by interaction between its *'intentions'* and the nature of the container where the object is located, as follows:

- if 'From' is a *clonable* container 'Object' is *copied* to 'To'
- if 'From' is a *unique* container 'Object' is *moved* to 'To'
- an agent is free to *wait* or *fail* while 'From' is *empty*

Roughly speaking, *containers* and *components* can be described in terms of any abstract data structure manipulating finite *dynamic* power sets. We will give here an executable specification of these operations in terms of affine linear logic, implemented in the subset supported by BinProlog [21]. When interaction of an agent is described, a `move/3` transaction is relativized into either a `get(Object,From)` or a `put(Object,To)` operation with the 'hand' of the agent seen as a container with its own attributes.

3.1   Containers on top of linear and intuitionistic assumptions

BinProlog's intuitionistic `assumei/1` adds temporarily a clause usable in subsequent proofs. Such a clause can be used an indefinite number of times, like asserted clauses, except that it vanishes on backtracking.

Its scoped versions `Clause=>Goal` and `[File]=>Goal` make `Clause` or respectively the set of clauses found in `File`, available only during the proof of `Goal`. Clauses assumed with `=>` are usable an indefinite number of times in the proof, e.g. `a(13) => (a(X),a(Y))` will succeed.

Linear `assumel/1` adds a clause usable *at most once* in subsequent proofs. Being usable *at most once* distinguishes *affine* linear logic from Girard's original framework where linear assumptions should be used *exactly* once. This assumption also vanishes on backtracking. Its scoped version `Clause -: Goal` or `[File] -: Goal` makes `Clause` or the set of clauses found in `File` available only during the proof of Goal. They vanish on backtracking and each clause is usable at most once in the proof, i.e. `a(13) -: (a(X),a(Y))` will fail. Note however, that `a(13) -: a(12) -: a(X)` will succeed with X=12 as alternative X=13 as answers, while its non-affine counterpart a(13) -o a(12) -o a(X) as implemented in Lolli or Lygon, would fail.

We can see the assumel/1 and assumei/1 builtins as linear affine and respectively intuitionistic implication scoped over the current AND-continuation, i.e. having their assumptions available in future computations on the *same* resolution branch.

Negotiating linear or intuitionistic behavior In various uses of linear assumptions as well as Linda operation it turned out that, most of the time, the intended behavior came out through a 'negotiation' between 'definition-time' and 'use-time' intents, possibly belonging to different agent components. We shall illustrate this in the case of our use of linear and intuitionistic assumptions, by going through the code needed to implement a basic set of MOO operations.

First, let us introduce some convenient notations[2].

```
% these operators introduce a more flexible
% Prolog syntax for our constructs
:-op(400,fx,(*)).
:-op(400,fx,(-)).    :-op(400,xfx,(-)).
:-op(400,fx,(?)).    :-op(400,xfx,(?)).

+X:-assumel(X). % linear assumption
*X:-assumei(X). % intuitionistic assumption
-X:-assumed(X). % use or consumption of an assumption
```

We are now able to express a typical instance of *negotiation*: the ability at *use* time to override some of the *definition time* intentions.

```
% This checks if assumed but refuses to consume even if linear!
?X:- -X, (\+ -X -> assumel(X) ; true).
```

Some more convenient notations:

```
X?Y:- ?contains(X,Y). % checks
X-Y:- -contains(X,Y). % consumes if linear!
```

Next, let us extract information about the nature of the assumptions and express how to enforce that a given type of assumption should be used:

```
if_assumed(X,How):-
   \+ (-X, -X)->How=linear
; \+ \+ -X -> How=intuitionistic
; fail.

assumed(X,How):- -X,
   ( \+ -X -> How=linear
   ; How=intuitionistic
```

---

[2] Actually, part of BinProlog starting with version 5.82.

```
).

assume(linear,X):- +X.
assume(intuitionistic,X):- *X.
```

Downward propagation of container properties At this point, we are ready to describe how properties of containers are inherited downward:

```
% creates a new Container inheriting
% the type of assumption from its parent
make_new(Container,Component,How):-
  if_assumed(contains(_,Container),How),
  make_name(Container,Component).

% make a new name for a component if necessary
make_name(_,Component):-nonvar(Component),!.
make_name(Container,Component):-var(Component),
  ( -counter(Container,Ctr)->NewCtr is Ctr+1
  ; NewCtr is 1
  ),
  + counter(Container,NewCtr),
  termcat(Container,NewCtr,Component).
```

3.2   Creating and moving components

Finally, let us introduce some 'user level' operations:

```
% creates Component as required by Container
Container<<Component :-
  make_new(Container,Component,How),
  put(Component,Container,How).

% move Component to Container, when allowed
Component>>Container :-
  get(Component,_,How),
  put(Component,Container,How).

% take and drop a component from/to a container
get(Component,From,How):-
  assumed(contains(From,Component),How).
put(Component,Container,How):-
  assume(How,contains(Container,Component)).
```

3.3   Comparison with Linda

The main difference with Linda [7] is that the *decision on blocking* is not solely left to the agent but also depends on the *nature of the container* where the agent acts.

The main inspiration comes from linear logic where the *future use* of a *resource* is decided at creation time. Not only this corresponds to more realistic assumptions about the structure of the interaction, but it also seems the simplest way to implement *physicality* constraints in the virtual world. For instance, in a container with 'gravity' or near a 'wall' the decision to block or unblock is not fully in the agent's hand. This also makes implementation of security mechanisms easier, by the ability to impose predefined behaviors on agents.

Moreover, by inheriting from complex 'container trees' (containers built of other containers and leaf components), the full power of an object oriented programming style becomes available. This promises to enhance 'procedure' oriented agent programming techniques with ability to reuse agent components.

A more refined protocol allowing to 'negotiate' behavior as a result of the agent's intentions and the constraints imposed upon them by the containers where they are 'located' as well as synchronization expressed in terms of Java's wait/notify primitives has been used in a prototype implementation.

3.4   Specifying MOO commands

Let us describe a basic set of MOO commands on top of our executable specification[3]:

```
login(Who):-
   new(avatar,Who), % adds avatar information
   lobby<<Who,
   +whoami(Who).

logout:- -whoami(_).

dig(P)  :- place<<P.

whereami(P):-
   ?whoami(Me),
   P?Me,
   is_place(P).
```

3.5   Agent scripts

A simple two-agent script looks as follows[4]:

```
go:-
   init, % creates prototypes 'unique' and 'clonable'
   prelude, % MOO initialization prelude
   login(wizard),
   dig(room),
```

---

[3] Combined with a few obvious intermediate predicate definitions.

[4] To fully emulate multi-threaded execution, a slightly more complex, continuation based scheduling mechanism can be used in BinProlog, as in [20].

```
 go(room),
 craft(flower),
 move(flower,lobby),
logout,
login(mary),
 clone(poem),
 take(poem,Clonable),go(room),
 drop(poem,Clonable),
logout.
```

Note that 'physicality' of an object like *flower* is inherited from 'unique' containers specified in terms of linear assumptions. On the other hand, an explicit 'clone' operation is defined to deal with 'overriding' such constraints in case of an 'informational' object like *poem*, which is intended to be disseminated indefinitely.

Note also that 'containers' are convenient abstractions which materialize as computer/path/server/database information very much as in the well known Windows'95 desktop which shows various system components in an uniform way. For mobile code, 'going through' various MOO components materializes as moving from one server to the other or from one database to the other on the same server.

4   Assumptions: Towards a unified view on local and distributed state

After working with various forms of assumptions/grammars, Linda based distributed programming or just plain assert/retract of Prolog we have found out that a unified view of all of them is possible through the following two primitives:

```
define_assumption(<clonable>,<backtrackable>,<local>,<before>,CLAUSE)
              |<unique>    |<committed>   |<remote>,|<after>

use_assumption( <as_is>,            <wait>,      GOAL)
               |<force_remove> |<fail>
               |<force_keep>
```

Our claim is that appropriate values for <flags> cover these operations in a unified framework, while hinting towards a code sharing in implementation technology. Informally, here are their intended meanings:

- a *clonable* assumption can be used an arbitrary number of times, with variables standardized apart on each use
- a *unique* assumption is intended to be consumed upon its first use with bindings propagating between the definition point and the point of use, through unification
- a *backtrackable* assumption is local to the current AND-continuation (resolution branch) while a *committed* is intended to be available on other branches by 'surviving failure'

- a *local* assumption ranges over the current process/thread while a *remote* assumption is considered to be *at* a (default) remote site (usually another computer/process/thread) in live communication with the local process/thread
- flags in `use_assumption` are intended to allow overriding/negotiation of definition time intents
  - *as_is* means that the definition time intent prevails
  - *force_remove* means that the assumption should be unavailable for future uses, whatever definition time clonable/unique properties were assigned to it
  - *force_keep* means that the assumption should be kept available for future uses, whatever definition time clonable/unique properties were assigned to it
- the *wait* flag (in practice wait(N) with N=wait timeout) indicates that the current process/thread should block until its intended definition or use time action can take place, while the *fail* flag indicates that immediate failure should be signaled

Here is (part of) the BinProlog code for `define_assumption` / `use_assumption`:

```
define_assumption(clonable,backtrackable,local,before,Clause):-!,
  assumeia(Clause).
define_assumption(clonable,backtrackable,local,after,Clause):-!,
  assumei(Clause).
define_assumption(unique,backtrackable,local,before,Clause):-!,
  assumela(Clause).
define_assumption(unique,backtrackable,local,before,Clause):-!,
  assumel(Clause).
define_assumption(unique,backtrackable,local,after,Clause):-!,
  assumel(Clause).
define_assumption(clonable,committed,local,before,Clause):-!,
  asserta(Clause).
define_assumption(clonable,committed,local,after,Clause):-!,
  assertz(Clause).
define_assumption(clonable,committed,remote,after,Clause):-!,
  out(Clause). % Linda operation
...........
define_assumption(RessourcePolicy,UndoPolicy,Extent,Position,Clause):-
  errmes(
    not_implemented(RessourcePolicy, UndoPolicy, Position, Extent),
    Clause
  ).

use_assumption(as_is,fail,Goal):-is_dynamic(Goal),Goal.
..........
use_assumption(force_remove,wait,Goal):-!,
  in(Goal). % blocking Linda operation
use_assumption(as_is,fail,Goal):-!,
  rd(Goal). % non-blocking Linda operation
..........
```

```
use_assumption(ForceResourcePolicy, BlockOrFail, Clause):-
  errmes(
    not_implemented(ForceResourcePolicy, BlockOrFail),
    Clause
  ).
```

Note that some flag combinations require restrictions on the nature of their data and that some have not yet been implemented in any LP languages we know of.

Clearly, this one-to-one mapping can be used backwards to support all the well-known operations through our proposed higher level operations. With respect to covering grammars, we refer to [21] for an emulation of the equivalent of (extended) Definite Clause Grammars in terms of Linear Assumptions.

Note that these general operations allow expressing our coordination logic as well as other aspects of assumptions as being local or remote and being backtrackable or not.

The key idea behind them is also the ability to express the negotiation between *definition time* and *use time* agent intentions, allowing a 'constructive' (and automated) dialog between *creators* and *users* of data. Note also that an implementation having `define_assumption` and `use_assumption` as primitives and emulating `assume/assert/Linda/grammars` in terms of them, would allow a very important amount of code reuse.

5   Related work

Virtual Worlds technologies pioneered by [2, 16, 24, 12] are becoming part of 'standard setting' applications like Netscape Communicator or Internet Explorer. Most of them concentrate on the interaction metaphor and/or visualization without a principled approach to the underlying coordination logic.

A growing number of sophisticated Web-based applications and tools are on the way to be implemented in LP/CLP languages. Among them, work with a similar emphasis on can be found in [5, 15, 6, 3, 17, 14, 23].

Among the most promising recent developments Luca Cardelli's Oblique project at Digital and mobile agent applications [1] and IBM Japan's aglets [11]. We share their emphasis on going beyond *code mobility* as present in Java, for instance, towards *control mobility*. We think that distributed containers with ability to negotiate with agents the resulting local and global behavior can offer a secure and flexible approach to Internet aware distributed programming.

6   Conclusion and future work

The proposed coordination logic can be seen as an adaptation of the Linda protocol to some of the challenges of agent programming in Virtual Worlds. Our

constructs emphasize an 'object based' approach, with synchronization information built in 'container objects' and allowing more flexible wait/notify negotiations between consumer/producer agent components, as well as inheritance and
agent component reuse.

The current BinProlog implementation had to go beyond our initial abstract
framework. The clonable/unique distinction is a very powerful one but in practice it is replaced by arbitrary filtering interpreters which can be customized to
support arbitrary negotiations with remote agents and are plugged in generic
servers. The practical implementation is built on proven client/server technology, on top of a generic socket package, while giving the illusion of a 'Web of
MOOs' with roaming mobile agents at the next level of abstraction.

A Java based Linda implementation, using a minimal set of logic programming components (unification, associative search) has been recently released (the
Java TermServer, available at http://clement.info.umoncton.ca/BinProlog). It
allows to communicate bidirectionally with the existing LogiMOO framework,
allowing creation of combined Java/Prolog programs. In particular, Java applets
can be used as front end in browser instead of the more resource consuming CGIs
currently LogiMOO is based on.

Intelligence and flexible metaprogramming on the logic programming side
combined with visualization and WWW programming abilities on the Java side
will allow easy component integration in various concrete containers.

Acknowledgment

We thank for support from NSERC (grants OGP0107411 and 611024), and from
the FESR of the Université de Moncton. Special thanks go to Daniel Perron for
long discussions helping to come out with the initial idea of LogiMOO, to Koen
De Bosschere for the implementation of the Multi-BinProlog Linda engine and to
Stephen Rochefort for his comments on the design and his help on implementing
LogiMOO's natural language component.

References

1. K. A. Bharat and L. Cardelli. Migratory applications. In *Proceedings of the
   8th Annual ACM Symposium on User Interface Software and Technology*, Nov.
   1995. http://gatekeeper.dec.com/pub/DEC/SRC/research-reports/abstracts/src-
   rr-138.html.
2. BlackSun. CyberGate. http://www.blacksun.com/.
3. P. Bonnet, L. Bressnan S., Leth, and B. Thomsen. Towards ECLIPSE Agents on
   the Internet. In Tarau et al. [22]. http://clement.info.umoncton.ca/ lpnet.
4. A. Brogi and P. Ciancarini. The concurrent language, shared Prolog. *TOPLAS*,
   13(1):99–123, 1991.
5. D. Cabeza and M. Hermenegildo. html.pl: A HTML Package for (C)LP systems.
   Technical report, 1996. Available from http://www.clip.dia.fi.upm.es.
6. D. Cabeza and M. Hermenegildo. The Pillow/CIAO Library for Internet/WWW
   Programming using Computational Logic Systems. In Tarau et al. [22].
   http://clement.info.umoncton.ca/ lpnet.

7. N. Carriero and D. Gelernter. Linda in context. *CACM*, 32(4):444–458, 1989.
8. K. De Bosschere, D. Perron, and P. Tarau. LogiMOO: Prolog Technology for Virtual Worlds. In *Proceedings of PAP'96*, pages 51–64, London, Apr. 1996. ISBN 0 9525554 1 7.
9. K. De Bosschere and P. Tarau. Blackboard-based Extensions in Prolog. *Software — Practice and Experience*, 26(1):49–69, Jan. 1996.
10. J.-Y. Girard. Linear logic. *Theoretical Computer Science*, (50):1–102, 1987.
11. IBM. Aglets. http://www.trl.ibm.co.jp/aglets.
12. Intel. Moondo. http://www.intel.com/iaweb/moondo/index.htm.
13. A. P. Kopylov. Decidability of linear affine logic. In *Proceedings, Tenth Annual IEEE Symposium on Logic in Computer Science*, pages 496–504, San Diego, California, 26–29 June 1995. IEEE Computer Society Press.
14. S. W. Locke, A. Davison, and S. L. Lightweight Deductive Databases for the World-Wide Web. In Tarau et al. [22]. http://clement.info.umoncton.ca/ lpnet.
15. S. W. Loke and A. Davison. Logic programming with the world-wide web. In *Proceedings of the 7th ACM Conference on Hypertext*, pages 235–245. ACM Press, 1996.
16. Sony. Cyber Passage. http://vs.sony.co.jp/VS-E/vstop.html.
17. P. Szeredi, K. Molnár, and R. Scott. Serving Multiple HTML Clients from a Prolog Application. In Tarau et al. [22]. http://clement.info.umoncton.ca/ lpnet.
18. P. Tarau. Logic Programming and Virtual Worlds. In *Proceedings of INAP96*, Tokyo, Nov. 1996. keynote address.
19. P. Tarau. BinProlog 5.40 User Guide. Technical Report 97-1, Département d'Informatique, Université de Moncton, Apr. 1997. Available from *http://clement.info.umoncton.ca/BinProlog*.
20. P. Tarau and V. Dahl. Logic Programming and Logic Grammars with First-order Continuations. In *Proceedings of LOPSTR'94*, Pisa, June 1994.
21. P. Tarau, V. Dahl, and A. Fall. Backtrackable State with Linear Affine Implication and Assumption Grammars. In J. Jaffar and R. H. Yap, editors, *Concurrency and Parallelism, Programming, Networking, and Security*, Lecture Notes in Computer Science 1179, pages 53–64, Singapore, Dec. 1996. Springer.
22. P. Tarau, A. Davison, K. De Bosschere, and M. Hermenegildo, editors. *Proceedings of the 1st Workshop on Logic Programming Tools for INTERNET Applications*, JICSLP'96, Bonn, Sept. 1996. http://clement.info.umoncton.ca/ lpnet.
23. P. Tarau and K. De Bosschere. Virtual World Brokerage with BinProlog and Netscape. In Tarau et al. [22]. http://clement.info.umoncton.ca/ lpnet.
24. Worlds. AlphaWorld. http://www.worlds.net/products/alphaworld.

Enhancement of Creative Aspects of a Daily Conversation with a Topic Development Agent

Kazushi Nishimoto, Yasuyuki Sumi, and Kenji Mase

ATR Media Integration & Communications Research Laboratories,
2-2 Hikari-dai, Seika-cho, Soraku-gun, Kyoto 619-02 Japan
Tel: +81 774 95 1442 Fax: +81 774 95 1408
email: {knishi/sumi/mase}@mic.atr.co.jp

Abstract. Daily informal conversations are highly creative activities. However, it is hard for most ordinary creativity support systems and discussion support systems to deal with daily conversations because they are done in environments characterized as free. In this paper, we propose a topic-development agent that is adaptable to daily conversations and that enhances the creative aspects of the conversations by entering them as an equal participant with the human participants and keeping the conversation lively. This agent autonomously detects novel directions in which new topics can be developed in conversations, and provides a piece of information which can likely form the seed of a new topic. From the experimental results, it is suggested that this agent can provide timely information to introduce a new topic and that the agent has the ability to effectively coordinate the creative aspects of daily conversations.

1 Introduction

A daily informal conversation can be a very creative activity. More specifically, we can obtain not only new information but also new ideas, inspirations and clues for solving difficult problems in a daily conversation with colleagues or friends. In this paper, we describe an agent that participates in on-line conversations as a normal participant, not as a moderator, and activates the conversations in order to enhance their creative aspects.

A daily conversation can be regarded as a mixture of divergent thinking and convergent thinking, which are two of the significant, but usually not distinguished, processes involved in human creative thinking [1]. Namely, in such a conversation, various pieces of information are first provided as the utterances of the participants (i.e., the divergent stage). Then, if a participant finds some relevance among some of the information or between some of the information and the participant's own knowledge (i.e., the convergent stage), the participant provides a new topic based on that relevance. Thus, the conversation progresses to a new phase, and this continues by alternating the divergent and convergent stages. Both the divergent thinking and the convergent thinking are done more deeply and broadly in lively conversations where many participants provide many utterances. Therefore, the creative aspects of conversations are especially remarkable in lively conversations.

Several CSCW systems which support the creative aspects of discussions have been developed. Such systems usually impose some special restrictions (or certain special attitudes) on the users. For instance, gIBIS [2] requests users to always declare the position of each utterance: support, objection and so on. DOLPHIN [3] requests users to group all of the opinions and to arrange the groups in a tree structure. Such requirements induce the effectiveness of the systems. On the other hand, however, the requirements isolate the system tasks from daily routine work and make it difficult for people to use the systems. Recently, to tackle this problem, it has been pointed out that creativity support systems should be more intimately linked with daily routine work and daily activities [4]. In particular, focus has been placed on daily conversations which are found in environment with a lot of freedom and few restrictions.

Hence, in order to support daily conversations, we should eliminate unusual restrictions as much as possible. Therefore, an agent named "conversationalist", which is described in this paper, was developed to play the role of a general participant, not a moderator. We think that the existence of a moderator causes a different atmosphere from that of a daily conversation. The agent supports the creative aspects of a conversation by autonomously providing pieces of information that might form the seeds of new topics; these pieces are normal utterances based on the situation of the conversation and the agent's own viewpoint. Boden pointed out that transformation of a conceptual space and exploration within the space are fundamental to human creativity, and that an agent can effectively help in this transformation and exploration [5]. The agent we describe in this paper supports humans in transforming and exploring the conversation space.

Section 2 describes conversation model which we assume in order to construct the conversationalist. In section 3, we mention the strategy to keep conversations lively. Section 4 describes the implementation of the conversationalist in detail. Section 5 shows an experimental conversation with the conversationalist and discusses the results. Section 6 shows methods to create conversation support agents with various characteristics. Section 7 gives brief conclusion and shows the future works.

2   Conversation Model

Since this research deals with daily conversations, neither the number of participants, nor the domains of topics are restricted, and the goal of a conversation need not be evident. We assume only the following conditions:

1. **A two-level structure of topics**

   We assume there are two levels of topics in our target conversation: a global topic and local topics. The global topic persists through the whole conversation, and each local topic is a partial topic under the global topic. A conversation, therefore, consists of successive local topics. It is assumed that a local topic does not have sub-topics.

2. **Cooperative conversation transition control**

   In a daily conversation (without a moderator), it often happens that a participant leads the conversation by focusing on a certain topic, and if the seed of a new topic is provided by another participant and the new topic is accepted by the others, a topic transition occurs and the participant who provided the new topic leads the conversation. Thus, we can regard all of the participants as cooperatively and individually watching and controlling the conversation transitions by successively taking turns as leader. Moreover, this cooperative work emerges nonintentionally. Each participant indirectly controls the conversation by providing pieces of information as normal utterances, not utterances for explicitly controlling the directions of the conversation.

Note that users need not be conscious of the assumptions in conversations with the conversationalist. There is no problem for users to use the conversationalist even if they think there is a nest-structure of topics in a conversation, or even if they have no idea about conversation transition mechanisms. The assumptions are needed only for the conversationalist to grasp the situation of a conversation and to decide how to act in each situation. Therefore, the assumptions do not obstruct the features of daily conversations, i.e., freeness and non-restrictiveness.

3   Strategy to Activate a Conversation

At least the following two conditions can be regarded as characteristics of a lively conversation:

1. Topics change often enough, and
2. Topics are compatible with the participants' interests.

The conversationalist always intends to ensure these two conditions.

To ensure that topics change often enough, the conversationalist always monitors the transition of topics. When a standstill is detected, the conversationalist intervenes in the conversation and provides a piece of information that can form the seed of a new topic.

To ensure that the introduced topics are of interest to the participants and to obtain information to help introduce new topics, the conversationalist continuously monitors the development structure of the topics. This structure effectively reflects the participants' interests. It is not good enough, however, for the extracted pieces of information to be only those directly relevant to the current topics. Such information does not help to change the topics but instead allows the conversation to stagnate. In order for the topics to change, some novel information must be introduced. Therefore, the conversationalist was developed to offer its own viewpoint. Consequently, it indicates novel directions of topic development by retrieving information based on both the development structure of topics and its own viewpoint.

4   Implementation

In this section, we describe the details of the implementation of the conversationalist. Since a daily conversation is not always well-structured and, moreover, it often spreads over several domains, it is not realistic for the conversationalist to have frame-knowledge of the conversation transitions or contents beforehand. Therefore, we apply a method of processing a conversation based on the surface information of each utterance.

Figure 1 shows the software structure of the conversationalist. The utterance-processing module morphologically analyses each input utterance and extracts weighted keywords by regarding the history of each keyword in a conversation. The conversation-structuring module arranges each utterance and keyword in 2-dimensional space based on a statistical method. Then the topic-development-recognition module searches for main topics and empty spaces in topics by using the space obtained by the conversation-structuring module based on an image processing method. On the other hand, the topic-transition-observation module observes topic transition by evaluating cohesion among utterances. If stagnation is detected in a topic, the topic-seeds-provision module is invoked and a piece of information is extracted which can form the seed of a new topic based on the topic development situation obtained by the topic-development-recognition module.

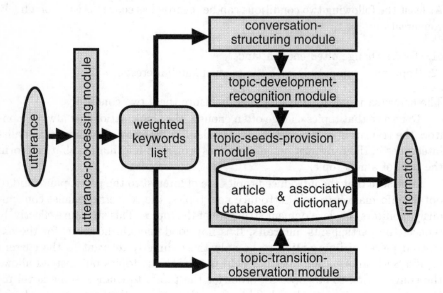

Fig. 1. Software structure of the conversationalist agent.

4.1   Utterance-Processing Module

The input data are the human participants' utterances as text data. We call the text data of each utterance an "utterance-object." This module analyzes an input utterance-object morphologically and determines the part-of-speech of each word. Nouns and unknown-part-of-speech words are then extracted as keywords of the utterance-object.

The weight $W_{w_i,n}$ of the keyword w_i at the n-th utterance is calculated by the following equation:

$$W_{w_i,n} = \frac{(1 + \frac{1}{1+e^{-f_{w_i,n}+F_l}})(1 + \frac{1}{1+e^{-i_{w_i,n}+I}})}{(1 + \frac{1}{1+e^{-f_{w_i}+F_g}})^2}, \qquad (1)$$

where f_{w_i} is the number of utterance-objects that include the word w_i until the $(n-1)$-th utterance-object, $f_{w_i,n}$ is the number of the word w_i in the n-th utterance-object, and $i_{w_i,n}$ is the blank duration in terms of the number of utterances made since w_i appeared last. The terms F_g, F_l, and I are constants, and their respective empirical values are 5,1, and 10. The weghting policy is as follows: A keyword appearing frequently throughout an entire conversation is a very general word used in all kinds of conversations, or a word related to the global topic of the conversation. Therefore, such words are not important for the utterance-object and weighted lightly. On the other hand, a keyword frequently used in a certain utterance-object and a keyword appearing in an utterance-object after a long unused period (or a first-appearing keyword) is important for the utterance-object, even if the word frequently appears throughout the whole conversation. Therefore, such words are weighted heavily.

4.2   Conversation-Structuring Module

We used the thought-space structuring method of Sumi et al. [6], in which relations between concepts (i.e., utterance-objects) and elements of concepts (i.e., keywords) are represented by spatially arranging the concepts and the elements.

For this spatial arranging, we applied the dual scaling method, which is a multi-variant statistical analysis method and which provides principal components of given data [7]. When an object set that consists of plural quantification attributes is given, the dual scaling method represents the relations of the attributes shared among the objects and the co-occurrent relations among the attributes as spatial relative relations, by quantitatively grading the object set and the attribute set.

In this research, we regarded keywords which are automatically extracted by the utterance-processing module as attributes of utterance-objects and regarded the weight of each keyword as its attribute value. As a result, the conversation-structure space which represents the relations among all of the utterance-objects and all of the keyword-objects (a keyword-object consists of a unique keyword) was obtained.

4.3   Topic-Development-Recognition Module

The conversation-structure space obtained by the conversation-structuring module usually provides several clusters that consist of several utterance-objects. Since highly relevant objects are placed close to each other in the conversation-structure space, we can assume that a cluster corresponds to certain contents. Therefore, we can know what kinds of contents compose the conversation and what the main contents are from the conversation-structure space. On the other hand, there are often "empty spaces" where no utterance-objects exist in the conversation-structure space.

This module divides the conversation-structure space into 16-by-16 cells. The number of utterance-objects is counted for each cell by smooth filtering, and this is regarded as the weight of each cell. After each utterance, this module searches for peaks of cell weights, and regards the peak cells as the main contents. At the same time, the distance of each 0 weighted cell from the boundary of clusters of non-0 weighted cells and that of the conversation-structure space are calculated based on a Euclidean distance transformation method [8]. If there are any clusters of 0 weighted cells which exceed a threshold distance (currently, a distance of 2 cells), this module regards them as empty spaces of the conversation at that time and regards the most distant region as the main empty space.

4.4   Topic-Transition-Observation Module

This module detects topic transition points in real-time by using two kinds of utterance cohesion – micro cohesion and macro cohesion – obtained from the morphological data and time transition data of the utterances [9]. The micro cohesion is determined by whether or not several specific expressions (e.g., clue-words, indicate-pronouns, synonyms, antonyms) are included in an utterance. The micro cohesion quantifies the cohesion between an utterance and the utterance just before it: strongly connected, weakly connected, or strongly disconnected. The macro cohesion is determined by the frequencies and intervals of nouns and synonyms included in utterances, and by the time since the last topic transition occurred. The macro cohesion at each utterance quantifies the tendency to maintain the topic so far talked about. Topic transitions are detected at the following utterances:

1. Utterances where the micro cohesion indicates a strong disconnection and the macro cohesion is not so strong, or
2. Utterances where the micro cohesion indicates a weak connection and the macro cohesion is very weak.

Since this method does not need any data from utterances after the current utterance, topic transition points can be detected in real-time. As a result, conversation stagnation can be detected. In the current prototype system, conversation stagnation is detected when a topic transition does not occur within twenty utterances.

4.5   Topic-Seeds-Provision Module

This module is invoked when the stagnation of a conversation is detected in the topic-transition-observation module. This module has a text object database that consists of many text objects. Beforehand, keywords are extracted from each text object in the same way that the utterance-processing module extracts keywords. All of the keywords, however, are weighted equally. A keyword vector of a text object is generated from extracted keywords and it is stored with its text object in the text object database. A piece of information is retrieved from the text object database and provided as the seed of a topic by one of the following two methods:

1. **When there are empty spaces in the conversation-structure space**
   According to subjective experiments in thought-space visualization, people often find new topics in empty spaces of the conversation-structure space [6]. Therefore, when empty spaces exist in the conversation-structure space, a piece of information included in the main empty space is retrieved from the text object database.
   First, a constant number of keywords are obtained by collecting keyword-objects in the order of their distance from the center of the main empty space, and a query keyword set W_q is generated from them. The weight I_{w_i} of each keyword $w_i (w_i \in W_q)$ is calculated by the following equation:

$$I_{w_i} = \frac{min(d_{w_j}; w_j \in W_q)}{d_{w_i}}, \tag{2}$$

   where d_{w_i} is the distance between the center of the target empty space and the keyword-object w_i. A query keyword vector $\mathbf{Q}$ is generated from the query keywords and their weights.
   The retrieval result is then determined by calculating the inner product of the query keyword vector and each keyword vector of each text object of the text object database. The result is the text object for which the inner product value is the highest. Such a piece of information can be expected to be located in the main empty space and to introduce a new topic.

2. **When there are no empty spaces in the conversation-structure space**
   One way to obtain information about a new topic when there are no empty spaces is to deal with the conversation-structure space in a higher dimension. The conversation-structuring module reduces the original very high dimensional space to a 2-dimensional space. Therefore, even if there are seemingly no empty spaces, there can actually be several empty spaces in a higher dimensional space. However, searching for empty spaces in the original dimensional space requires a very high calculation cost. We therefore use a different method: linear transformation of the system of coordinates based on a specific viewpoint.
   In this method, a new topic development direction is obtained by linear transformation of a query keyword vector. The topic-seeds-provision module is equipped with an associative dictionary generated beforehand from a

collection of text objects in a certain knowledge domain. The dictionary is constructed as follows [10]. Keywords are extracted from each text object in the same way that keywords are extracted in the utterance-processing module, but all of the keywords are weighted equally. A keyword vector of the text object is generated from the extracted keywords. Then, by using a method based on Associatron [11], one of the associative memory techniques, a self-correlation matrix is calculated from each keyword vector, and an associative memory matrix $\mathbf{M}$ (i.e., the associative dictionary) is obtained by accumulating all of the self-correlation matrices. This associative memory matrix $\mathbf{M}$ thus describes the co-occurring relations between all of the keywords included in the text objects, and it represents the viewpoint that is expressed by the text object set.

This module searches for the main topic cell closest to the newest utterance-object, obtains a constant number of keywords by collecting keyword-objects in the order of their distance from the main topic cell, and generates a query keyword set. The weight of each keyword is calculated in the same way as when empty spaces exist. As a result, a keyword vector $\mathbf{Q}$ is generated, and this vector is linearly transformed by using the associative dictionary; that is the associative memory matrix $\mathbf{M}$:

$$\mathbf{R} = \mathbf{MQ}, \tag{3}$$

where $\mathbf{Q}$ is a vertical $N \times 1$ vector and we assume that the matrix $\mathbf{M}$ is an $N \times N$ matrix. If the dimensions of matrix $\mathbf{M}$ and vector $\mathbf{Q}$ are different, their dimensions should be adjusted to the larger dimension. Equation (3) is the associative recalling procedure of Associatron. By this linear transformation, the original system of coordinates is transformed into another system of coordinates by distorting, rotating, and shifting the original system, and the original keyword vector is mapped onto the transformed system. Finally, the inner product between the obtained (recalled) vector $\mathbf{R}$ and each keyword vector of each text object in the text object database is evaluated, and the text object that has the highest inner product value is extracted as the retrieval result.

Since the associative matrix $\mathbf{M}$ is constructed from a specific knowledge domain, it can be said that this process is a re-grasping of the meaning of the original topic from the conversationalist's viewpoint. As a result, the conversationalist can introduce a new viewpoint and a new direction. We have already confirmed that the associative method described above has such an effect [10]. Thus, the conversationalist can provide the seed of a new topic even if no empty spaces exist.

5   Experiments

5.1   Process of the Experiment and Results

We applied the conversationalist to an experimental conversation in which four participants discussed, as the global topic, whether or not a "kangaroo-bar", i.e., a bar equipped on a car which protects the car when the car and a kangaroo come into contact, should be prohibited in Japan. The conversationalist's knowledge (the text object database and the associative dictionary) was generated from articles of "Gendai Yougo no Kiso Chishiki '93 (A Japanese dictionary of contemporary vocabulary in 1993, by Jiyuu Kokuminsha Co.). The number of articles in the article database was 10,406 and the number of keywords in the associative dictionary was 37,502.

Figure 2 shows the conversation situation when 30 utterances have so far been provided by the human participants. The right window shows the utterances with their user-IDs and the left window shows the conversation-structure space. Each icon in the left window corresponds to each utterance in the right window. Figure 3 shows the topic-development structure obtained by the topic-development-recognition module based on the conversation situation of the left window in Figure 2. Cells marked "T" represent main topic locations, and "E" represents the center of an empty space. In Figure 3, we can see that there are three main topics and the right lower empty space is the largest. The main topics are: about car safety equipment (in the upper-left direction), about the relation between a kangaroo-bar and fashion trends (in the downward direction), and about experimental data on the dangers of a kangaroo-bar (in the upper-right direction).

The topic-transition-observation module detected a topic transition at the eleventh utterance. After that, however, no topic transition was detected until the thirtieth utterance after twenty utterances. Thus, the topic-transition observation-module detected a stagnation in the conversation and invoked the topic-seeds-provision module. The topic-seeds-provision module retrieved the text object database by using keywords based on the largest empty space. The piece of information extracted was as follows and the conversationalist provided it as its utterance.:

U-curve shape of personal consumption: According to a survey on consumers of expensive cars in the USA, a U-curve shape consumption tendency (i.e., not only people in the upper income bracket but also people in the lower income bracket tend to spend much money on expensive goods) was observed. The same tendency can be observed in Japan, too. This tendency is caused by the following reason: although people in the middle income bracket tend to spend much money on housing and education for their children, young single people spend all of their income on themselves in spite of their low income. In particular, such a tendency can be observed for people with hobbies, e.g., a car, audio equipment, and leisure activities.

This information was plotted where the largest empty space used to be, by the conversation-structuring module.

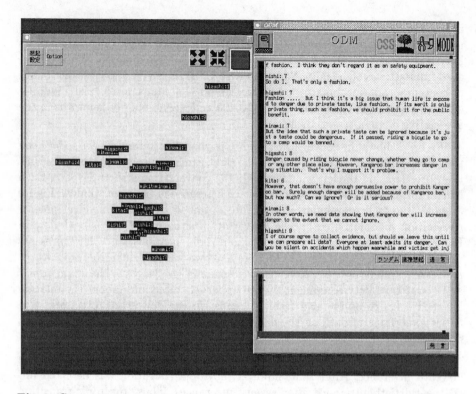

Fig. 2. Conversation situation when 30 utterances had so far been provided by the human participants.

5.2   Discussion

The main empty space the conversationalist used for obtaining query keywords was surrounded by topics on experimental data of the dangers of a kangaroo-bar and the relation between a kangaroo-bar and fashion trends. The piece of information (the conversationalist's utterance) was about survey data relating to cars, although it did not relate to a kangaroo-bar. The information mentioned that young single people tend to spend a lot of money on cars as a hobby. The piece of information can therefore be semantically regarded as information in the main empty space.

The kind of consumers who tend to install a kangaroo-bar on their cars had not been referred to in the conversation until the 30th utterance. The piece of information provided by the conversationalist, however, let the participants know that young single people tend to spend unreasonable amounts of money on fashionable things as a hobby, and that there is a high possibility that young people would like to install kangaroo-bars on their cars. Consequently, the participants were able to notice that they should consider such a consumption tendency and life-style when thinking about the kangaroo-bar problem. Thus, it

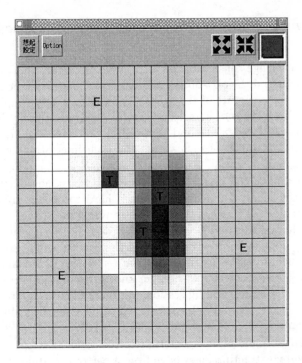

Fig. 3. Topic-development structure based on the conversation situation of the left window of Figure 2.

can be expected that a conversation will develop in a new direction with the conversationalist.

We asked another subject who did not attend the conversation to read the log file of the conversation. After reading it, the subject gave us the impression that the conversation went in circles before the intervention. That is, although the conversation seemed lively with its many utterances, it was actually in stagnation. Therefore, the conversationalist's intervention was appropriate and timely.

Furthermore, we found that the conversationalist's intervention had mental effects as well as semantic effects. The participants were very excited by their discussion, but when the conversationalist provided a very objective piece of information, the excited conversation tended to calm down. This effect can be expected to help a conversation stay reasonable.

Consequently, we can say that the conversationalist effectively and timely introduced a new topic and a new viewpoint to the conversation as expected. Moreover, the conversationalist's opinion can keep a conversation from becoming emotional and thus help keep it reasonable.

6   Creating Agents With Various Characteristics

The agent's knowledge consists of the associative dictionary that represents the agent's viewpoint and the text-object database that represents the agent's memory. Moreover, the structure of the agent's knowledge is very simple. Therefore, agents with various types of knowledge can be constructed easily by combining various associative dictionaries and text-object databases. In this section, we introduce several examples of such agents and their interesting applications.

The first example is an outsider agent, or an agent who has domain knowledge different from that of the users. People who have the same domain knowledge often share fixed ideas. Therefore, it is often hard to obtain diverse pieces of information outside the frame of the fixed ideas even if they have a brainstorming session. In such a case, experience tells us that it is effective for an outsider who has a different domain knowledge to attend the brainstorming session. We can easily create such an agent by providing an associative dictionary and a text-object database constructed from domain knowledge different from that of the participants in the brainstorming session. We have already confirmed that such an agent can obtain pieces of information which have not only direct relevance but also hidden relevance to an input query text [10].

The second example is an agent that is the agent of a specific person. It can be created by extracting knowledge from a person's writings (e.g., novels or technical/scientific papers). Such an agent provides pieces of information reflecting the person's knowledge. Thus, we can simulate a discussion with the person by talking with the agent not only if the person is simply absent but even if the person died hundreds of years ago. For example, by constructing an agent's knowledge from Shakespeare's writings or Newton's papers, we can virtually talk with them. Additionally, a user can create an agent of himself/herself and give the agent knowledge through his/her writings. By talking with this self-agent, the user can recall what he/she used to think, and, moreover, can find new relevance among pieces of information that he/she knows.

The third example is an agent that has heterogeneous knowledge. There are two methods for obtaining heterogeneous knowledge. One method is to combine an associative dictionary and a text-object database whose knowledge domains are not the same. For example, by combining an associative dictionary generated by Newton's or Shakespeare's writings and a text-object database of contemporary information, it is possible to create an agent with contemporary information but reflecting an ancient person's viewpoints. The other method is to combine plural associative dictionaries of different knowledge domains. This can be done easily by multiplying associative memory matrices. By using such a multiplied associative dictionary, it is possible to obtain new relevance that cannot otherwise be obtained by using each associative dictionary individually. This method can thus be used to create an agent that is a multi-domains expert. Moreover, by multiplying the associative dictionaries of more than one person (for example, the user's own associative dictionary and Newton's associative dictionary) a very interesting viewpoint for the user could be generated.

Thus, various agents characterized by various combinations of various knowledge can be created very easily. By preparing agents with specific knowledge on demand, we can be expected to be able to converse much more creatively.

7 Conclusion

We described a topic-development agent that enters a daily conversation as an equal participant with human participants in order to keep the conversation lively. This agent grasps the relevance of utterances as spatial arrangements, detects a novel direction in which a new topic can be developed, and provides an appropriate piece of information which might likely form the seed of a new topic. In this process, the agent deconstructs and reconstructs conversational topics and contents based on the agent's own viewpoint. Hence, the agent can be regarded as an "emergence agent" in a conversation environment, which is different from the emergence agent of [12] which deconstructs and reconstructs geometrical objects.

From the experimental results, it is suggested that this agent can provide timely information that introduces a new topic. Moreover, it is also suggested that the agent has the ability to refresh the atmosphere of a conversation. Thus, the agent has the ability to effectively coordinate creative aspects of conversations without imposing any of the special restrictions which most ordinary creative discussion systems place on participants. This feature makes it possible to apply the agent to daily conversations that are held in environments characterized as free.

We are planning to apply this agent to various kinds of conversations in order to confirm the effects of conversation activation. Furthermore, we are planning to build agents that have various kinds of characters and to experiment with them.

Acknowledgment

The authors would like to thank Dr. Yasuyoshi Sakai, chairman of the board and Dr. Ryohei Nakatsu, president of ATR MI&C Laboratories for their support of this work. The authors would also like to thank Mr. Osamu Sato, Mr. Makoto Takahashi, Mr. Naotaka Mitsui, and Ms. Miwa Daitoh for their contributions in constructing the experimental system.

References

[1]   Imai, K., Nonaka, I., and Takeuchi, H.: Managing the New Product Development Process, in 75th Anniversary Colloquium Productivity and Technology, Harvard Business School, Mar. (1984) 28–29

[2]   Conklin, J. and Begeman, M. L.: gIBIS: A Hypertext Tool for Exploratory Policy Discussion, Proc. of CSCW'88, (1988) 140–152

[3]   Streitz, N. A., Geibler, J., Haake, J. M., and Hol, J.: DOLPHIN: Integrated Meeting Support across Local and Remote Desktop Environments and Live-Boards, Proc. of CSCW '94, (1994) 345–358

[4]   Hori, K.: A model to explain and predict the effect of human-computer interaction in the articulation process for concept formation Information Modelling and Knowledge Bases, vol. 7, 1996.

[5]   Boden, M. A.: Agents and Creativity, Communications of The ACM, Vol. 37, No. 7, (1994) 117–121

[6]   Sumi, Y., Ogawa, R., Hori, K., Ohsuga, S., and Mase, K.: Computer-aided communications by visualizing thought space structure, Electronics and Communications in Japan, J79-B-II, (1996) 1120–1129

[7]   Nishisato, S.: Analysis of Categorical Data: Dual Scaling and Its Applications, Univ. of Toronto press, (1980)

[8]   Saito, T., and Toriwaki, J.: New Algorithm for Euclidean Distance Transformation of An n-Dimensional Digitized Picture with Applications, Pattern Recognition, Vol. 27, No. 11, (1994) 1551–1566

[9]   Nishimoto, K., Abe, S., and Mase, K.: Realtime topic transition detection for a free style dialog of an unspecified domain, Proc. of Symp. on Natural Language Processing Applications, Vol. 95, No. 6, Information Processing Society of Japan, (1995) 41–48 (in Japanese).

[10]   Nishimoto, K., Abe, S., and Mase, K.: Effectively-heterogeneous information extraction to stimulate divergent thinking, Proc. of Intl. Symp. of Creativity and Cognition 2, (1996) 156–163

[11]   Nakano, K.: Associatron – A Model of Associative Memory, IEEE Trans. on S.M.C., SMC-2,3, (1972) 381–388

[12]   Edmonds, E. A., Candy, L., Jones, R., and Soufi, B.: Support for Collaborative Design: Agents and Emergence, Communications of The ACM, Vol. 37, No. 7, (1994) 41–47

Coordinating Human and Computer Agents

Keith S. Decker

Department of Computer and Information Sciences
University of Delaware, Newark, DE 19716
decker@cis.udel.edu

Abstract. In many application areas individuals are responsible for an agenda of tasks and face choices about the best way to locally handle each task, in what order to do tasks, and when to do them. Such decisions are often hard to make because of *coordination problems*: individual tasks are related to the tasks of others in complex ways, and there are many sources of uncertainty (no one has a complete view of the task structure at arbitrary levels of detail, the situation may be changing dynamically, and no one is entirely sure of the outcomes of all of their actions). The focus of this paper is the development of support tools for distributed, cooperative work by groups (collaborative teams) of human and computational agents. We will discuss the design of a set of distributed autonomous computer programs ("agents") that assist people in coordinating their activities by helping them to manage their agendas. We describe several ongoing implementations of these ideas including 1) simulated agents and tasks, 2) a real multi-agent system for financial portfolio management, and 3) a real mixed human and computational agent system for concurrent engineering design.

1 Introduction

One operational vision of concurrent engineering is one of a *network* of workstations that enable *concurrent* and *distributed* requirements assessment, design generation, and analysis. It envisions that *groups* of humans and computational 'agents' will *cooperatively* create, resource, evaluate, execute, and monitor design processes or manufacturing plans. Work to date has not directly addressed the problems and *opportunities* that arise from a truly distributed and cooperative environment. The focus of this paper is the development of support tools for distributed, cooperative work by groups of human and computational agents. Patterns of *interrelated task structures* that are partially shared by multiple agents with mixed initiative tasking appear in many military and commercial environments (air campaign planning, concurrent engineering, hospital scheduling, manufacturing scheduling, coordinating large software development efforts). These interrelationships provide not only potential problems to avoid (such as forgetting a required task) but also opportunities to take advantage of (such as doing a task needed by more than one other agent first, or doing a favor for another agent).

The remainder of this paper is organized as follows. First, the overall vision of where we are headed, including an extended example. Next, Section 2 discusses our formal approach to representing coordination problems, called TÆMS, and our approach to interagent scheduling coordination, called GPGP. We have also developed an agent problem-solving environment simulator that allows us to analyze scheduling and coordination algorithms for average performance characterisitcs, the ability to deal with different levels of uncertainty, etc. Section 3 decribes one application of these ideas to a multi-agent system for multi-agent portfolio management. Finally, Section 4 describes an application, just beginning, of these ideas to a mixed human and computational agent system for concurrent engineering design of composite helicopter body panels.

1.1   Where we are Heading: An example

In general, each person and computational agent involved in such distributed cooperative work has a set of tasks before them that currently need to be done (identifying targets in several areas, collecting intelligence on each of several disparate targets, etc.). The tasks may come from a local initiative, may be assigned by a superior, or may just be subtasks needed to accomplish current goals. The tasks may be initially perceived as unrelated. We propose to assist users in task selection by developing a User Coordination Assistant Agent (UCAA) that keeps track of a workstation user's current agenda of tasks and presents a possible schedule (ordering) of these tasks according to user- and domain-directed preferences. The idea is not to force a user into the schedule, but rather to provide the user with up-to-date, relevant information so that the user can make an informed decision. Such an agenda is not developed in isolation, but rather through a distributed coordination process using multiple coordination mechanisms triggered by the *coordination relationships* between the task structures of the different agents involved. We also are developing an Agent Coordination Module (ACM) that can be linked-in to provide agenda management services for the coordination of computational agents in accord with the human agents' task-order preferences (see Figure 1).

Such a set of tools will allow the development of systems that can truly support cooperative work involving people at multiple workstations and computational agent assistants by helping to manage and organize the workloads of these agents. Certain tasks will be dependent on other tasks *and* be time critical, and such information for differentiating tasks could be lost in critical situations if only ad hoc coordinating mechanisms are used. It is useful to communicate more information than simply task assignments and task coordination relationships. For example, users and computational agents can request possible due dates for potential tasks before assignment (allowing both better time estimates and load balancing) and request *commitments* to complete certain time-critical tasks (in effect, supporting inter-agent negotiation protocols). Our approach of tying coordination mechanisms to the particular kinds of coordination relationships that exist in a particular task environment provides for a reusable tool foundation (the UCAA and its interactive human interface, the ACM and its interface to a computational agent) and a customizable set of coordination mechanisms for a particular application environment (since no single coordination mechanism would be useful across different environments with different task coordination relationships).

We have already mentioned that one vision of concurrent engineering is of groups of humans and computational 'agents' that will cooperatively create, resource, evaluate, execute, and monitor design processes or manufacturing plans. The technologies that we are developing are aimed squarely at supporting this vision by providing mechanisms to effectively and efficiently *coordinate* such a distributed system. As envisioned, the entire system allows both concurrent activities (carried out by humans and computer programs), and mixed-initiative tasks. Either of these implies there is no fixed, static control of all the human and computational agents in the system. All agents, both human and computational, will be expected to perform multiple tasks—certainly more than one task at a time—in a potentially high pressure, time-sensitive environment. To make things harder, the tasks will not be independent but will be related in potentially complex ways—not only by hard relationships like "A must precede B" but also by softer relationships such as "A would facilitate B", where completing task A will help B by making it easier (quicker) to do, or by making a higher quality result possible, or both.[1] Relationships include not only computational relationships between tasks, but other resources as well. Exclusive access is only one possible resource relationship. Another example is the appearance of diminishing returns in the use of compute servers for large engineering simulations or software design programs, leading to the need for automated load balancing mechanisms.

Figure 1 shows a high-level view of the system described here, with two human user workstations and one autonomous, computational agent (which could be running on either a user's workstation or on a third hardware processor/server).

1.2   Air Campaign Planning Example

We will describe a system in the Air Campaign Planning Domain that consists of several planning tools used concurrently by a JFACC (Joint Forces Air Component Commander), his staff, and associated humans, computational agents, and smart databases, based on information in [2,5][2]. Coordination assistance technology has applications in many areas besides military command and control of course. For example, in an office or concurrent engineering environment, both independent computerized agents (usually controlling access to resources) and intelligent assistants to office workers can exist [25]. In real offices, activity is taking place semi-autonomously, and centralized control and detailed global views are rarely available or socially possible [21,26]. In the intelligent office

---

[1] For example, imagine that your task is to find a new book in a library, and you can do this either before or after the new books are unpacked, sorted, and correctly shelved.

[2] This example was originally presented at Concurrent Engineering '95.

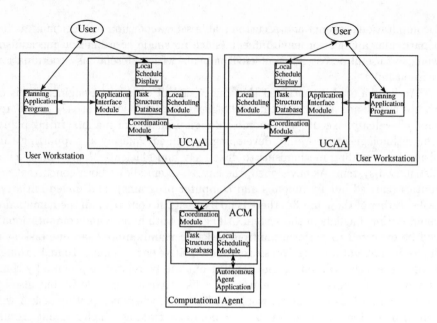

Fig. 1. Architectural overview of a cooperative, mixed human and computational agent system based on User Coordination Assistant Agents (UCAAs) and Agent Coordination Modules (ACMs)

assistant domain, then, coordination algorithms can be applied to providing guidance to an office worker (for instance, a computer programmer) about how to prioritize tasks ("what are the most important things to do next?"), given known and discovered relationships between one worker's tasks and the tasks of others. Coordination algorithms do not supply a solution for problems of negotiating outcomes or resolving disparate views, but rather try to avoid negative interactions between agent goals or planned actions (avoiding conflicting actions or inter-agent action sequences), and recognize positive or helpful interactions (such as the potential to do another agent a favor, or send some preliminary, predictive information)[33]. Often the coordination process triggers a process of negotiation.

Figure 2 shows a portion of the global task structure for the air campaign planning environment. No one human or computational agent (from here on, referred to simply as 'c-agent') is responsible for all of these tasks, and this global view is never actually constructed—not only would it be expensive to construct in terms of time and communication resources, but it would very likely be both incomplete and out-of date very quickly. Instead, the UCAA that advises each human operator will have a *partially global* view of what's going on (we'll show this in Figures 3 through 4). The complete scenario expressed by Figure 2 concerns the JFACC developing several objectives, identifying a course-of-action for each objective, and then assigning the objective and course-of-action to a planning staff member at their own workstation to develop detailed targeting plans. The development of target sets will in turn involve the work of other staff members, who are working on tasks involving the areas of intelligence, weather, logistics, etc.

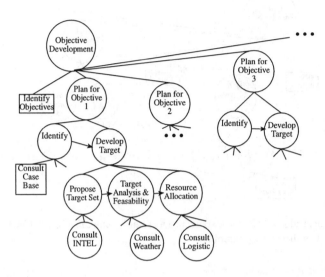

Fig. 2. Part of the global task structure in the Air Campaign Planning environment. Typically, no single agent would ever actually construct such a complete global view.

We'll begin with the JFACC, who is using air campaign planning tools to refine general objectives into the selection of specific objectives, and a course-of-action for achieving the objective (such as disrupting aircraft manufacture). Inherent in this process is the analysis of enemy strengths and vulnerabilities [2]; such analysis is tied to ongoing situation analysis and assessment done remotely and by the JFACC intelligence staff (at remote workstations). Along with the air campaign planning tools, the JFACC has a window on his workstation that displays his current agenda of tasks. For the JFACC, who is basically initiating work, the agenda is simple and unordered. From the point of view of the UCAA, the JFACC's task structure may look something like that in Figure 3, where the JFACC is primarily responsible for the grey tasks. The UCAA is still of great use to the JFACC, however. As the JFACC completes a plan objective and course-of-action specification, he can query the UCAA as to the current status of the work of his planning staff (without bothering them directly)—this information, brought about by communication between the JFACC's UCAA and the UCAAs assigned to each planning staff workstation, is used by the JFACC to make informed decisions about dividing work among his staff members. This is an important point about tools that support group planning—they bring the up-to-date, high-quality information needed to make good human tasking decisions to the user (in this case, the JFACC) when they are needed.[3]

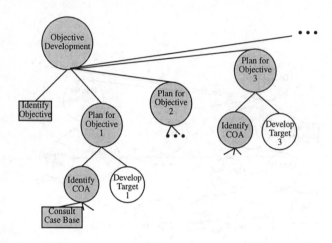

Fig. 3. The local view of the task structure as seen by the JFACC's UCAA. Grey tasks are the JFACC's direct responsibility.

Let us assume that the JFACC has identified three detailed objectives so far, and that the task of target development for objective 1 has been assigned to staff planner A, and objectives 2 and 3 to staff planner B. During the first phase of developing a target set, staff planner A begins by finding the 'Center Of Gravity' (COG) of the enemy positions around the objective. Staff planner A's UCAA communicates with the other staff planners' UCAAs to discover if any overlapping work exists—indeed, planner A's UCAA discovers that staff planner B has an objective very close to that of planner A's objective. The COG calculation currently underway by planner A will *facilitate* the COG calculation by planner B. The task structure from the view of planner A's UCAA looks very much like Figure 4 (again, the grey tasks are the responsibility of planner A). The discovery of this relationship was done by the Coordination Modules of the UCAA, using a coordination mechanism we call 'developing non-local views' (we'll discuss coordination mechanisms in more detail in Section 2). The soft relationship as discovered has implications for the scheduling of tasks at planner A's and B's workstations—since B has two tasks to do, and no other reason to order them, B should work on objective 2 first so that B can use the result of planner A's calculations later on in developing targets for objective 3. The Local Scheduling Display for planner B indicates this to him, and the Local Scheduling Display for planner A indicates that B is now depending on the result of his COG calculations (so he shouldn't just delay the task for no good reason). Thus the

---

[3] It is possible to automate this sort of task partitioning for computational agents.

UCAAs, via their coordination and local scheduling components, have allowed the two staff planners to do their work more efficiently and quickly.

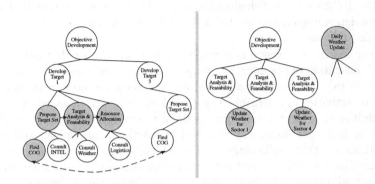

Fig. 4. On the left, the local view of the task structure as seen by the UCAA of member 'A' of the JFACC's planning staff (responsible for the left side grey tasks). On the right, the local view of the task structure as seen by the UCAA of the JFACC staff member in charge of weather forecasting who is responsible for the right side grey tasks.

The reader might raise an objection in the last paragraph that the JFACC should have assigned both objectives 1 and 3 to the same staff planner. Perhaps— but there is plenty of reason to *not* do this as well. For example, one objective might have been taking out an aircraft manufacturer, and the second a disruption of communications, and the staff planners may have different areas of expertise. Or perhaps objective 1 is quite hard, long, and involved, and for load balancing the JFACC assigned the other two objectives to staff planner B. In any case, the point is that the technology we are building for use by humans (the UCAA) does not *force* humans into certain actions. At this point in time it would not be realistic to imagine a computer system that could second guess command decisions. Instead the UCAA provides the information needed to make an informed decision, and once it is made, propagates the consequences.

Finally, let's look at a third member of the JFACC staff, the weather forecaster. From the point of view of planning staff members A and B, the weather forecaster is providing a service; these staff members have the choice of using the current weather forecast for an area, or of requesting a more up-to-date forecast (but which will take time). Perhaps an autonomous weather forecasting computational agent is also available that can give updated forecasts more quickly, but with lower accuracy. The planners can use their UCAAs to see the estimated time to get an updated forecast—such a request is handled by the weather staffer's UCAA and the weather c-agent's ACM. Again, this allows the planner to make an up-to-date, informed decision about whether to go with the out-of-date forecast or wait for the new one.

From the point of view of the weather forecasting agent (human or computational) information about task requests coming in can be used to help the agent schedule their activities. Figure 4 shows the local UCAA's view of the weather staffer's tasks. Notice that the tasks include both those requests from planners for updated forecasts, and standing orders to keep all forecasts not too far out of date. The UCAA's Local Schedule Display will indicate to the user that several tasks are depending on an updated forecast for area 1, and so that might be the best task to do next.

To summarize, our vision is to provide direct support for the goal of concurrent, mixed-initiative planning by groups of humans and computational agents. We will do this by providing an interface that helps the user to schedule their agenda of activities in a sensible way given how those activities interrelate with the activities of other humans and agents in the system. Our support will help make sure tasks get done, and that bad interactions are avoided and positive interactions are taken advantage of. The interface will also enable users to get up-to-date information on the loads of other users and computational agents, so that users who allocate tasks to other users can make better decisions.

2   Approach

Coordination is the process of managing interdependencies between activities. If we view an agent as an entity that has some beliefs about the world and can perform actions, then the coordination problem arises when any or all of the following situations occur: the agent has a *choice* of actions it can take, and that choice affects the agent's performance; the *order* in which actions are carried out affects performance; the *time* at which actions are carried out affects performance. The coordination problem of choosing and temporally ordering actions is made more complex because the agent may only have an incomplete view of the entire task structure of which its actions are a part, the task structure may be changing dynamically, and the agent may be uncertain about the outcomes of its actions. If there are multiple agents in an environment, then when the potential actions of one agent are related to those of another agent, we call the relationship a *coordination relationship*. Each coordination mechanism we describe in Section 2.2 is a response to some coordination relationship.

Developing and applying a domain independent approach to mixed initiative human and computer agent coordination involves developing a language to express agent task structures and potential coordination points (TÆMS); a modular, parameterized, and adaptable approach to the coordination activities themselves (GPGP); and a sophisticated local scheduling mechanism capable of dealing with multiple, dynamically changing evaluation criteria ("design-to-time"[19, 18] or "design-to-criteria" [34] scheduling). This section will discuss TÆMS and GPGP. A secondary issue that is also important to keep in mind is the "open systems" nature of our underlying approach. We do not propose to construct a global view of the evolving task structure—most agents will only have a fairly local (or global but abstract) view. Only tasks that have direct relationships need to be understood between agents, and scheduling criteria (or the schedulers themselves) can be different at each agent (and can change over time). Newly developed Coordination mechanisms can be tailored to the agent (human or computational) and task environment at hand.

2.1   A Framework for Modeling Task Environments: TÆMS

In order to construct a general approach to coordination, it is necessary to have an underlying framework that can represent the wide diversity of activities/tasks and the properties and relationships that need to be represented and understood in order to arrive at effective coordination among activity structures of different human or c-agents in a wide variety of domains.

The TÆMS framework (Task Analysis, Environment Modeling, and Simulation) [11] represents coordination problems in a formal, domain-independent way. We have used it to represent coordination problems in distributed sensor networks, hospital patient scheduling, airport resource management, distributed information retrieval, pilot's associate, local area network diagnosis, etc. [9]. For the subject of this paper, there are two unique features of TÆMS. The first is the explicit, quantitative representation of task interrelationships that describe the effect on performance of activity choices and temporal orderings. The second is the representation of task structures at multiple levels of abstraction. The lowest level of abstraction is called an executable *method*, or a basic *action*. A *method* or *action* represents a schedulable entity, such as a blackboard knowledge source instance, a chunk of code and its input data, or a totally-ordered plan that has been recalled and instantiated for a task. A method or action could also be an instance of a human activity at some useful level of detail, for example, "take an X-ray of patient 1's left foot". A *task group* contains all tasks that have explicit computational interrelationships. There may be physical resource relationships between task groups.

A coordination problem instance (called an *episode* **E**) is defined as a set of task groups, each with a deadline $D(\mathcal{T})$, such as $\mathbf{E} = \langle \mathcal{T}_1, \mathcal{T}_2, \ldots, \mathcal{T}_n \rangle$. Figure 5 shows an objective[4] task group and agent A's subjective view of that same task group. Note that no agent ever gains an objective view, but by communicating with other agents, it can expand its subjective view with non-local information, developing a partial global view (see the next section). We use objective-level models in simulation to study the effects on algorithm performance of the presence, absence, or uncertainty associated with certain types of task information. The simulator supports the graphical display of generated task structures, agent actions, and statistical data collection via CLIP[35] in CLOS (the Common Lisp Object System) on various Unix workstations. In real agent systems (Section 3 and 4), of course, only subjective information exists.

The goal of the agent or agents is to maximize the sum of the quality achieved for each task group before its deadline. A task group consists of a set of tasks related to one another by a **subtask** relationship that forms an acyclic graph (here, a tree). Tasks at the leaves of the tree represent executable *methods*, which

---

[4] The word 'objective' refers to the fact that this is the true, real structure as viewed by 'nature'.

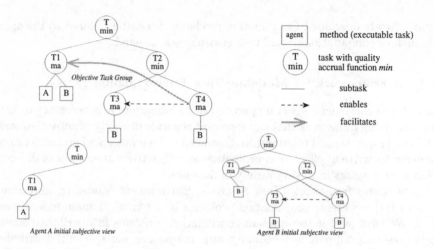

Fig. 5. Agent A and B's subjective views (bottom) of a typical objective task group (top)

are the actual instantiated computations or actions the agent will execute that produce some amount of quality (in the figure, these are shown as boxes). The circles higher up in the tree represent various subtasks involved in the task group, and indicate precisely how quality will accrue depending on what methods are executed and when. The arrows between tasks and/or methods indicate other task interrelationships where the execution of some method will have a positive or negative effect on the quality or duration of another method. The presence of these interrelationships make this an NP-hard scheduling problem; further complicating factors for the local scheduler include the fact that multiple agents are executing related methods, that some methods are redundant (executable at more than one agent), and that the subjective task structure may differ from the real objective structure. The relationships between tasks may also depend on physical resources. This notation and associated semantics are formally defined in [11, 9].

A Hospital Scheduling Example We have taken a preliminary look at the application of the described technology to hospital patient scheduling. Let's look at a brief example of a task structure model of this environment expressed with TÆMS, our framework for reasoning about multi-agent task environments (see Section 2.1) The following description is from an actual case study [29]:

> *Patients in General Hospital reside in units that are organized by branches of medicine, such as orthopedics or neurosurgery. Each day, physicians request certain tests and/or therapy to be performed as a part of the diagnosis and treatment of a patient. [...] Tests are performed by separate, independent, and distally located* ancillary departments *in the*

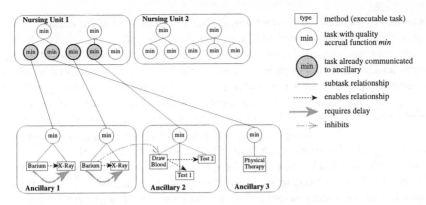

Fig. 6. High-level, subjective task structure for a typical hospital patient scheduling episode. The top task in each hospital ancillary is really the same objective entity as the unit task it is linked to in the diagram.

hospital. The radiology department, for example, provides X-ray services and may receive requests from a number of different units in the hospital.

Furthermore, each test may interact with other tests in relationships such as enables, requires−delay (must be performed after), and inhibits (test A's performance invalidates test B's result if A is performed during specified time period relative to B). Note that the unit secretaries (as scheduling agents) try to minimize the patients' stays in the hospital, while the ancillary secretaries (as scheduling agents) try to maximize equipment use (throughput) and minimize setup times.

Figure 6 shows an subjective TÆMS task structure corresponding to an episode in this domain, and the subjective views of the unit and ancillary scheduling agents after four tests have been ordered. Note that quite a bit of detail can be captured in just the 'computational' aspects of the environment—in this case, the tasks use peoples' time, not a computer's. However, TÆMS can model in more detail the physical resources and job shop characteristics of the ancillaries if necessary [9]. Such detail is not necessary for us to analyze the protocols developed by [29], who propose a primary unit-ancillary protocol and a secondary ancillary-ancillary protocol.

In this type of environment, scheduling agents would interact with nurses and each other, using the mechanisms, facilities, and tools suggested here, to assist in the efficient and effective scheduling of patient tests and treatments. Similar applications of our technology occur in manufacturing scheduling applications.

2.2 A Framework for Coordination: GPGP

Many researchers have shown that there is no single best organization or coordination mechanism for all environments. Thus, in order to effectively handle the wide range of possible environments, we have developed an extendable family of coordination mechanisms, called Generalized Partial Global Planning (GPGP), that form a basic set of coordination mechanisms for teams of cooperative computational agents. The important features of this approach include a set of modular coordination components called "mechanisms" (any subset or all of which can be used in response to a particular task environment); a general specification of these mechanisms involving the detection and response to certain abstract coordination relationships in the incoming TÆMS task structure that are not tied to a particular domain; and a separation of the coordination mechanisms from an agent's local scheduler that allows each to better do the job for which it was designed. Each component or mechanism can be added as required in reaction to the environment in which the agents find themselves. An individual algorithm in the family is defined by a particular set of active mechanisms and their associated parameters. In [12] we discuss the interactions between these mechanisms and how to decide when each mechanism should be used, drawing data from simulation experiments of multiple agent teams working in abstract task environments.

The GPGP approach specifies three basic areas of the agent's coordination behavior: how and when to communicate and construct non-local views of the current problem solving situation; how and when to exchange the partial results of problem solving; how and when to make and break *commitments* to other agents about what results will be available and when. The GPGP approach of recognizing and reacting to the characteristics of certain coordination relationships is shared with Von Martial's work on the *favor* relationship [33]. The use of commitments in the GPGP family of algorithms is based on the ideas of many other researchers [3, 1, 22]. Each agent also has a heuristic local scheduler that decides what actions the agent should take and when, based on its current view of the problem solving situation (including the commitments it has made), and a utility function. The coordination mechanisms supply non-local views of problem solving to the local scheduler, including *what* non-local results will be available locally, and *when* they will be available. The local scheduler creates (and monitors the execution of) schedules that attempt to maximize group quality through both local action and the use of non-local actions (committed to by other agents).

One way to think about this work is that the GPGP approach views coordination as *modulating* local control, not supplanting it—a two level process that makes a clear distinction between coordination behavior and local scheduling. This process occurs via a set of coordination mechanisms that post constraints to the local scheduler about the importance of certain tasks and appropriate times for their initiation and completion. This indirect aspect is extremely important for a system that will integrate both human and computational agents—when dealing with a human agent, the process is necessarily one of providing the correct information at the proper time to the human decision-maker, as opposed to direct control. By having separate modules for coordination and local scheduling, we can also take advantage of advances in real-time scheduling algorithms to produce cooperative distributed problem solving systems that respond to real-time deadlines. We can also take advantage of local schedulers that have a great deal of domain scheduling knowledge already encoded within them. Finally, we can rely on humans as well in making local scheduling decisions.

The way that we specify the family of algorithms in a general, domain-independent way (as responses to certain environmental situations, interactions with a local scheduler, and decisions made by a human or computer) is very important. It leads to the eventual construction of libraries of reusable coordination components that can be chosen (customized) with respect to certain attributes of the target application. It is from this perspective that we feel we can customize our UCAA and ACM to the requirements of the specific application domain. The observation that no single organization or coordination algorithm is 'the best' across environments, problem-solving instances, or even particular situations is a common one in the study of both human organizational theory (especially contingency theory) [24, 17, 31] and cooperative distributed problem solving [16, 14, 13, 10]. Key features of task environments demonstrated in both these threads of work that lead to different coordination mechanisms include those related to the structure of the environment (the particular kinds and patterns of **interrelationships** or dependencies that occur between tasks) and environmental **uncertainty** (both in the *a priori* structure of any problem-solving episode and in the outcome's of an agent's actions; for example, the presence of both uncertainty and concomitant high variance in a task structure). This makes it important for a general approach to coordination (i.e., one that will be used in many domains) to be appropriately parameterized so that the overhead activities associated with the algorithm, in terms of both communication and computation, can be varied depending upon the characteristics of the application environment.

The Coordination Module The role of the coordination mechanisms is to provide constraints to the local scheduler that allow the local scheduler to construct objectively better schedules. The mechanisms fulfill this role for an agent by (variously) communicating private portions of its task structures, communicating results to fulfill non-local commitments, and making commitments to respond to coordination relationships **between** portions of the task structure controllable by *different* agents (as in the JFACC assigning tasks to his staff example) or **within** portions controllable by *multiple* agents (as in the case of the overlapping tasks in the JFACC example).[5]

The five mechanisms we described in [12] form a basic set that provides similar functionality to Durfee's original partial global planning algorithm [15]. Mechanism 1 exchanges useful private views of task structures; Mechanism 2 communicates results; Mechanism 3 handles redundant methods; Mechanisms 4 and 5 handle hard and soft coordination relationships. More mechanisms can be added, such as a load balancing mechanism. The mechanisms are independent in the sense that they can be used in any combination. If inconsistent constraints

---

[5] We say a subtree of a task structure is *controllable* by an agent if that agent has at least one executable method in that subtree.

are introduced, the local scheduler would return at least one violated constraint in all its schedules, which would be dealt with so as to maximize subjective utility [12]. Since the local scheduler is boundedly rational and satisfices instead of optimizing, it may do this even if constraints are not inconsistent (i.e. it does not search exhaustively).

3   Multi-agent Financial Portfolio Management

One implementation of these ideas has been in a system named WARREN for financial portfolio mangement [32]. WARREN gives a concrete, working implementation of some of the ACM ideas discussed earlier in this paper. The internal architecture of each agent was designed to be compatible with the TÆMS and GPGP approaches discussed above, but for our initial implementation we have replaced the GPGP coordination module with a simpler HTN task reduction planner. The WARREN system is *open*, meaning agents can come and go at any time. A WARREN organization consists of a portfolio interface agent for each user, two task agents for fundemental stock analysis and price-news graphing, a news information agent for Dow-Jones and Clarinet news, several different stock ticker information agents, and two EDGAR information agents assigned to the SEC's electronic archives for quarterly and annual reports. Organizational information agents include a "matchmaker" or yellow-pages agent that helps an information requestor find the appropriate information server in the dynamic, open system. One important requirement was robustness, so that when any WARREN agent leaves the system (or crashes) the remaining agents reorganize so as to carry on as effectively as possible. We have conducted an analysis of various features (privacy, efficiency, robustness, etc.) for both matchmade and brokered open agent organizations [7].

In particular, "information agents" that are one step above raw data sources have a stylized set of reusable behaviors that make them easy to create [6] [6]. The main function of an information agent and hence its dominant domain-level behaviors are: retrieving information from external information sources in response to *one shot* queries (e.g. "retrieve the current price of IBM stock"); fulfilling requests for *periodic* information (e.g. "give me the price of IBM every 30 minutes"); monitoring external information sources for the occurrence of given information patterns, called *information monitoring* requests, (e.g. "notify me when IBM's price increases by 10% over $80"). An information agent's reusable behaviors are facilitated by its reusable agent architecture, i.e. the domain-independent abstraction of the local infobase schema, and a set of generic software components for knowledge representation, agent control, and interaction with other agents. The generic software components, based on DECAF [12, 27], are common to all classes of information agents as well as to the task and interface agents we have built.

The control process for information agents includes, *communication* of planning goals, *planning* to achieve internal or external goals, *scheduling* the actions

---

[6] There is always the problem of building a consistant, shared ontology [23, 4, 20]).

within these plans, actually carrying out these actions (see Figure 7), and *monitoring action execution*. This entire "metacontrol" sequence (communicate, plan, schedule, monitor) happens at *every* monitoring point (at the very least, upon completion of each executed action). Thus the architecture allows the interleaving of planning and execution, and allows the agent to quickly adapt to new information and unexpected outcomes. In addition, the agent metacontroller has a shutdown and an initialization process. At startup, the agent executes the initialization process which bootstraps the agent by giving it initial goals, i.e. to poll for messages from other agents and to advertise itself with a matchmaker or broker. The shutdown process is executed when the agent either chooses to terminate or receives an error signal. The shutdown process sends messages from the terminating agent to any current customers and the matchmaker or broker informing them of service interruption.

An information agent's external goals, i.e. answering a one-shot query, setting up periodic queries and monitoring information changes are communicated to it in KQML messages originating from other agents. The communication module receives and parses messages, extracts the information goals and passes them to the planner.

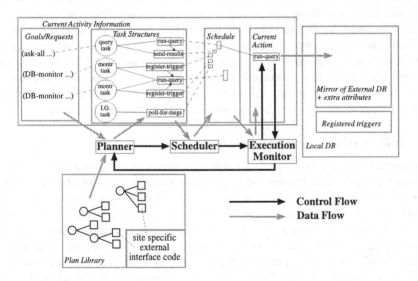

Fig. 7. Overall view of data and control flow in an information agent.

3.1 Planning

The agent planning process is based on a hierarchical task network (HTN) planning formalism. It takes as input the agent's current set of goals, the current set of task structures, and a library of task reduction schemas. A task structure is a partially instantiated task network, including inter-task information flow and other coordination relationships and descriptions of potential task outcomes (See [36] for a complete description of the WARREN task structure representation). Since arrival of goals, planning and execution are on-going and interleaved, the planning process modifies the current set of task structures—by removing tasks, further reducing existing tasks, or instantiating new tasks—to account for any changes to the agent's goals. Task reduction is incremental, and is interleaved with execution.

3.2   Scheduling

The agent scheduling process takes as input the agent's current set of task structures, particularly the set of all primitive actions, and decides which primitive action, if any, is to be executed next. This action is then identified as a fixed intention until it is actually carried out (by the execution component).

3.3   Execution Monitoring

The execution monitoring process takes the agent's next intended action and prepares, monitors, and completes its execution. The execution monitor prepares an action for execution by setting up a context (including the results of previous actions, etc.) for the action. It monitors the action by optionally providing the associated computation-limited resources—for example, the action may be allowed only a certain amount of time and if the action does not complete before that time is up, the computation is interrupted and the action is marked as having failed. Upon completion of an action, results are provided to downstream actions by provision links in the task network, and statistics collected.

3.4   Information Agent Behaviors

An information agent behavior is a particular approach to accomplishing a goal. Behavior instances are represented by a task instance, a set of sub-tasks or primitive action instances, and the information-flow relationships between them. As described above, the task structure for a given goal is instantiated incrementally and dynamically by the planner. The scheduler then determines when individual action instances should be executed, depending on their deadline and on the availablity of required information. As actions are executed and new information is produced, it is routed (as stipulated by information-flow links in the task structure) to other tasks. Thus, the control flow of individual actions within a behavior is determined by information flow. Some of these behaviors are shared in part by agents in WARREN that are *not* information agents—in general these other agents have both reusable and unique behaviors.

Information agent behaviors include:

Advertising: Upon startup, every agent creates an internal goal to advertise itself. An agent advertises itself by sending a matchmaker or broker its infobase schema, which contains all the information needed for describing the information services that the advertising agent can provide.

Message Polling: Message Polling is the simplest information agent behavior. The information agent initialization process asserts a goal for the agent to collect and process incoming KQML messages.

Answering Simple Queries: A simple query is one that is simply applied to the agent's infobase and the results returned to the query-initiator. The query might be a one-shot question or it might be a request for periodic query applications with a given frequency. A task to respond to a simple query consists of two actions: running the query and sending the results to the query-initiator; the running action enables the sending action. The only difference between one-shot and periodic simple queries is whether the constituent actions are themselves periodic.

Information Monitoring: An information monitoring query is one that is interpreted as expressing a condition that when true will trigger the transmission of a selected record or records.

Cloning: Cloning is one of an information agent's possible responses to overloaded conditions. An information agent could recognize via self-reflection that it is becoming overloaded. To do this, it uses a simple model of how its ability to meet new deadlines is related to the characteristics of its current queries and other tasks. It compares this model to a hypothetical situation that describes the effect of adding a new agent. If this evaluation suggests that adding a new agent would be beneficial, the agent removes itself (temporarily) from actively pursuing new queries (by "unadvertising" its services to the matchmaker) and creates a new information agent that is a clone of itself. In this way, the information agent can make a rational meta-control decision about whether or not it should undertake a cloning behavior. A formal presentation of the cloning criteria and the results of empirical evaluation can be found in [8].

4   MADEsmart: Coordination Support for Manufacturing and Design Engineering

We are currently working with a group implementing the UCAA/ACM vision of coordination support as a part of the MADEsmart project at Boeing Helicopters [28]. MADEsmart seeks to partially automate the integrated product teams used to organize design engineers through the use of multi-agent approaches. For example, associated with each human engineer in an integrated product team is a UCAA agent that can interact with that engineer. Other agents, using ACM technology, wrap around existing computationally intensive resources such as composite fiber placement simulations and the COSTADE design cost analysis tool, which uses an existing FORTRAN-based model.

For this project, the core agent architecture components are being integrated using GBB, a commercial blackboard system. If you look at Figure 7, you can see how the goal, planned task structure, schedule, and domain-dependent data structures could be stored on levels of an agent blackboard, and that the major control components (coordination, planning, scheduling, and the domain actions themselves) could be blackboard knowledge sources and their instances. A graphical task structure specification tool allows programmers to create and edit agent-executable task structures (behaviors), including the flows of information between executable methods / basic actions.

In the initial implementation, the UCAA has little scheduling to do, mostly due to the fact that only one project is being worked on, and the initial task structures have been purposely kept quite spartan. We plan to eventually apply our scheduling technologies to intelligent user interfaces (via the Local Schedule Display in the UCAA). The UCAA will help a user to schedule his or her activities at the workstation and display that schedule (using the Local Schedule Display) in a meaningful and expressive form that can be queried and explained. In most cases, the user will have significant freedom in the ordering of their activities—the purpose of the Local Schedule Display is to make sure that tasks are not forgotten, that time critical or critical enabling tasks are identified to the user, and that facilitating or other soft-related tasks are also identified.

5   Conclusions and Future Work

The most important thing to be clear about the results of our approach is that we are *not* building tools for solving a particular domain problem like crisis management or cost analysis—we are building tools to support the use of domain-level tools by *groups* of people and computational agents to solve large, interrelated problems concurrently. Our results will enable people and c-agents to coordinate their activities so that:

Problems get solved completely. No one drops the ball on an important component for which they are responsible. This is especially important in high pressure situations, and where there has not been enough training.

Problems get solved in a timely manner. Schedules for human and c-agent activities allow for estimates on the completion of important tasks. Humans need to know which tasks on their agendas are time critical. C-agents can use modern resource-bounded reasoning techniques to accomplish tasks by certain deadlines with certain minimal qualities—and to notify others as appropriate when problems develop.

Problems are solved in efficient ways that are dynamically adapted to the current situation. One example is load balancing—more than one agent is capable of solving a subtask, but one can get to it sooner than the other or one has more expertise and is likely to produce a higher quality solution. Another example is exploiting soft task relationships such as where one task facilitates another (but is not necessary), or where one agent could do a 'favor' for another agent (temporarily extending the agent's responsibilities at a low cost). Both positive and negative relationships can exist between tasks, and are usually dealt with through separate mechanisms.

Some important research questions to be answered in this work include the question of how accurate task duration estimates have to be, and how important task monitoring is. We are also looking into automatically learning task duration models, and proper sets of coordination mechanisms [30]. Other important questions include the representation and impact of formal and informal organizational roles when assessing the value of potential schedules.

Our vision of concurrent engineering environments includes intelligent, autonomous computational agents, and agentifying wrappers for existing databases (such as WARREN information agents), that will accept tasks from users or other agents. These tasks could be as 'simple' as one-shot, periodic or database monitoring queries or as complex as the development of initial contingency plans for a certain situation. In a mixed-initiative system we can expect some c-agents to initiate tasks as well (perhaps even to humans). The results of our research will enable these agents to also take advantage of the human user's coordination and scheduling mechanisms so that each agent can intelligently order its tasks, meet deadlines, and take advantage of soft coordination relationships when possible.

References

1. C. Castelfranchi. Commitments:from individual intentions to groups and organizations. In Michael Prietula, editor, *AI and theories of groups & organizations: Conceptual and Empirical Research*. AAAI Workshop, 1993. Working Notes.
2. CHECKMATE. Air campaign planning—an approach for the future. White Paper.
3. Philip R. Cohen and Hector J. Levesque. Intention is choice with commitment. *Artificial Intelligence*, 42(3):213–261, 1990.
4. C. Collet, M.N. Huhns, and W. Shen. Resource integration using a large knowledge base in Carnot. *Computer*, pages 55–62, December 1991.
5. ISX Corporation. ACPT—the air campaign planning tool. White Paper.
6. K. Decker, A. Pannu, K. Sycara, and M. Williamson. Designing behaviors for information agents. In *Proceedings of the 1st Intl. Conf. on Autonomous Agents*, pages 404–413, Marina del Rey, February 1997.
7. K. Decker, K. Sycara, and M. Williamson. Middle-agents for the internet. In *Proceedings of the Fifteenth International Joint Conference on Artificial Intelligence*, Nagoya, Japan, August 1997.
8. K. Decker, M. Williamson, and K. Sycara. Intelligent adaptive information agents. In *Proceedings of the AAAI-96 Workshop on Intelligent Adaptive Agents*, 1996. AAAI Press Tech Report WS-96-04.
9. Keith S. Decker. *Environment Centered Analysis and Design of Coordination Mechanisms*. PhD thesis, University of Massachusetts, 1995.
10. Keith S. Decker and Victor R. Lesser. An approach to analyzing the need for meta-level communication. In *Proceedings of the Thirteenth International Joint Conference on Artificial Intelligence*, pages 360–366, Chambéry, France, August 1993.
11. Keith S. Decker and Victor R. Lesser. Quantitative modeling of complex computational task environments. In *Proceedings of the Eleventh National Conference on Artificial Intelligence*, pages 217–224, Washington, July 1993.
12. Keith S. Decker and Victor R. Lesser. Designing a family of coordination algorithms. In *Proceedings of the First International Conference on Multi-Agent Systems*, pages 73–80, San Francisco, June 1995. AAAI Press. Longer version available as UMass CS-TR 94-14.

13. E. H. Durfee and T. A. Montgomery. Coordination as distributed search in a hierarchical behavior space. *IEEE Transactions on Systems, Man, and Cybernetics*, 21(6):1363–1378, November 1991.

14. Edmund H. Durfee, Victor R. Lesser, and Daniel D. Corkill. Coherent cooperation among communicating problem solvers. *IEEE Transactions on Computers*, 36(11):1275–1291, November 1987.

15. E.H. Durfee and V.R. Lesser. Partial global planning: A coordination framework for distributed hypothesis formation. *IEEE Transactions on Systems, Man, and Cybernetics*, 21(5):1167–1183, September 1991.

16. Mark S. Fox. An organizational view of distributed systems. *IEEE Transactions on Systems, Man, and Cybernetics*, 11(1):70–80, January 1981.

17. J. Galbraith. *Organizational Design*. Addison-Wesley, Reading, MA, 1977.

18. Alan Garvey, Marty Humphrey, and Victor Lesser. Task interdependencies in design-to-time real-time scheduling. In *Proceedings of the Eleventh National Conference on Artificial Intelligence*, pages 580–585, Washington, July 1993.

19. Alan Garvey and Victor Lesser. Design-to-time real-time scheduling. *IEEE Transactions on Systems, Man, and Cybernetics*, 23(6):1491–1502, 1993.

20. T.R. Gruber. Toward principles for the design of ontologies used for knowledge sharing. Technical Report KSL-93-4, Knowledge Systems Laboratory, Stanford University, 1993.

21. Carl Hewitt. Offices are open systems. *ACM Transactions on Office Information Systems*, 4(3):271–287, July 1986.

22. N. R. Jennings. Commitments and conventions: The foundation of coordination in multi-agent systems. *The Knowledge Engineering Review*, 8(3):223–250, 1993.

23. W. Kim and J. Seo. Classifying schematic and data heterogeneity in multidatabase systems. *Computer*, pages 12–18, December 1991.

24. Paul Lawrence and Jay Lorsch. *Organization and Environment*. Harvard University Press, Cambridge, MA, 1967.

25. Thomas W. Malone. What is coordination theory? In *Proceedings of the National Science Foundation Coordination Theory Workshop*, February 1988.

26. Sergei Nirenburg and Victor Lesser. Providing intelligent assistance in distributed office environments. In Alan H. Bond and Les Gasser, editors, *Readings in Distributed Artificial Intelligence*, pages 590–598. Morgan Kaufmann, 1988.

27. Tim Oates, M. V. Nagendra Prasad, Victor R. Lesser, and Keith S. Decker. A distributed problem solving approach to cooperative information gathering. In *AAAI Spring Symposium on Information Gathering in Distributed Environments*, Stanford University, March 1995.

28. L. Obrst, M. Woytowitz, D. Rock, S. Lander, K. Gallagher, and K. Decker. Agent-based integrated project teams. Submitted, 1997 ASME Design Engineering and Computers in Engineering Conference; Engineering Information Management Symposium, 1997.

29. P. S. Ow, M. J. Prietula, and W. Hsu. Configuring knowledge-based systems to organizational structures: Issues and examples in multiple agent support. In L. F. Pau, J. Motiwalla, Y. H. Pao, and H. H. Teh, editors, *Expert Systems in Economics, Banking, and Management*, pages 309–318. North-Holland, Amsterdam, 1989.

30. M.V. Nagendra Prasad and V.R. Lesser. Learning situation-specific coordination in generalized partial global planning. In *AAAI Spring Symposium on Adaptation, Co-evolution and Learning in Multiagent Systems*, Stanford, March 1996.

31. Arthur L. Stinchcombe. *Information and Organizations*. University of California Press, Berkeley, CA, 1990.

32. K. Sycara, K. Decker, A. Pannu, M. Williamson, and D. Zeng. Distributed intelligent agents. *IEEE Expert*, 11(6):36–46, December 1996.
33. Frank v. Martial. *Coordinating Plans of Autonomous Agents*. Springer-Verlag, Berlin, 1992. Lecture Notes in Artificial Intelligence no. 610.
34. T. Wagner, A. Garvey, and V. Lesser. Complex goal criteria and its application in design-to-criteria scheduling. In *Proceedings of the Fourteenth National Conference on Artificial Intelligence*, Providence, July 1997.
35. D.L. Westbrook, S.D. Anderson, D.M. Hart, and P.R. Cohen. Common lisp instrumentation package: User manual. Technical Report 94–26, Department of Computer Science, University of Massachusetts, 1994.
36. M. Williamson, K. Decker, and K. Sycara. Unified information and control flow in hierarchical task networks. In *Proceedings of the AAAI-96 workshop on Theories of Planning, Action, and Control*, 1996.

Coordination in Workflow Management Systems - A Rule-Based Approach

G. Kappel, S. Rausch-Schott, and W. Retschitzegger

Department of Information Systems
University of Linz, A-4040 Linz, Austria
email: {gerti,stefan,werner}@ifs.uni-linz.ac.at

Abstract. Coordination is a key requirement of software systems where different parts have to be adjusted in order to reach a common goal. A prominent example thereof are workflow management systems (WFMS). They in particular require flexible mechanisms to realize different kinds of coordination, which are called coordination policies. This need for flexibility emerges from the fact that coordination policies in WFMS are subject to frequent changes caused by the business environment. Flexibility is required in different directions, ranging from a dynamic evolution of existing policies to proper reactions to unpredictable situations. Active object-oriented database systems (AOODBS) along with their basic mechanism in terms of Event/Condition/Action (ECA) rules seem to be a promising technology in order to cope with these requirements. ECA rules allow for an event-driven realization of context- and time-dependent behavior which constitutes a major property of coordination policies. By encapsulating coordination policies within ECA rules, general knowledge can be represented independently from specific business processes. This both eases modification of coordination policies and enhances their reusability. To demonstrate the power of this approach, the paper identifies various coordination policies required within different areas of WFMS and outlines their mapping to ECA rules.

1 Introduction

In recent years, there has been growing interest in questions about how activities of complex systems can be coordinated. These include not only computer systems but also human, biological and economical systems. In fact, coordination is necessary in all systems where some interdependencies between the different elements constituting the system exist [23]. Before discussing coordination in the context of a particular system, let us shortly explain what we understand by the term *coordination*. Following [29] coordination is the "integration and harmonious adjustment of individual work efforts toward the accomplishment of a larger goal". According to [23], coordination can be achieved by managing *dependencies* between activities which usually can be done by using different *coordination policies*. These dependencies exist, for example, when using shared resources, in case of producer/consumer or task/subtask relationships, and when synchronization constraints have to be enforced. Two forms of coordination, namely *concurrency* and *cooperation*, can be distinguished [25]. Concurrency prevents indeterminism and inconsistencies, e.g., by using a "first come/first serve" coordination policy or another one based on priorities. In contrast, coordination policies for cooperation establish, e.g., a producer consumer relationship between two processes by enforcing a logical order. A prominent application area where both forms of coordination are required are workflow management systems.

A workflow management system (WFMS) supports the design, execution and monitoring of in general long-lasting business processes that typically involve multiple activities and multiple collaborating persons in a distributed environment. By making the business process explicit, WFMS promise to increase the efficiency of business processes and, consequently, to raise productivity and the competitive edge of an organization. In this respect, the *coordination* of the various *activities* as well as of the several *resources* needed to perform these activities plays a central role. In fact, the business process itself may be seen as a metaphor for a specific form of coordination that controls the access of several agents to different shared resources [28]. In this paper, we focus on coordination policies necessary in WFMS and in particular on their flexible realization by means of active mechanisms.

The remainder of the paper is organized as follows. Section 2 provides a concise introduction into areas of WFMS requiring coordination policies and motivates their realization by means of active mechanisms. Section 3 proposes several useful coordination policies and describes their mapping to ECA rules. The architecture of our research vehicle TriGS$_{flow}$ realizing this approach is presented in Section 4. Finally, Section 5 discusses related work and Section 6 points to ongoing research.

2 Application Areas for Coordination Policies in WFMS

As already mentioned, coordination is of major concern for WFMS irrespective of the domain for which they are applicable, like office automation, reservation management, or computer integrated manufacturing (CIM). Although the concrete design of the processes themselves may vary considerably from domain to domain and even within a single domain, the dependencies which have to be managed in order to realize these business processes, and thus required coordination policies, can be subsumed in a few basic application areas.

As a prerequisite for identifying the areas in WFMS requiring coordination policies, the basic model of our research vehicle TriGS$_{flow}$, a WFMS based on an active object-oriented database system, is sketched in the following [19, 20].

The model used in TriGS$_{flow}$ to represent a business process comprises a number of classes within an object-oriented setting. It is generic in the sense that different kinds of workflows such as product maintenance, reimbursement of business trips, and reordering of goods can be modeled by simply specializing and instantiating the corresponding object classes. Note, that the object classes

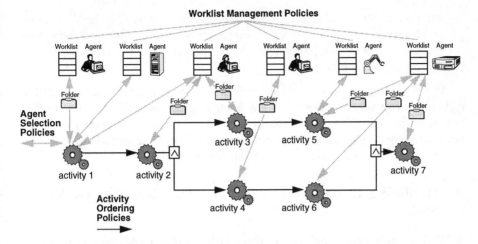

Fig. 1. Application Areas for Coordination Policies

used in this paper are described on the fly. For a description of the complete object-oriented model it is referred to [20].

In TriGS$_{flow}$, similar to [17], a business process among others is characterized by the following aspects. The *functional and operational aspects* describe *activities* that are part of the business process by means of consumed and produced resources, the services used, and their nesting. The *behavioral aspect* defines relationships between activities, i.e., the control flow of the process by means of an *activity net*, while the *informational aspect* deals with the data flow between activities, which is realized by means of folders. The *organizational aspect*, finally, describes organizational entities, like *human agents* or *software agents* and *roles*, as well as the assignment of activities to them based on *worklists*. In other words, while the functional and operational aspects of business processes deal with a single activity, which is either atomic or composed of further activities, the other aspects describe relationships between activities and between activity and agent, respectively.

Based on this workflow model, different areas can be identified, where coordination is necessary. It has to be emphasized that these application areas, which are depicted in Figure 1, are orthogonal to each other.

1. *Activity Ordering*: Activities which are part of a certain workflow have to be coordinated with respect to their execution order by means of *activity ordering policies*.
2. *Agent Selection*: An agent which is able to perform a certain activity has to be selected for actually executing the activity by means of *agent selection policies*.
3. *Worklist Management*: Similar to activity ordering policies which coordinate the execution order of activities which are part of a certain workflow, *worklist management policies* coordinate the execution order of several activities

assigned to a certain agent. These activities can be part of a single workflow or of several workflows. Worklist management policies are necessary since business processes and therefore also single activities are often subject to temporal constraints [9].

It is important to mention that some kind of coordination is also needed to control the concurrent access of several agents/activities to shared data residing in folders. Since TriGS$_{flow}$ is based on a database system, concurrency control is automatically covered by the transaction mechanism of the underlying database system. Thus, this issue is not further discussed in this paper.

3   Realizing Coordination Policies by Means of ECA Rules

A WFMS, on the one hand, has to cope with the individual needs of organizations and, on the other hand, has to dynamically react to frequently changing requirements or unpredictable situations [10]. A powerful means to meet these requirements for flexibility of coordination policies are active object-oriented database systems (AOODBS) [7, 18]. The realization of coordination policies by means of Event/Condition/Action (ECA) rules, which represent the most prominent basic mechanism of such active systems, leads to various advantages.

To start with, ECA rules enable the system to monitor certain situations and to react to them automatically in a predefined way. With this, they not only provide a uniform and natural description of *context- and time-dependent behavior* which is inherent to coordination policies but also free the system from continuously checking *when* to apply a certain coordination policy since it is driven by events.

Another important benefit of using AOODBS is that coordination policies are specified and stored separately from a business process as part of the database schema, thus achieving some kind of *knowledge independence* [4]. The power of knowledge independence is that coordination policies expressed by rules can be automatically shared by and therefore imposed on several business processes. Furthermore, as with all other levels of independence, evolution - in this case evolution of coordination policies - is much more feasible and controllable. Points of change can be easier localized and modifications can be done locally, i.e., without affecting other system components. It is possible to change or extend coordination policies dynamically by merely modifying existing rules or defining new rules. Finally, since coordination policies are encapsulated within rules, *reusability* of existing policies is alleviated.

Up to now we have identified the application areas for coordination policies in WFMS. In the following, different coordination policies and their realization by means of ECA rules are outlined for each of these application areas. Since the mapping of coordination policies to rules is quite similar for different kinds thereof, the resulting rules are not described explicitly. Rather, to get a better understanding of the basic idea of this mapping process, its differences and similarities for various policies are factored out and described in detail. Examples used to illustrate rules realizing coordination policies are all taken from a simple product maintenance process which is based on customer feedback. Note, the generic components of these rules are factored out into so-called *rule patterns*, thus realizing a framework of business process independent primitives for coordination policies. For a discussion of the rule pattern approach it is referred to [21].

3.1 Activity Ordering Policies

The control flow between activities in our model is specified by means of an *activity net* relating activities to each other on the basis of different activity ordering policies. The basic activity ordering policies supported in TriGS$_{flow}$ can be classified along two dimensions:

- *Kind of Control Structure.* Three different kinds of control structures similar to those described in [6] and [26] are supported, namely sequencing, branching, and joining.
- *Kind of Dependency.* Orthogonal to the control structure, the starting point(s) of the successor activities may be defined as either the *end* of the predecessor activity (which is default), or the *start* thereof. In more detail, the *end-start dependency* specifies that the successor activity may not start before the predecessor activity has been finished, thus blocking the successor activity. This is especially useful if the execution of the successor activity completely depends on the result of the predecessor activity. In contrast, the *start-start dependency* specifies, that already the start of the predecessor triggers the successor activity, which can lead to a parallel execution of these activities, thus increasing concurrency. This kind of dependency makes sense in all those cases, where the successor activity does not need any result of the predecessor except that it has been started.

By combining these two dimensions, seven different activity ordering policies, which are illustrated in Figure 2, emerge.

Logical Operators. Whereas the sequence policies are already specified completely, for branching and joining a logical operator still has to be defined. TriGS$_{flow}$ supports the three logical operators AND ($\wedge$), exclusive OR ($\times$), and inclusive OR ($\vee$). Consequently, three different kinds of branching as well as of joining are distinguished. *ExOR-branching* specifies that only one of the specified successor activities may be triggered by the predecessor activity. *AND-branching* means that all of the specified successors are triggered. *InOR-branching* defines that a subset of the specified successors is chosen. Analogously, an *AND-join* specifies that the common successor cannot be performed until all predecessor activities have been started or finished, depending on the kind of dependency. In contrast, an *exOR-join* specifies that the successor activity can be performed as soon as one of the predecessors has been started or finished. Last but not least, an *inOR-join* specifies that a subset of the predecessor activities has to be started or finished before the successor activity is enabled. Note, that in Figure 2 branching and joining have just two successors or predecessors, respectively. In general however, the number of successors/predecessors may be arbitrary.

While for most of these policies their differences are obvious, this might not be the case for the two policies *start-start sequence* and *end-start branching*. At a first glance, they look similar since activity1 and activity2, and activity2 and activity3, respectively, can be executed in parallel. However, the difference is that while in the start-start sequence, activity2 is causally depending on the start of activity1, the corresponding activities in the AND-branching construct, which are activity2 and activity3, are rather at the same level and have no direct causal relationship to each other.

Higher-Level Policies. The basic activity ordering policies described above can almost arbitrarily be combined to some form of higher-level coordination policies. The only combination not allowed is an ExOR-branching followed by an AND-join. This is because, since the ExOR-branching activates only a single successor, the precondition for the AND-join would never be satisfied.

Example. To illustrate a useful combination, in the following a higher-level policy called "Future Synchronizer" is briefly described (cf. Fig. 3).

The usefulness of this policy is motivated by the fact that during execution of a certain activity activity1, the agent performing this activity needs the result of another activity activity2 performed by another agent in order to proceed. To increase concurrency, activity2 is not requested when its result is actually needed but already at the start of activity1. Thus, activity2 is able to produce its result in parallel to the execution of activity1. Upon needing the result, i.e., sometimes in the future, activity1 has to synchronize with the end of activity2. For this, activity1 is partitioned into two subactivities representing the parts that can be executed before (activity1.2) and after (activity1.2) the result is available, respectively. Synchronization is done by means of an AND-join. The applicability of this policy, of course, is based on the assumption that activity2 does not need any data produced by activity1.

Mapping Activity Ordering Policies to Rules. In the following, the introduced activity ordering policies are mapped to the basic components of ECA rules. As already mentioned, instead of listing all resulting activity ordering rules, the basic mapping process is outlined in detail.

First, according to the various *kinds of control structure*, six different cases can be identified for this mapping:

1. a relationship representing a *sequence* is mapped to a single rule
2. all relationships taking part in an *AND-branching* are mapped to a single rule
3. all relationships taking part in an *AND-join* are mapped to a single rule containing a composite event, i.e., an event combining other events by means of logical operators [7]
4. each relationship taking part in an *OR-branching* (exclusive OR or inclusive OR) is mapped to a separate rule
5. each relationship taking part in an *ExOR-join* is mapped to a separate rule

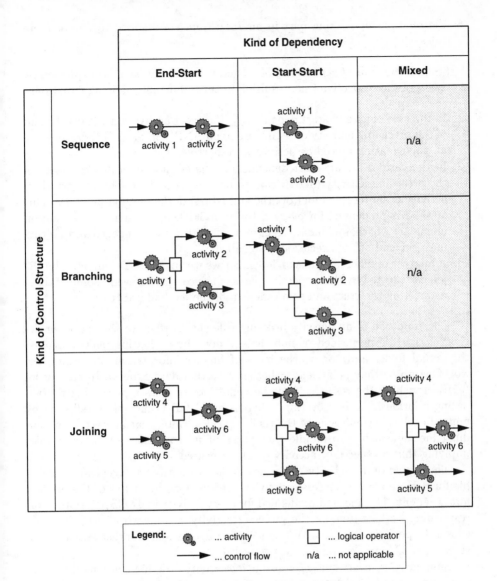

Fig. 2. Basic Activity Ordering Policies

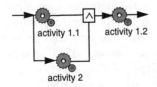

Fig. 3. A Higher Level Coordination Policy - The "Future Synchronizer"

6. the relationships taking part in an *InOR-join* are mapped to one or more rules

Second, the *kind of dependency* of an activity ordering policy is expressed by the *event* of the respective rule, resulting in three different mapping situations:

1. In the case of an end-start dependency, the event always constitutes the end of the preceding activity or — in case of an AND-join or an InOR-join — of all participating preceding activities, respectively.
2. In the case of a start-start dependency, the event constitutes the start of the preceding activity (activities). To be more specific, the event part of an activity ordering rule monitors the end (start) of the method `perform`. This method is predefined for every activity in TriGS$_{flow}$ starting its execution no matter whether a human agent or a software agent is engaged and waiting until the end of the execution is signalled.
3. A mixture of different kinds of dependencies within an AND-join or an InOR-join is reflected by the respective parts of the composite event, some of them monitoring the start and some the end of the method `perform`.

The *condition* of an activity ordering rule checks whether the successor activity has to be performed or not. This is done by evaluating queries against the actual folder and/ or on the basis of further information concerning the workflow up to that point, e.g., whether a certain date expired. In case of an InOR-branching the result sets of the conditions of rules representing participating relationships may overlap, whereas an ExOR-branching is reflected by mutual exclusive conditions of the realizing rules. Note, that an exception handling mechanism has to handle the case that all conditions evaluate to false implying that no successor activity can be executed.

The *action* of an activity ordering rule has to notify the agent(s) responsible for performing the successor activity. This is done by means of the method `notifyAgent`. This method predefined for every activity in TriGS$_{flow}$ puts a corresponding worklist item for the successor activity into the worklist of the agent chosen to perform this activity (for selecting agents and worklist management cf. Section 3.2 and Section 3.3, respectively).

Summarizing, every rule responsible for activity ordering contains the methods `perform` and `notifyAgent` in its event part and action part, respectively.

Example. In the following, an example is given to illustrate the mapping of activity ordering policies to rules. A part of the activity net of our running example describing a product maintenance workflow is depicted in Figure 4.

The figure illustrates an ExOR-branching between the predecessor activity "analyze reports" and the successor activities "redesign", "recommend new service instructions" and "create report". Each of these activities is realized as an instance of a predefined class of the object-oriented class model of TriGS$_{flow}$ called `Activity`. The realization of this policy requires three rules responsible for triggering either of the successor activities upon end of the activity "analyze reports".

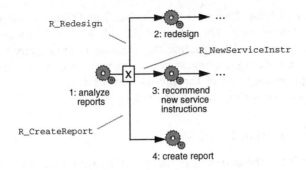

Fig. 4. ExOR-branching of Activities

The rules named R_Redesign, R_NewServiceInstr, and R_CreateReport are activated for the same instance of class Activity, namely a_analyze_reports by means of its guards. A guard represents a logical predicate further restricting the events able to trigger the rule. That is, after the method perform has been executed (denoted by the keyword POST) on that instance (depicted by the keyword trgObj), all three rules are triggered.

```
DEFINE RULE R_Redesign
    ON POST (Activity, perform: actFolder) [trgObj==a_analyze_reports] DO
    IF ((actFolder docNamed: 'analysis report') errortype = 'conceptual')
       and:
       (actFolder docNamed: 'analysis report') percentage > 10] ] THEN
    EXECUTE a_redesign notifyAgent: actFolder
END RULE R_Redesign.

DEFINE RULE R_NewServiceInstr
    ON POST (Activity, perform: actFolder) [trgObj==a_analyze_reports] DO
    IF ((actFolder docNamed: 'analysis report') errortype = 'conceptual')
       and:
       (actFolder docNamed: 'analysis report') percentage <= 10] ] THEN
    EXECUTE a_new_service_instr notifyAgent: actFolder
END RULE R_NewServiceInstr.

DEFINE RULE R_CreateReport
    ON POST (Activity, perform: actFolder) [trgObj==a_analyze_reports] DO
    IF ((actFolder docNamed: 'analysis report') errortype = 'other') THEN
    EXECUTE a_create_report notifyAgent: actFolder
END RULE R_CreateReport.
```

The conditions of these rules are complementary, checking on the basis of the analysis reports whether a redesign is necessary (which is assumed to be the case if the percentage of conceptual errors, i.e., errors of type 'conceptual', is above 10 percent), new service instructions are to be recommended (percentage of conceptual errors is less than 10 percent and the percentage of errors of type 'maintenance' is high), or whether the error reports cannot be reacted upon properly at time (type of error is 'other') and, thus, are reported to the management, respectively. The action of the rule for which the condition evaluates to true is executed by sending the message notifyAgent to the respective instance (a_redesign, a_new_service_instr, or a_create_report) of class Activity representing one of the mutual exclusive successors of the activity a_analyze_reports within the activity net.

3.2 Agent Selection Policies

For each activity of the activity net described in Section 3.1, an agent has to be selected which has to perform the activity at hand.[1] For this selection process again different forms of coordination called *agent selection policies* can be applied during workflow execution [2] TriGS$_{flow}$ supports the following basic kinds of agent selection policies:

- *Agent Related Selection.* The simplest form of agent selection policies directly selects a certain agent by means of its identifier. Since this selection policy establishes a very tight coupling between agent and activity, it is totally inflexible against changes in the personnel of the organization. Thus, for human agents it will usually be used in combination with one of the policies below, realizing some kind of higher-level agent selection policy, similar to higher-level activity ordering policies.

- *Role Related Selection.* This kind of policy selects all agents currently playing a certain role. For example, an activity "reordering parts" necessary for manufacturing some product might be executed by any clerk within the purchasing department, i.e., any agent that plays the role "clerk" for that department. With this policy the tight- coupling of an agent related policy is neutralized since roles usually remain stable even if the personnel changes. In case that this policy leads to the selection of more than one agent for a certain activity since they all play the same role, an additional agent selection policy has to be applied. The set of selected agents may be heterogeneous, i.e., it may comprise both, human agents as well as software agents.

- *Workflow Related Selection.* The last category of agent selection policies takes workflow-related data into consideration. Selection criteria of these policies can be based on various data about actual or previous workflows such as "who has performed a certain activity sometimes in the past", "who started this workflow", or "which agent has the least worklist items".

Mapping Agent Selection Policies to Rules. Realizing agent selection policies by means of ECA rules provides the possibility to implement different agent selection policies for a single activity and, in particular, to switch between

---

[1] Note, that similar to [2], TriGS$_{flow}$ also allows to identify more than one agent to perform a certain activity [19]. In this case, coordination is required at the end of activity execution. Examples for such coordination policies are "select the result of the fastest agent" or "select the best result". In order to reduce complexity, however, we assume that only one agent is selected in the remainder of this paper.

them dynamically by simply activating and deactivating the corresponding rule at activity instance level. With this it can be reacted easily to, e.g., unpredictable state changes of agents during workflow execution.

In the following the generic components of agent selection rules are briefly outlined. For all agent selection rules the *event* specifies that the selection process should start, i.e., the rule should be triggered, right before an activity is distributed into the worklists of agents. The *condition* in fact is responsible for realizing the desired kind of basic policy or a combination thereof. For this, queries are posed against the actual folder and/ or other workflow relevant data analogous to the condition of activity ordering rules. The *action* simply assigns the condition result, i.e., the selected agent, to the corresponding activity.

Example. The example in Figure 5 illustrates a higher-level agent selection policy for the activity a_create_report by combining a role-related policy with a workflow-related one. In particular, first, the agents playing the role of a "clerk" are selected. Out of these agents, that agent with the minimal workload is finally chosen to perform the activity at hand. The following rule named R_MinWorkload realizes this higher-level policy. The event of R_MinWorkload is signaled before the method notifyAgent: of class Activity is executed (denoted by the keyword PRE) on the instance a_create_report.

```
DEFINE RULE R_MinWorkload
    ON PRE (Activity, notifyAgent: aFolder) [trgObj==a_create_report] DO
    IF (AllAgents roleOf:Clerk) selMinWorkload THEN
    EXECUTE (trgObj actAgRoles) assignAgent: conditionResult
END RULE R_MinWorkload.
```

The condition determines the agent with the least number of worklist items (selMinWorkload) out of the set of agents playing the role "clerk". The selected agent is passed to the action of the rule (cf. keyword conditionResult).

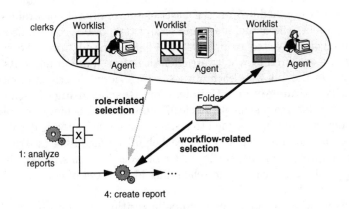

Fig. 5. Agent Selection

The action of the rule assigns the query result to the instance variable actAgRoles of the triggering object (trgObj), i.e., the receiver of the message that triggered the rule. Since in this example, the rule is activated for the activity a_create_report by means of a guard, only, the policy is valid just for that activity.

3.3   Worklist Management Policies

In the previous section, different policies for selecting an agent to execute an activity have been proposed. Requesting an agent to execute the activity, however, does not mean that the activity is started immediately. This is since for activities which have to be executed worklist items are inserted into the worklists of the selected agents, which realize some kind of *asynchronous communication*. These worklist items are coordinated by worklist management policies for each worklist separately. This coordination would not be necessary if the items of the worklists of every agent would be processed in a fixed order. However, usually a business process has to meet certain temporal constraints that may affect its activities as well [9]. Consequently, activity-specific temporal constraints and worklist management policies taking them into account are required. Examples for such temporal constraints are [30]:

- the entire business process has to be *finished before* a certain date
- an activity may be started *at the earliest* at some specified point in time or time period after a preceding activity
- an activity *cannot be performed later than* a certain point in time
- an activity should start *immediately after* its predecessor has finished
- the succeeding activity must be done *some specified time period after* one/the last of its preceding activities

In fact, there are three basic forms of worklist management policies that support these temporal constraints. First, as soon as a new worklist item arrives at a certain worklist, the execution order of existing worklist items including the new one is re-scheduled on the basis of the temporal constraints. Second, for human agents the actual start and end of temporally constrained activities is monitored and reacted to in case of violations. And third, the start of an activity to be executed by a software agent is enforced according to its temporal constraints. In the following each of these categories is described in more detail.

Worklist Management Policies for Rescheduling. Rescheduling by means of worklist management policies is necessary to achieve an optimal execution order of activities assigned to a single human or software agent according to their temporal constraints. The idea behind rescheduling in TriGS$_{flow}$ is a dynamic adaptation of the partial order of worklist items. Note, this is similar to the problem of short-term scheduling in the area of computer integrated manufacturing [27].

In the following, a simple rescheduling algorithm as supported by TriGS$_{flow}$ is outlined: First, activities *with* temporal constraints have higher priority than activities *without*. Second, among constrained activities, those that have to be started or finished at a certain (absolutely or relatively specified) point in time, are considered with higher priority than those with an earliest or latest start/end defined. Third, the priority of activities that have to be started or finished at the latest at a certain deadline increases the nearer they get to that point in time. Finally, to avoid "starving" of unconstrained worklist items for worklists that always include some temporally constrained worklist item, the priority of any worklist item waiting for execution increases with every change of the worklist. Every time a new worklist item arrives,[2] these priorities including that of the newly arrived one are used as basis for computing a new partial order between them.

The realization of this rescheduling policy by means of the *action* of an ECA rule allows to easily exchange it with a different one. The *event* of this rule monitors the arrival of new worklist items, indicated by the predefined method insert of class Worklist of TriGS$_{flow}$. Note, a *condition* is not needed for this specific policy.

Worklist Management Policies for Human Agents. Since WFMS are people systems [10], i.e., human agents are engaged in business processes, a temporal constraint cannot be enforced for them. Thus, an important question is how to react if the constraint is violated. The following policies are supported by TriGS$_{flow}$:

1. *Remind the agent.* Agents could be reminded of overdue activities. If the agent does not react to this reminder after a certain period, the agent can be either reminded further times periodically, or policy (2) or policy (3) could be applied.
2. *Delegate to another agent.* An alternate agent which is ready for performing the activity immediately might be selected and assigned to the activity, i.e., the activity might be delegated. If no alternate agent can be found, policy (3) can be chosen.
3. *Notify the workflow administrator.* This policy has to be chosen if either none of the previous two policies works, or if the kind of reaction cannot be decided automatically, or if a different reaction requiring some kind of human intervention is necessary. The workflow administrator may then, for example, redistribute the overall workload by manually reassigning activities among available agents, interrupt or stop running activities, cancel scheduled activities, etc.

These different kinds of reaction are realized by further rules that monitor the violation of temporal constraints. The major advantage of using ECA rules in this context is that the system does not have to poll for violations periodically

---

[2] Note, that agents are notified about activities they will have to perform sometimes in the future as soon as possible. Thus, the worklist item for an activity constrained to an earliest processing time is deactivated for execution upon insertion into the worklist. As soon as the earliest processing time is valid, the worklist item is activated, and the agent is notified about it.

but rather can be notified about them event-driven. According to the examples for temporal constraints given above, the *event* represents an absolute time event or a time event that is relative to the execution times of some preceding activity, and thus indirectly to the notification time of the agent. The *condition* has to check whether the constraint is violated. A temporal constraint is violated if at the specified point in time - which is the triggering time for the rule - the activity has not yet been started. For this, the status of the corresponding worklist item is examined by the condition. If no corresponding worklist item can be found, the execution of the activity either has already been finished, or the activity has been reassigned to another agent. Since no reaction is required, in both of these cases the condition evaluates to false. The *action* of a temporal constraint rule has to implement the desired reaction strategy as described above.

Example. Consider the following example, realizing a reminder policy in that the agent which has been selected to perform activity a_create_report is reminded in case that (s)he has not started executing this activity within a period of 5 days.

```
DEFINE RULE R_Remind5Days
    ON REL(POST(Activity, notifyAgent:) [trgObj==a_create_report], 5D) DO
    IF ((trgObj actAgRoles) statusOf: trgObj) ~= 'started' THEN
    EXECUTE (trgObj actAgRoles) remindStartOf: trgObj
END RULE R_Remind5Days.
```

Worklist Management Policies for Software Agents. Whereas for human agents, temporal constraints cannot be enforced, this is possible for software agents to a certain extent. The processes realizing software agents can be controlled by ECA rules on the basis of the partial order of the worklist items as follows. First, instead of reminding an agent to start or finish the processing of some activity, rules are able to automatically start the processing of worklist items for a software agent on the basis of the agent's processing status and the temporal constraints specified for the worklist items. Second, similar to a human agent, in case of overloaded software agents, a worklist item may be delegated to another software agent or, if appropriate, even to a human agent. And third, unlike with human agents, the number of resources, i.e., of software agents, may be controlled automatically, by starting additional parallel processes representing these software agents and stopping them as necessary. Worklist items then may be distributed between the dynamic number of software agents, resulting in an optimal utilization of software resources.

Concerning the mapping to ECA rules, the *event* is the same as for worklist management policies in the context of human agents. Unlike them, a *condition* part is not needed and the *action* simply realizes the policies described above.

4 System Architecture of TriGS$_{flow}$

In this section we describe the architectural components of the TriGS$_{flow}$ prototype, as illustrated in Figure 6. The prototype has been implemented as a layer on top of the object-oriented database system GemStone, extended by the active system TriGS providing ECA rules and a module providing roles. Currently, two frontend tools named MasterTOOL and AgentTOOL are being developed providing a graphical user interface for the workflow modeling phase and the workflow execution phase, respectively. We will now describe each layer of the architecture in more detail.

The data model of *GemStone* [3] is based on the *GemStone Smalltalk* programming language, which is a derivate of Smalltalk-80 [14]. In addition to Smalltalk, *GemStone Smalltalk* provides some predefined classes in order to realize database functionality. Considering query facilities, *GemStone Smalltalk* provides a limited query language allowing associative access to objects residing in a single collection. To speed up the retrieval of objects, identity indexes as well as equality indexes can be defined. Concerning concurrency control, GemStone supports optimistic as well as pessimistic mechanisms.

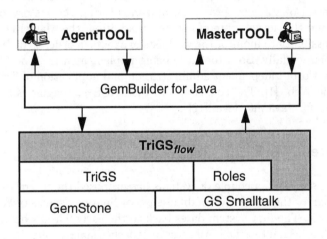

Fig. 6. Architecture of TriGS$_{flow}$

The Roles module used in our prototype is based on the work of [15]. A role hierarchy can be specified orthogonal to the class hierarchy permitting GemStone objects to learn and forget roles, i.e., behavior, dynamically and to play several roles at the same time. In TriGS$_{flow}$, roles are used to specify capabilities and duties of agents, consequently supporting the assignment of activities to agents. For details of the role model of TriGS$_{flow}$ we refer to [20].

The active component of TriGS$_{flow}$ is based on TriGS (=Trigger System for GemStone) [18]. TriGS has been implemented on top of GemStone and makes explicit use of objects, message passing, inheritance, and overriding to provide a seamless integration between rules and the object-oriented data model of GemStone. TriGS rules consisting of events, conditions, and actions monitor the behavior of objects and can be attached to specific object classes or defined independently of any object class hierarchy. Rules can be (de)activated at different levels of granularity ranging from the instance level to the object class level. Moreover, since rules and its components are first-class objects they can be dynamically defined, modified, and extended independently of any application.

In order to be able to use TriGS$_{flow}$ in an efficient and comfortable way, it is essential to provide proper graphical user interfaces which take into account the idiosyncrasies of a high-level design environment for business process applications incorporating rules. With respect to this requirement, two frontend tools named AgentTOOL and MasterTOOL are being developed providing graphical user interfaces for both agents and WFMS administrators. The *Agent-TOOL* will support agents during workflow execution by displaying the agent's worklist, managing selection and rejection of worklist items, starting available workflow types, monitoring the current state of a certain workflow, and communication with other agents, to mention just a few. The *MasterTOOL* will provide functions for design and administration of business processes including organizational modeling, activity modeling and folder modeling, authorization of human agents, control of software processes, and monitoring the history of workflow execution and the actual state of agents. In addition, the MasterTOOL should have the possibility to monitor the worklists of agents in order to distribute tasks between them equally. Both tools are being implemented in Java [11] thus allowing a platform-independent administration and application of TriGS$_{flow}$ via World Wide Web [1]. The connection to the TriGS$_{flow}$ engine is based on the GemBuilder for Java interface [12].

5 Related Work

For the last six years, a couple of systems has proposed the use of ECA rules as a mechanism for the realization of different coordination aspects of WFMS [2, 4, 5, 8, 13, 24, 25]. The first system dates back to the early 90ies, when research on AOODBS has been intensified. All these approaches mainly differ in the degree of rule employment. In the following, the different approaches are surveyed - based on available literature - with respect to their application areas for rules and compared to the concepts realized in TriGS$_{flow}$. Figure 7 summarizes the surveyed approaches, comparing their implementation environment, their employment of roles and their application areas for rules.

The approach of long running activities [5] was one of the first approaches that introduced the use active mechanisms for the realization of coordination. Coming from the area of AOODBS, the authors proposed EA rules for the realization of the control flow between "procedures" and "transactions", including integrity constraint checking and handling of exceptional conditions. Operations on folders or time points are specified as events for these rules, while actions comprise arbitrary procedural statements invoking further procedures.

The system ActMan [25] employs ECA rules for coordination policies which are most similar to worklist management policies in TriGS$_{flow}$. First, rules are used for checking so-called "execution conditions", i.e., some kind of precondition, for "interactive activities", i.e., activities performed by a human agent. For those, the selection of the activity from the worklist represents the event, whereas the condition is responsible for checking the execution conditions by referring to parameters and regarding the execution environment of the activity. If the condition is not satisfied, e.g., due to access right restrictions, the activity might be postponed. The action of the ECA rule comprises data preparation, initiation of the activity, and post analysis routines of the activity. Concerning "batch activities", i.e., activities executed by software agents, similar to $TriGS_{flow}$, their start is automatically enforced as soon as the activity is inserted into the worklist.

	Implementation Environment	Roles	Application Areas for ECA Rules		
			Activity Ordering	Agent Selection	Worklist Management
Long Running Activities	RDBS HiPAC	-	✓	-	-
ActMan	RDBS	-	-	-	✓
InConcert	C++, RDBS	✓	-	-	✓
Bußler et al.	C++, RDBS	✓	-	-	-
Panta Rhei	RDBS Oracle	✓	✓	✓	-
IDEA	AOODBS Chimera	-	✓	✓	-
Geppert et al.	AOODBS SAMOS	✓	✓	-	✓
$TriGS_{flow}$	AOODBS TriGS	✓	✓	✓	✓

Legend: ✓ ... supported   RDBS   ... relational database system including rules
           - ... not supported   AOODBS ... active object-oriented database system

Fig. 7. Role Support and Rule Employment in Related Approaches

InConcert [24] allows to attach EA rules to significant events that are recorded within an audit log. Examples for such events are state changes of activities such as "ready" or "overdue", document check-out/check-in, as well as user-defined events. These events may trigger the start of a new workflow, notification of a user via e-mail or invocation of application-supplied procedures external to the workflow engine via remote procedure calls. In contrast to $TriGS_{flow}$, triggers are executed independently from the actual execution of a workflow, which itself does not rely on trigger concepts.

Although having introduced powerful organizational concepts, Bußler and Jablonski [2] do not employ rules for agent selection policies as is done in $TriGS_{flow}$. Instead agent selection policies are maintained and ensured by a policy resolution manager implemented in a conventional programming language environment. ECA rules in [2] are only applied for so-called agent synchronization, i.e., for synchronizing a number of agents executing a single activity. These rules are triggered upon actions of agents performed on their worklist items. Conditions and actions are defined as relational operations against a table containing the status of the activity corresponding to the worklist item, respectively. Their approach for agent synchronization is very flexible and extensible. For example, new synchronization policies can be introduced by extending the set of conditions and actions as necessary and specifying new ECA rules.

Another approach which also restricts the application of ECA rules to control flow aspects has been introduced in [13]. A workflow in [13] is modeled as a set of brokers providing several services. Brokers correspond to cooperating (human or software) agents implemented as objects on top of the active database system SAMOS. Note, that brokers do not communicate asynchronously by means of worklists, but rather synchronously request services from other brokers and reply to other requests. Services correspond to applications realizing the functionality of activities. Similar to TriGS$_{flow}$, control structures such as sequence, AND-join and OR-join between services are mapped to ECA-rules by using primitive or composite events, respectively. Conditional execution may depend on parameters of the previous activities as well as further values accessible within their broker/service environment. Unlike in other approaches, the event(s) for such a rule is (are) raised explicitly by the service(s) implementing the preceding activity (activities) upon its (their) termination. The action requests a service from a specific broker corresponding to the successor activity. Temporal dependencies between activities, like the execution of an activity due to some deadline reached, are also considered as control flow and are mapped to rules triggered by temporal events. In TriGS$_{flow}$, these dependencies are mapped to worklist management policies for human agents. The application of rules for further worklist management policies and agent selection policies are not considered. Concerning role support, [13] uses a slightly different notion of roles compared to others. Roles are defined within the confines of a broker, i.e., an agent, denoting the broker's responsibilities within an organization during some point in lifetime, while usually roles are specified apart from agents.

The approaches within the IDEA project [4] and of Panta Rhei [8] exploit ECA rules as convenient mechanism for workflow enactment. They are quite similar, since both allow to generate a workflow schema as well as ECA rules semi-automatically out of a formal conceptual specification of the workflow type. For this generation, both approaches use predefined rule templates, i.e., generic rule specifications, which are translated into fully specified rules when the workflow specification is translated. As already mentioned, a similar mechanism, called rule patterns, has been introduced for TriGS and can be applied for any kinds of rules in TriGS$_{flow}$, too [21]. In contrast to TriGS$_{flow}$, the workflow schema is stored together with run-time information within the underlying database within so-called workflow description tables [4] or as forms together with status tables [8], respectively. ECA rules react to reads and updates of these tables and forms, and respond by means of their action with inserts into and updates of them. In particular, [4] distinguishes rules for the control flow of activities (schema interpretation rules), agent selection policies (task assignment rules), exception handling (exception management rules), and derivation of historical data (administration rules). In [8], on the other hand, rules are applied for realizing control flow, agent *synchronization* policies, checking of postconditions of tasks, and optional before- as well as after-procedures for tasks which, e.g., can be used for data conversions. Especially the approach of [8] is interesting, since the whole WFMS consists of the set of rules, only. Concerning role support, Panta Rhei defines a role similar to InConcert [24] as place-holder for a user or a program. While in InConcert an activity has to be assigned to a role in any case, Panta Rhei in addition allows to directly assign activities to users/programs already at specification time of the workflow. If a role has been specified, only one agent playing that role is selected at run-time, similar to InConcert.

6 Conclusion and Outlook

In this paper, various coordination policies necessary for business processes have been outlined and categorized according to the three major application areas activity ordering, agent selection, and worklist management. To realize these policies in a flexible way, active object-oriented database systems have been proposed as a powerful mechanism. The mapping process of the various coordination policies to ECA rules has been described and illustrated by means of examples.

A topic which has not been discussed so far but which is of major importance in the area of coordination in WFMS is the problem of coordinating the transactions embedding the activities which have to be performed. In Section 2, it was mentioned that the underlying database system will take care about that. However, especially WFMS usually require more sophisticated transactional mechanisms compared to the transactional support of most database systems. Among others, serializability is not applicable as a global correctness criterion to enforce overall consistency for workflows, since they are not serial in their nature. Activities, e.g., may again represent workflows consisting of further activities.

One step towards more cooperation is achieved by the *nested transaction model*, where a transaction may be decomposed into several subtransactions, "cooperating" with their parent transaction by accessing shared data [16]. In this way, the nested transaction model is able to support cooperation between a single predecessor activity and several parallel, but causally dependent successor activities (cf. start-start dependency in Subsection 3.1). As soon as more than one predecessor activity start a common successor activity, however, the nested transaction model is too restrictive. This is due to the fact that the nested transaction model does not provide any concept to relate several transactions to a single subtransaction. What is actually required is that the successor activity can be performed within a *subtransaction of more than one so-called parent transaction* representing the predecessor activities, and, that the subtransaction is able to cooperate with them when accessing shared data [22]. Consequently, the structure of a nested transaction no longer resembles a tree, but a directed acyclic graph. We are currently extending the nested transaction model of [16] in this direction since these extensions allow combining the reliability and flexibility of the nested transaction model with the flexible coordination mechanisms used in TriGS$_{flow}$.

References

1. T. Berners-Lee, "WWW: Past, Present, and Future", in *IEEE Computer*, vol. 29, October 1996.
2. C. Bußler and S. Jablonski, "Implementing Agent Coordination for Workflow Management Systems Using Active Database Systems", in *Proceedings of the 4th International Workshop on Research Issues in Data Engineering (RIDE '94): Active Database Systems, IEEE-CS*, eds. Jennifer Widom, Sharma Chakravary, Houston, Texas, 1994.
3. P. Butterworth, A. Otis and J. Stein, "The GemStone Object Database Management System", in *Communications of the ACM*, vol. 34(10), October 1991.
4. F. Casati, S. Ceri, B. Pernici and G. Pozzi, "Conceptual Modeling of WorkFlows", in *Proceedings of the 14th International Conference on Object-Oriented and Entity-Relationship Modeling (OOER'95), Springer LNCS 1021*, ed. M.P. Papazoglou, Gold Coast, Australia, December 1995.
5. U. Dayal, M. Hsu and R. Ladin, "Organizing Long-Running Activities with Triggers and Transactions", in *Proceedings of the 1990 ACM SIGMOD Int. Conference on Management of Data*, Atlantic City, NJ, 1990.
6. V.De Antonellis, B. Zonta, "Modelling Events in Data Base Applications Design", in *Proceedings of the 7th International Conference on Very Large Data Bases (VLDB '81), IEEE Computer Society Press 1021*, eds. C. Zaniolo and C. Delobel, Cannes, France, September 1981.
7. K.R. Dittrich, S. Gatziu and A. Geppert, "The Active Database Management System Manifesto: A Rulebase of ADBMS Features", in *Proceedings of the 2nd Workshop on Rules in Databases (RIDS)*, ed. T. Sellis, Springer LNCS 985, Athens, Greece, September 1995.
8. J. Eder and H. Groiss, "Ein Workflow-Management-System auf der Basis aktiver Datenbanken", in *Geschäftsprozeßmodellierung und Workflow-Management: Modelle, Methoden, Werkzeuge*, eds. G. Vossen, J. Becker (eds.), Thomson Publishing, 1995 (in german).
9. C.A. Ellis, S.J. Gibbs and G.L. Rein, "Groupware - Some Issues and Experiences", in *Communications of the ACM*, vol. 34(1), 1991.
10. C.A. Ellis, K. Keddara and G. Rozenberg, "Dynamic Change Within Workflow Systems", in *Proceedings of the Conference on Organizational Computing Systems*, eds. N. Comstock et al., ACM Press, Milpitas, 1995.
11. D. Flanagan, *Java in a Nutshell*, O'Reilly & Associates, 1996.
12. *GemStone Reference Manual, GemBuilder for Java*, O'Reilly & Associates, 1997.
13. A. Geppert, M. Kradolfer and D. Tombros, "Realization of Cooperative Agents Using an Active Object-Oriented Database Management System", in *Proceedings of the 2nd International Workshop on Rules in Database Systems (RIDS '95), Springer LNCS 985*, ed. T. Sellis, Athens, Greece, Sept. 1995.
14. A. Goldberg and D. Robson, *Smalltalk-80 The Language*, Addison-Wesley Reading, 1989.
15. G. Gottlob, B. Röck and M. Schrefl, "Extending Object-Oriented Systems with Roles", in *ACM Transactions on Information Systems*, vol. 14, July, 1996.

16. T. Härder, K. Rothermel, "Concurrency Control Issues in Nested Transactions", in *VLDB Journal*, vol. 2(1), 1993.

17. S. Jablonski, "Workflow-Management-Systeme: Modellierung und Architektur", in *Thomsons Aktuelle Tutorien (TAT)*, 9, Thomson Publishing, 1995.

18. G. Kappel, S. Rausch-Schott, W. Retschitzegger and S. Vieweg, "TriGS: Making a Passive Object-Oriented Database System Active", in *Journal of Object-Oriented Programming (JOOP)*, vol. 7(4), July/August 1994.

19. G. Kappel, B. Pröll, S. Rausch-Schott and W. Retschitzegger, "TriGS$_{flow}$ - Active Object-Oriented Workflow Management", in *Proceedings of the 28th Hawaiian International Conference on System Sciences (HICSS '95)*, Maui, Hawaii, Jan. 1995.

20. G. Kappel, P. Lang, S. Rausch-Schott and W. Retschitzegger, "Workflow Management Based on Objects, Rules, and Roles", in *IEEE Bulletin of the Technical Committee on Data Engineering*, vol. 18(1), March 1995.

21. G. Kappel, S. Rausch-Schott, W. Retschitzegger and M. Sakkinen, "From Rules to Rule Patterns", in *Proceedings of the 8th International Conference on Advanced Information Systems Engineering (CAiSE '96)*, ed. Y. Vassiliou, Springer LNCS 1080, Heraklion, Crete, May 1996.

22. G. Kappel, S. Rausch-Schott and W. Retschitzegger, "A Transaction Model For Handling Composite Events", in *Proceedings of the Third International Workshop of the Moscow ACM SIGMOD Chapter on Advances in Databases and Information Systems (ADBIS '96)*, ed. Y. Vassiliou, Moscow, September 1996.

23. T.W. Malone and K. Crowston, "The Interdisciplinary Study of Coordination", in *ACM Computing Surveys*, vol. 26(1), March 1994.

24. D.R. McCarthy, S.K. Sarin, "Workflow and Transactions in InConcert", in *IEEE Bulletin of the Technical Committee on Data Engineering*, vol. 16(2), June 1993.

25. B. Reinwald, *Workflow Management in verteilten Systemen: Entwurf und Betrieb geregelter arbeitsteiliger Anwendungssysteme*, Teubner, 1993 (in german).

26. A.-W. Scheer, *Wirtschaftsinformatik - Referenzmodelle für industrielle Geschäftsprozesse*, 4. Auflage, Springer, 1994 (in german).

27. J. Schultz, M. Weigelt and P. Mertens, "Verfahren für die rechnergestützte Produktionsplanung - Ein Überblick", in *Wirtschaftinformatik*, vol. 37, 1995 (in german).

28. K. Schwab, "Koordinationsmodelle und Softwarearchitekturen als Basis für die Auswahl und Spezialisierung von Workflow-Management-Systemen", in *Geschäftsprozeßmodellierung und Workflow-Manangement*, eds. G. Vossen, J. Becker, Thomson Publishing, 1996 (in german).

29. B. Singh, *Invited talk on coordination systems at the Organizational Computing Conference*, Austin, Texas, Nov. 13-14, 1989.

30. R. Zicari, M.G. Fugini and R. Maiocchi , "Time Management in the Office-Net System", in *Office Knowledge: Representation, Management and Utilization*, ed. W. Lamersdorf, Elesevier Science Publishers, North Holland, 1988.

A Framework and Mathematical Model for Collaboration Technology

Clarence A. Ellis **.

Department of Computer Science
University of Colorado
Boulder, Colorado, USA

Abstract. This document presents a functional framework for group-ware, with examples of how it can be used to understand and analyze collaboration technologies. The document also introduces a new mathematical model for groupware architecture called Team Automata. Emerging from the model is a new, mathematically rigorous definition of the terms "cooperation" and "collaboration" which clearly separates these terms. The paper concludes by illustrating the application of this model to the analysis of real time shared application groupware. We observe that there are design alternatives for shared application groupware suggested by the model which have mostly gone unexplored.

1 Introduction

Within our societies, we see technologies which appear to greatly advance the human condition (e.g. water purification technology), and others which seem to be questionable in their societal effect (e.g. television technology). Convergence of technologies recently has appeared to bring the world closer together, both physically, and conceptually. For example, transportation technology has progressed tremendously, so that physically, we can travel to more places, more safely, in less time, with less effort. Conceptually, the telephone and other communication technologies have made it possible for families, communities, and interest groups to feel closer together although they may be separated by great distances. Groupware is an emerging technology with great promise of bringing people closer together conceptually. Whether people are in the same conference room or scattered around the world, groupware can potentially help them to coordinate, collaborate, and cooperate. However, like many emerging technologies, if not carefully directed, applied, and assessed, it can impose significant negative societal effects. *Groupware* is the generic name for technologies that support groups of people working (and playing) together. The term was first defined and published by Johnson-Lenz [21] to refer to computer-based systems plus the social group processes that the systems support. In this paper, we follow the definition published in a groupware overview paper [11] that defines group-ware as "computer based systems that support groups of people engaged in a

---
** This work was partially supported by NSF grant IRI-9307619

common task or goal, and that provide an interface to a shared environment."
We use the notion of group in its general sense, and we use the terminology
of *Collaboration Technology* to be synonymous with groupware. It is important
to note that the system and the group are intimately interacting entities. This
paper puts forth a framework, and a mathematical model for description and
analysis of collaboration technology.[1]

Examples of groupware range from meeting room technology [29] which is
typically used by a group at the same time, same place, to electronic mail technology [25] which is typically used by a group at different times, different places.
This time space taxonomy of groupware has been discussed by numerous authors
[20, 11]. In Section 2 of this paper, we introduce and explain a new and different
paradigm for viewing the groupware space upon which we base our architectural
building blocks. In Section 3, we present a general set of groupware architectural
building blocks, and in Section 4, a mathematical formalism which we apply
to a salient groupware example in Section 5. In our conclusions (Section 6), we
argue that this model and formalism can be quite useful for exploring the space
of alternative groupware architectures, and suggest some directions for further
work.

2   Groupware Paradigms

In this section, we offer and motivate a new, functionally based taxonomy of
groupware components. This taxonomy, which categorizes groupware as keepers,
coordinators, communicators, and agents, is useful to elucidate and understand
the spectrum of groupware products currently on the market, and to suggest useful groupware directions which have not yet emerged. We also give explanation
and examples of groupware in each category. Although it is useful to understand groupware functionality in terms of these "pure" categories, in reality,
many groupware systems are, and should be, a mixture of the above categories.
The concept of "spheres of collaboration" is introduced in this section; it turns
out that each category of the taxonomy is naturally associated with different
spheres of collaboration. There is a bewildering array of possibilities for sharing and interaction within a groupware system. Among other considerations,
users may collaborate by sharing data, control, communication, and context.
This taxonomy helps to remove some of the bewilderment from this array. The
interaction among various design choices can also be quite confusing to users,
and the spheres of collaboration can simplify some of this complexity.

The taxonomy that we offer in this paper is a functional taxonomy. It classifies according to the type of generic function that a system provides. Other tax-
onomies based upon different criteria have been discussed in the literature, and
found useful for understanding and analysis within the groupware area. Closely
related is the classification of groupware according to perspectives [11]. This can
be contrasted with the time - space taxonomy [20], the typology of group tasks

---

[1] Preliminary versions of some of the ideas within this paper have been published over
time in conferences [12].

[26], the organizational structures taxonomy [27], the office models taxonomy [28], and others. In this document, we also illustrate how our taxonomy can be mathematically modeled, and applied at the architectural (middleware) layer of groupware.

2.1 The Keeper

One of the functional categories of our groupware taxonomy is the function of the "keeper of the artifact." When a group of designers are working on a complex design, a primary means of interaction for them is to interact through the design artifact. Consider, for example, a group CAD (Computer Aided Design) system which allows a group of designers to concurrently view and edit design diagrams. One designer might say "I implemented a super low cost solution to our cross-over noise problem. Take a look at the auto-CAD." The second designer, upon hearing this might bring up the appropriate working diagram, study it, and understand exactly what the first designer did. Note that this detail was communicated via the auto-CAD diagram - by the work artifact itself. Thus, the groupware system acts primarily as a repository for, and a controller of access to the artifact. Other examples include group discussion tools such as NetNews where the artifacts are bulletin boards, concurrent engineering design tools, and group CASE tools, where the artifacts are code, specifications, and documentation.

Associated with a keeper is an explicit or implicit object model. This is a description of the repositories, the information items (or types), and the operators on these that the system provides. One can view the artifact as a database of objects, and the keeper as the manager of these objects. As an example, the gIBIS hypertext system is a keeper of design rationale [6]. It is based upon the IBIS theory that the design process, and design rationale can be usefully structured and captured as a conversation involving various issues, various designers positions on those issues, and a set of arguments for and against those positions. Thus the gIBIS system is a keeper of design nodes that are of type issue, position, or argument. These are this keeper's object classes, and operators that can be invoked by users include create node, edit node, link nodes, unlink nodes, and view nodes.

Generally, object oriented databases and shared hypermedia systems fall into this keeper category. We insist that systems falling into this category are for groups' shared usage; these systems pose some different challenges than single user systems [31]. It has, for example, been pointed out that groupware systems impose different requirements, and are built upon a different philosophy than typical database systems. Databases employ mechanisms such as locking and transactions to insure that simultaneous users are undisturbed by each other; in contrast the philosophy of groupware is to encourage cooperation by making it known and instantly apparent to all who is sharing what with whom. We find that correctness criteria such as database serializability are no longer the appropriate criteria, and need to be re-thought [8]. Thus, notions of simultaneous access and shared editing of the artifact play a much more central role within groupware.

Keepers are typically concerned with access and sharing within the *data space*. Each participant in a groupware interaction can be considered to have multiple spheres of data access within the data space. One sphere may surround those data points that the participant can read; another surrounds those points that the participant can write. Overlap of spheres of different participants indicate sharing possibilities. An interesting example of this is the group document editor which is designed to allow multiple participants in different locations to simultaneously edit a document. In this case, the document = the artifact = the data space. Different editors have different object classes (e.g. text paragraphs, diagrams, pages, lines, or words), and different operations (e.g. read, append, insert, replace, copy, paste, or delete). In the ShrEdit group editor [30], all participants can read the entire document, but at any particular instant, no two users can write into the same region. ShrEdit uses "selection locking." Thus if user A selects region X on her screen, then user B cannot write into region X until user A has released it. Figure 1a shows a two dimensional picture of a ShrEdit data space with two participants, A and B. At any instant in time, the write spheres of these two users, A_*write* and B_*write* , are always disjoint.

It is useful to contrast the data space of Figure 1a with the more complex data space of the GROVE group editor [9] shown in Figure 1b. GROVE allows participants to open multiple windows onto a document - these windows may be public (readable by all), shared (among a subgroup), or private (readable by only one participant). Thus there can be parts of the text edited by A that B cannot read, or even that B cannot know about its existence. This editor allows multiple users to edit the same text item at the same time, and uses a transformational concurrency control algorithm to maintain consistency [8]. The data space is the document being edited; points in the rectangle of Figure 1b represent items of the document that can potentially be edited, depending upon the current access control settings for the item. For a particular participant, e.g. user A, the spheres of data access are concerned with write access (labelled A_*write* in Figure 1b), read access (labelled A_*read*), and existence access (labelled A_*exist*). In Figure 1b, note that the write spheres intersect. This means that data points inside of the intersection of ovals A_*write* and B_*write* can be freely edited by both users A and B. A text item that is inside of A_*write* , but outside of B_*write* , can be edited by A but not by B. The existence spheres indicate that a person or subgroup can be working on an appendage of the document, and be assured that others do not even get notified that the appendage exists. Thus, a text item outside of the sphere A_*exist* is not even known to exist by user A. Finally, a participant who can edit an item, also can always read that item. Similarly, a participant who can read an item always knows of the existence of that item. Thus the sphere A_*write* is always wholly within the sphere A_*read* , which in turn is always within the sphere A_*exist* . The same is true for participant B and all other participants.

In summary, ShrEdit and GROVE made particular, and very different choices for sharing. This all suggests that there are many other possible designs for group document editors that could be fruitfully explored. There are emerging two primary technical issues with which keepers must deal. One is the issue of dealing with concurrent access - for groups, this is much more important than it is for single user systems. A second issue is concerned with group memory - its storage mechanisms and its access. This is particularly crucial in groups and organizations which change frequently.

2.2   The Coordinator

Another functional category of groupware is the function of "coordinator of the group activities" where activities are work tasks or procedure steps. In many group situations, the work or task of one person cannot be started until another person's task is completed. For example, yearly income tax cannot be calculated until after total year's income has been reported. Activities are frequently defined within the context of a procedure which is some partial ordering of work steps. The notion of precedence of activities within a procedure, together with parallelism and coordination, are primary concerns of the coordinator. CSCW systems which typically fall into this category include passive groupware such as PERT chart programs, and active groupware such as workflow systems. A PERT chart program describes graphically which activities must precede or follow which others, and can calculate quantities such as critical path [33]. Although this program has no knowledge of the information objects used by the various activities (its not a keeper!), the precedence information imbedded in its display makes the PERT charter a useful coordinator. Coordinators such as workflow systems actually utilize the precedence information to synchronize the enactment (execution) of the associated activities. A workflow system that has a specification of activity x precedes activity y may have a feature which inhibits the users from processing activity y on their computers until activity x has been completed and terminated. This feature, depending upon the situation, may be very helpful or a barrier to productive work. For example, if the largest, most important customer requests that her work order be expedited, the fact that the system prevents activities x and y from being done concurrently may be a severe barrier. We see goal based workflow as a means of avoiding some of these problem. We further discuss this issue, and other workflow criticisms elsewhere [11].

Coordinators encapsulate control flow. Associated with a coordinator, there is always an explicit or implicit coordination model. This is a description of the activities, and the precedence relation between them. Some of these coordination models allow parallel activity execution and some do not. Some rely upon and utilize nesting of activities. Finally, some explicitly represent fork, join, choice, and decision making. Most of these models are static - i.e. they do not allow change of this structure during execution. In a related paper, we discuss in detail the issue of dynamic change in workflow systems [10].

As shown in Figure 1c, coordinators are concerned primarily with control space. There are many control issues arising in CSCW systems which do not arise in single user systems. For example, real time groupware systems may support entities such as group windows and telepointers. Decisions must be made as to who can manipulate these entities, and when. Another important issues is "Who is in control of change to the synchronization specification?" Points in the control space represent control rights such as the previously mentioned change control, floor control, control of the group telepointer, or access to the scroll bar in a group window. For example, if the point in control space representing scroll bar access is within the intersection of A and B in Figure 1c, then users A and B both have the right to scroll the group window at any time. In this case, potential conflicts may be mediated primarily by social protocol. We find varied and complex control issues here that do not currently have clear-cut solutions. Coordinators are especially concerned with A-B and B-A, and how points move from one of these subspaces to another.

Figure 1a - ShrEdit Data Space

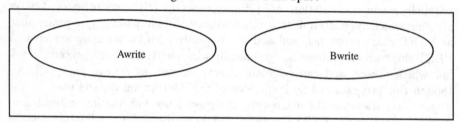

Figure 1b - GROVE Data Space

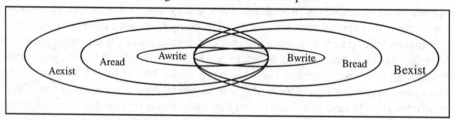

Figure 1c - Coordinator Control Space

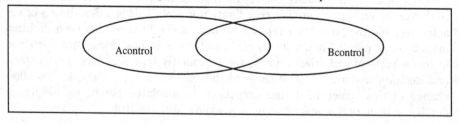

2.3   The Communicator

A third category is the communicator. More than other categories of our taxonomy, communicators recognize the importance and pre-eminence of humans in groupware, and specifically support human to human communications. Groupware systems are people systems! Somehow groupware must support and enhance people communicating with people. Communicators implement a communications paradigm. In these systems, instead of the user thinking in terms of control flow (coordinator) or data repositories (keeper), she typically thinks in terms of communication messages, and operations such as call, send and receive. A salient example is electronic messaging systems (e-mail) which typically allow users to send and reply to text messages asynchronously. It is primarily concerned with getting messages from people to people. As with the other paradigms presented it can be used for other functionality, but this is subsidiary. E-mail may also be used as a keeper by storing and organizing information as messages. It may also be cleverly used as a coordinator if specific activities are associated with specific messages; the messages can help to control the order of those activities. Nevertheless, the dominant paradigm and the primary built-in functionality of an e-mail system is communication.

There are numerous other examples of communicators including "old" technology of telephone and facsimile. Real time videoconferencing systems fall within this category because they are explicitly designed, built, and bought for communication among people. Even for people involved in a large face to face meeting, technology is available to help them communicate [29]. Video windows and desktop conferencing systems [18] are interesting examples of creative communicators. An important subset is the category of context communicators. The Xerox shared video coffee room [17] was an example of this - it employed continuous running video cameras and video monitors in the coffee rooms of two Xerox research labs in two different states. This allowed people at remote locations to meet and informally interact with fellow employees. As another example, the Cruiser system enabled researchers to electronically scan the offices of coworkers whenever they wanted to formally or informally have a conversation [1]. Office rooms were equipped with video cameras and video windows on the workstation screens of researchers. Each participant could choose to set their video door to open (available to talk,) closed (unavailable,) or partially open (in office, but busy.) Whenever someone chose to go cruising from their own office, they would see a few seconds of scan of each office that was connected and could optionally choose to remain in contact with some office, and start an audio visual conversation. Note that a good communicator is useful for both formal and informal communication; it delivers social as well as technical information.

Associated with each communicator is an (implicit or explicit) model of communication which specifies classes of communication possible (see for example [14].) This model may include, among other things, senders, receivers, possible message types, and the set of available operations. Typical operations include send, receive, and possibly edit. These apply to messages, to packets, to frames, or to some other units of transmission. Specializations of the send operation such as reply and forward are prevalent in e-mail systems. If appropriate, display, print, and delete may be available. Transmission of the information, which we said may be text, voice, video, etc., will be synchronous or asynchronous, and may be implemented using concepts such as mail servers, addresses and routes, envelopes, multicast groups, message headers, and message bodies. One example of a model of this type is the model specified by the ISO 4000 messaging standard; many other models have emerged in recent years.

Communicators are primarily concerned with the *communication space* within our spheres of collaboration. Points within this space represent potential communication acts. Suppose that as a student, I am not authorized to initiate a long distance phone call in my office, but any professor within my university can call long distance. Then there will be a point in the communication sphere of the professor to allow this communication, but no point within my sphere. In the communication space there may be points labelled reply, commit, change rights, open video channel, etc. A point may have a list of potential correspondents attached to it. A point must specify what type of communication, with whom, and via which medium. In general, communicators for users A and B must be concerned with all points of A union B within the communication space.

2.4   The Team Agent

There are numerous important aspects of group interaction which are not primarily task related (e.g. team building, socialization over coffee), and which are spontaneous and unstructured (e.g. problem solving, exception handling, friendly persuasion.) The fourth category, which encompasses technology for all of these aspects, is called team agents. Agents perform specialized functions within a group setting. Besides groupware modules which must be concerned with operation of the entire groupware system, there are frequently modules which are built to perform specific non-global subtasks. These frequently involve specialized domain knowledge; we call these modules team agents. Examples include the "performance specialist" within a software engineering team, and the "social mediator" within an electronic meeting. Neither of these examples is concerned with the overall workings of the system, but each contributes useful functionality in a specialized domain as part of a group. Thus, each is a groupware agent which typically implies certain characteristics such as autonomy, distribution, encapsulation, high level interface, and pro-active interaction. As with other categories, we insist that modules falling into this category are for groups, not individuals. Thus they are designed to play a specific role within the group, or within the groupware architecture.

As another example, the notion of a critic has been introduced into the literature as a knowledge based software subsystem which acts as an intelligent automated co-worker who offers some criticism of work which it has been asked to evaluate. In some cases, the criticism may be inappropriate, and humans are free to ignore the criticism. Fischer [13] writes about the "kitchen critic" which is a software system imbedded in a larger building design aid system. When a team of architects design a kitchen for the home of a client, they specify placement of ovens, sink, etc., within the space of the kitchen. The automated kitchen critic will then look at the design and compare what was specified to its many rules of good kitchen design. It may notice that the oven was placed directly below the window, which is a violation of one of its tenants of good kitchen design. The system interacts with the designers to present this finding to the designers, and to arrive at a satisfactory solution for this specific case. An important aspect of this agent is that it is designed to interact with a *group*, so it tries to follow the electronic conversation, and to contribute in synergistic, socially acceptable ways. Because the conversation is not face to face, it becomes natural for the group to accept the critic as "one of the group members."

Systems such as critics clearly do not fit neatly into one of the categories of keeper, coordinator, or communicator, but they clearly are groupware. The category of agent is a fitting place for this type of system, because it is a distributed autonomous subsystem, concerned with a specialized domain rather than the general concern of the total design. Some of the typical operations associated with agents are assert, observe, and update knowledge. Numerous papers about agents are available in the artificial intelligence literature; especially distributed AI.

There are numerous categories of agents; one of particular emerging interest is the "social agent" which has a potential for greatly enhancing group cohesion, cooperation, satisfaction, and success. The computer is being used more and more as a medium for human to human communication; the social agent is specifically concerned with the quality of this communication, and the social psychology of successful collaboration. Just as the emergence of highly interactive personal computer user interfaces has greatly benefitted from a close coupling with psychology (HCI field), the emergence of effective group user interfaces should be closely coupled with sociology and related fields.

Research in the area of Human-Computer interaction (HCI) has produced useful theories, models, architectures, and studies to assist in our understanding of how people can, and naturally do, interact successfully and easily with their computerized environment. For example, the GOMS theory puts forth a cybernetic theory of how people interact with computers; the HIPAC model puts forth a layered architecture which separates the user interface clearly from the application and communication modules. The clear next question that we are raising is "How can computers assist and enhance group collaboration?" Analogs to the above HCI results are mostly lacking in the social agent arena; we see a need for research and development to help develop these types of results.

We foresee that in the future, group user interface modules will be studied and implemented as separate modules just as user interface modules have emerged as separate entities (UIMSs.) This is the logical place in groupware systems for knowledge of how and why people interact well to reside. In the future, my social agent will mediate my personal goals with others; our group social agent will mediate my group goals with other groups, and with the organization wide goals, etc. This must be done in such a way that users are not overloaded - so group user interfaces must be designed to hide irrelevant information and activity, as well as to present context in a useful, natural, and non-distracting manner. Thus the notion of context must be expanded to go beyond presentation of state of the artifact, to present state of the total project, of other participants, and of social / organizational context.

Social agents are interested in the social context, and thus are concerned with the *context space* within our spheres of collaboration. Points in the context space denote context items. The intersection of the context spheres of user A and user B represents their shared context (or their common ground.) A context item in the intersection may be a shared previous social experience, affiliation to the same organization, common knowledge of a technical field or fact, or shared physical context. All of these may play a role in the effectiveness of the collaboration. A social agent is especially concerned with A_*context* intersect B_*context* . For all of these examples, if the group has more than two participants then the intersection (or other operation) is among all participants.

GroupAnalyzer [23] is one of the few existing CSCW systems that is an example of a successful social agent. It is a system for dynamic analysis of group interaction that has been used in conjunction with the Capture Lab, an electronic meeting room at the Center for Machine Intelligence in Ann Arbor, Michigan. This social agent relies upon coders, social scientists trained in observation of meetings, to input observed actions that occur during the meeting. From this input, GroupAnalyzer dynamically generates social field diagrams, meeting split graphs, and time series analysis of the meeting interactions. These generated outputs are then (optionally) fed back to meeting participants.

The underlying social psychological theory and coding method upon which GroupAnalyzer was based is SYMLOG (A System for the Multiple Level Obser-vation of Groups). There is a large body of literature [2] which describes theory, research, and findings associated with SYMLOG. This work has been praised as "among the most consistent and robust findings in the field." [26] Group-Analyzer was tested by coding 65 meetings in real time in the Capture Lab. Losada reports that "the effect of feedback on groups that used the technology was highly significant in terms of changing interactive behavior considered more conducive to collaborative work."

3   The Architectural Model

The above taxonomy can also be fruitfully applied at the middleware level. At this level, we are concerned with groupware building blocks and collaboration technology architectures and components. In this section, we discuss groupware building blocks of keeper components, coordination components, communica-tion components, and agent components. We show how these components can precisely describe many architectural variations within the groupware spectrum.

There are a number of important and outstanding issues that must be faced in the design and implementation of groupware [11]. Some of these issues, such as distribution, privacy, notification, and group control, fall within the domain of Groupware architecture. Our group at the University of Colorado has implemented a variety of types of groupware, and strongly believes that a groupware architecture model is needed for (at least) two reasons. First, the implementation of these systems becomes quite complex, and algorithms that have been implemented to solve problems have been elusively inadequate. A model is much needed to reason about the correctness and performance of these implementations. Secondly, there is a need to understand the underlying commonalities of these implementation constructs. A model such as this can suggest general constructs, elucidate the spectrum of implementation possibilities, and help lay the groundwork for a general and verifiable "groupware implementation language and toolkit."

3.1 Architectural Building Blocks

Within our framework, one composes a groupware system (modeled as a *team automaton*), by creating instances of one or more of the four basic building blocks (modelled as component automata), and hooking them together in a loosely coupled or tightly coupled fashion. This aggregate can then, in turn, be used as a component in a larger groupware system. The four basic classes of automata are:

1. Keeper Automata (which capture the information structures or the DBMS),
2. Coordination Automata (which perform synchronization activities),
3. Communication Automata (which represent message distribution, network protocols and transmission buffering), and
4. Agent Automata.

Within the agent automaton category, there are many types. Two important types of agents are:

4a Application Automata (which capture the computations on application objects), and
4b User Interface Automata (which capture the info presentation and user input aspects).

These building blocks can be considered as classes; multiple instances of each can then be combined in various configurations to form various architectures. For example, a fundamental design decision is concerned with the centralized versus distributed storage of data, which is modelled by having one versus multiple instances of the keeper automaton within an architectural specification. Further specification concerning the replicated versus partitioned nature of the data storage within the set of keepers is modelled well by specifying the internal operation of each keeper using an automata theoretic formalism. Similarly, various configurations of centralized versus decentralized versus totally distributed control can be modelled by various organizations of coordination automata connected by various structures of communication automata. The inner details of these modules can be described very precisely by automata formalisms, and their interconnection specifications are captured formally by our novel Team Automata definitions.

3.2   Asynchronous Groupware Example

One of the highly visible, popular, and challenging types of groupware products is called Workflow Management Systems. Workflow systems are groupware designed to model and coordinate organizational processes [19]. These systems, which typically have a modeling module and an enactment module, allow managers and analysts to graphically describe the procedures that are carried out within their distributed organizations, to mathematically analyze those procedures, and then to enable the networked computer system to coordinate and help the various participants to actually carry out the procedures. The aim is to perform the procedures more efficiently and effectively. The workflow system can provide needed information, reminders, protection structures, audit summaries, and the system can even perform steps of the procedure which are automatable. Most workflow products are implemented as server client architectures. Figure 2 shows the enactment module of a typical workflow system architecture as described using our building blocks.

Figure 2 - WORKFLOW Architectural Model

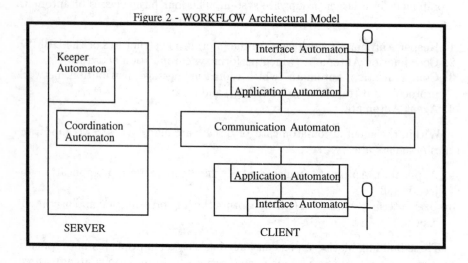

This diagram shows a keeper module within the server. The keeper module keeps the workflow description as generated by the modeling component. This includes procedures, steps of procedures, actors who perform steps, precedence among steps, etc. The coordination module, also within the server, uses this information to decide who does what, and when. After this decision is made, the communications module distributes needed information to the appropriate client(s). Figure 2 also shows an application module within each client where the real work of performing each step of the procedure gets done. This work is typically done by a combination of user activity and client software computation. Thus, each client has a user interface module for communication with the person doing the current activity. When activities are completed, notification is sent to the server, so that the coordinator module can initiate the next procedure step(s).

3.3 Synchronous Groupware Example

The essence of successful collaborative functioning is the ability of the group to act as a team with a certain amount of shared context and shared goals. It then becomes possible and productive to conceptualize the group as a coherent cognitive unit. Task models and social models are emerging which view the group or organization or community as a single coherent cognitive unit [32]. Our mathematical model, described in Section 4 of this document, goes beyond previous automaton models to specifically include a tightly coupled shared action mechanism to help model this group collaboration aspect which frequently occurs in synchronous groupware. We see examples of this notion of group action when we watch a professional basketball team work together, or listen to a good classical music orchestra. The experience is one in which the participants are not doing separate sequential activity, but the whole is precisely shaped in an ongoing manner by the simultaneous activity of each participant. Indeed, these are experiences that substantiate the saying that "the whole is greater than the sum of its parts." No one person could create these effects alone.

Models within the distributed systems literature typically allow system elements to coordinate via either message passing or via shared memory. Our model uses neither of these mechanisms! Our team automaton models collaborate and cooperate by "joint actions."

In our model, we have a 2-pronged mechanism, which can be used to model a spectrum of synchronous to asynchronous group interactions. One prong is a master/slave mechanism in which the master automaton performs an "output action" forcing the slave automaton to concurrently perform the related "input action." Under this mechanism, the master is never blocked waiting for a slave. The output action of the master proceeds even if the slave is not in a state of readiness to perform the input action.

The second prong of our model is a peer-to-peer mechanism in which all automata involved in a joint action are equal participants. The set of actions (actually, its a single joint team action) cannot occur unless all of the participants are in a state of readiness to perform the action. Thus, blocking can occur in this case. We call the master/slave mechanism *passive cooperation*, and contrast this to the peer-to-peer mechanism which we call *active collaboration*, this is an important distinction.

Definition 1. *Cooperation*
A Team Automaton is defined to be *cooperating* if it is structured so that one of the automata is the active master, and all others are passive slaves.

Definition 2. *Collaboration*
A Team Automaton is defined to be *collaborating* if it is structured so that all of the automata are active peers.

In fact, the peer-to-peer mechanism is implemented by having an action with two or more masters doing output actions simultaneously. Likewise, this action could also have two or more slaves doing input actions, so it is really a single (2-pronged) mechanism, and various hybrids of master/slave mixed with peer-to-peer are possible. See the example in the next section for details.

There are numerous examples of groupware systems which can usefully and naturally be modelled as peer-to-peer joint actions. Consider a decision making meeting among a management team. This may be an important real-time face-to-face event that can usefully be augmented by groupware technology. The actual happenings at the meeting may involve ad-hoc, semi-structured activity that is quite dissimilar to the pre-planned structured workflow example. This example might be modelled as joint actions, and this may help to encourage acceptance of decisions made at the meeting to be viewed by all as jointly owned "team decisions."

In the meeting there may, for example, be voting. There are a plethora of different voting schemes, and meeting room voting technology can help to make this quick and accurate. Voting can nicely be modelled as a peer-to-peers type joint action of the group.

At the middleware implementation level, we can look inside of the typical groupware keeper. Because groupware is concerned with allowing free team access and flexible sharing, a simple keeper may be structured as four modules, as shown in Figure 3, which simultaneously do verification checks and information delivery when a participant accesses the keeper's database. This is an example of a four way peer-to-peer action.

Figure 3 - The Keeper

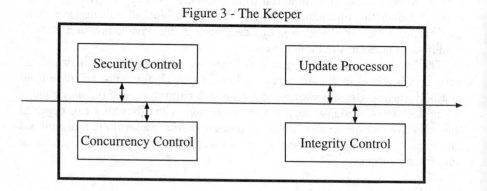

The above examples have illustrated that our architectural components can be used to model both synchronous and asynchronous systems. In the next section we explain the formalism behind these architectural building blocks, and our method for combining the building blocks.

4 The Formalism

We have presented an intuitive overview, with motivated groupware examples, of our Team Automata model. In this section, we give the formal definition of Team Automata, followed by a simple example.

4.1 Team Automata Definition

Team Automata are mathematical compositions of a set of Component Automata. They are a variation of the Input/Output Automata conceived by Professor Nancy Lynch at MIT, and elucidated in her 1996 book [24]. They are nondeterministic; they interact via "shared actions;" they can have an infinite number of states; they can be iteratively nested to form composite automata which satisfy the same definitions; and they can be used to specify simultaneous group operations. Our model has similarity to, but significant differences from, Petri nets [3], Vector Controlled Concurrent Systems [22]. and other models of concurrency [15]. The primary embellishment to the Lynch model is the addition of a mechanism allowing peer-to-peer shared action as occurs within many types of groupware sessions.

The automata defined by Lynch represent a mathematical automata theoretic specification, rather than a high level language specification such as Hoare's CSP or Forman's Raddle [16] or the n-party interaction [15]. They are known to be adequate to specify shared memory systems, and message passing systems, although they are neither. They have the power to specify synchronous or asynchronous, blocking or nonblocking systems. Their utility is primarily derived from mathematical tractability and machine processability, rather than from human readability. Although this model is inappropriate for capturing some aspects of group activity (particularly social aspects and informal unstructured activity,) we show in the next section of this document that we can usefully and succinctly capture the inner workings of significant classes of groupware systems. Although the author is not completely contented with the model, a large body of literature, theorems, and proof techniques on automata theory is available, and applicable to this model; this has been quite useful.

The automata are rather ordinary, but their interconnection strategy is intriguing because, as we mentioned, it is neither shared variable nor message passing. Lynch classifies the actions which take an automaton from one state to another into three categories:

1. input actions (from other automata),
2. output actions (to other automata),
3. internal actions (strictly local visibility).

Thus the automaton interconnection strategy is "shared action" in which one or more automata specify, within their input action sets, the same action as one or more other automata specify within their output action sets.

Definition 3. *Component Automaton*

A component automaton C consists of the following four mathematical entities:

1. a nonempty state set, $S(C)$,
2. a nonempty initial state set, $I(C)$ contained in $S(C)$,
3. an action signature, $A(C)$,
4. a transition relation, $F(C)$ contained in $S(C) \times A(C) \times S(C)$.

[I/O automata as defined in [24] also include a fifth component, an equivalence relation part (C) which is used for describing fair executions. Since it is not needed in this paper, it is omitted from the current definition. Likewise it is sometimes convenient within our user interface automata to specify an output function which controls the display of information to the users. That is a different topic, and omitted from this paper.]

An action signature A is an ordered triple consisting of three pairwise disjoint sets of actions. We write $in(A)$, $out(A)$, and $int(A)$ for these three components and refer to the actions in the three sets as input actions, output actions, and internal actions of C, respectively. In the system being modeled, the distinctions are that input actions are not under the local system's control and are caused by another non-local component, the output actions are under the system's control and externally observable by other components, and internal actions are under the local system's control but are not externally observable.

A component automaton is considered to start in some initial state of $I(C)$, and to execute instantaneous transitions into other states of $S(C)$. Note that the state sets need not be finite. This means among other things, that one can model asynchronous message passing systems with unbounded buffer capacity. The transition relation relates a state and an action to another state. If the triple (s_1, a, s_2) is in the relation, then this is interpreted to mean that the automaton, when in state s_1 and presented with the action a, can transition into state s_2 . We refer to (s_1, a, s_2) as a step of C. An execution of C is a finite (also can be extended to infinite) sequence $s_0, a_1, s_1, a_2, \ldots, a_n, s_n$ of alternating states and actions of C such that s_0 is contained in $I(C)$, and (s_i, a_{i+1}, s_{i+1}) is a step of C for every i.

Definition 4. *Team Automaton*

Given a collection, $\{C_i\}$ of component automata, a team automaton T consists of the following four mathematical entities:

1. a nonempty state set, $S(T) = \Pi(S_i)$ where Π denotes the cartesian product,
2. a nonempty initial state set, $I(T) = \Pi(I_i)$ where Π denotes the cartesian product,
3. an action signature, $A(T) = (Ai)$ where A denotes the action signature composition operation described below,
4. a transition relation, $F(T)$ containing all admissible triplets (s, a, s') such that s and s' are members of $S(T)$ and a is a member of $A(T)$.

If there are n component automata being combined to compose a team automaton T, then the state set $S(T)$ is composed of states which are n-tuples or n element state vectors, one element from each of the contributing C_i . On the other hand, the action signature, $A(T)$, is composed of all single actions from any one of the component automata, not vectors of actions. An action is executed by this team automaton by finding all component automata which can execute the action from their given state at the given time, and requiring them all to simultaneously do it. All component automata which do not recognize that action are dormant during that cycle. A requirement for a set of component automata to be composed is that their internal action sets be disjoint. Then the internal action set of T is the union of the internal action sets of the components. Also the T output action set is the union of the component automata output sets, and the T input action set is the union of all component inputs minus the set of all component outputs.

4.2   Team Automaton Example

To illustrate these concepts and definitions, a simple example is next presented of three component automata, U, V, and W which each have two states and three actions as shown diagrammatically in Figure 4. All actions except the joint action J are internal actions. Notice that the composed team automaton, $T = U\Pi V\Pi W$, has one output action, J, and no input actions. Here, Π denotes a team building relation that is different from a cartesian product, see the definition of T below. The definitions of U, V, W, and T are as follows:

Definition 5. Component Automaton U:

$$S = \{s_{u1}, s_{u2}\}$$
$$I = \{s_{u1}\}$$
$$A = \{a_{u1}, a_{u2}, J\}$$
$$F = \{(s_{u1}, a_{u1}, s_{u2}), (s_{u2}, a_{u2}, s_{u1}), (s_{u1}, J, s_{u2})\}$$

$<$ note that J is the only output action for U $>$

Definition 6. Component Automaton V:

$$S = \{s_{v1}, s_{v2}\}$$
$$I = \{s_{v1}\}$$
$$A = \{a_{v1}, a_{v2}, J\}$$
$$F = \{(s_{v1}, a_{v1}, s_{v2}), (s_{v2}, a_{v2}, s_{v1}), (s_{v1}, J, s_{v2})\}$$

$<$note that J is the only output action for V $>$

Definition 7. Component Automaton W

$$S = \{s_{w1}, s_{w2}\}$$
$$I = \{s_{w1}\}$$
$$A = \{a_{w1}, a_{w2}, J\}$$
$$F = \{(s_{w1}, a_{w1}, s_{w1}), (s_{w2}, a_{w2}, s_{w2}), (s_{w1}, J, s_{w2})\}$$

<note that J is the only input action for W >

Definition 8. Team Automaton T:

$$S = \{[s_{ui}, s_{vj}, s_{wk}]\} < i, j, k = 1, 2 >$$
$$I = \{[s_{u1}, s_{v1}, s_{w1}]\}$$
$$A = \{a_{ui}, a_{vj}, a_{wk}, J] < i, j, k = 1, 2 >$$
$$F = \{[(s_{u1}, a_{u1}, s_{u2}), (), ()], [(s_{u2}, a_{u2}, s_{u1}), (), ()],$$
$$[(), (s_{v1}, a_{v1}, s_{v2}), ()], [(), (s_{v2}, a_{v2}, s_{v1}), ()],$$
$$[(), (), (s_{w1}, a_{w1}, s_{w1})], [(), (), (s_{w2}, a_{w2}, s_{w2})],$$
$$[(s_{u1}, J, s_{u2}), (s_{v1}, J, s_{v2}), (s_{w1}, J, s_{w2})]\}$$

<empty parentheses represent dormant automata>

Braces $\{\}$ denote sets; parentheses $()$ denotes relations, brackets $[]$ denote vectors, and angular brackets $<>$ denote comments.

In this example, all of the actions are local except for the one which involves J. This action is peer to peer between U and V because J is an output action of both. (This is not allowed in the Lynch model.) Thus the action J will not occur unless both U and V are in their initial states, and both voluntarily decide to execute J. Also, W is involved in J as a slave automaton if it is in its initial state because J is an input action to W. Thus, W is stuck in state s_{w1} until its two masters agree to both execute action J. At this time, W is forced to transition into state s_{w2}. In this state, W does not respond to action J, although J may occur many times. (This is also not allowed in the Lynch model.) Thus, W is now free of its two masters; and also W can never return to its initial slave state.

4.3   Comparison to I/O Automata

As noted above, component automata deviate from Lynch's definition of I/O automata by not requiring that there must exist a transition for every combination of state and input action. Thus our automata are not forced to be input enabled, and an algorithm can choose to ignore (not be interrupted by) certain input actions while in certain states. Team automata deviate from Lynch's definition of composition of automata by not requiring that the output actions of the component automata be disjoint. This allows the modeling of peer-to-peer group operations that mirror the ways that tightly coupled well coordinated groups work.

Figure 4 - Team Automaton T

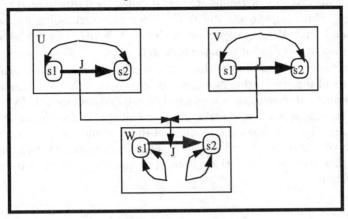

5   Shared Application Example

There is a general category of groupware called real time shared application groupware which we explain and explore in this section. It typically requires a coordination module which we can succinctly model as a component of a team automaton. This example shows some of the power and elegance of our model. There is a large space of design choices for the coordination module, and our model elucidates this, and suggests some design choices that would not be otherwise apparent, and that do not currently appear in commercially available shared application groupware.

5.1   The Shared X Server

There is a type of groupware (we call it shared X) which seems to have been simultaneously invented by a number of groupware research groups at the same time. It was an immediate high leverage tool easily implemented on top of the X window manager system. Indeed, it was co-invented by many (including the author) immediately after the release of the X window protocol. The X window protocol clearly separated all user interface considerations and code from all application considerations and code. At that time (the mid-1980s), the X window system was a breakthrough because it allowed the user interface subsystem to easily execute on a different machine (e.g. the user's workstation) from the applications.

The groupware idea that occurred to many developers at that time was to capture the outputs of the application (which was well specified by the X window protocol), and send them to multiple users' workstations rather than only to one. Thus, the group of users, who might be at quite distant locations, all see an identical user interface to the application on their workstation screens, and all get (approximately) real time simultaneous screen updates. This is an example of the category of groupware that is called "real time shared application groupware" which implements the WYSIWIS concept, standing for "what you see is what I see." The high leverage of shared X is that absolutely no change to the application is needed to make it shared.

This groupware does require the creation of another module which receives the outputs of the application and forwards a copy to each user's display screen (or X-terminal.) However this is a relatively small and easy module to implement given the enormous leverage of making any and all applications into shared group applications. Figure 5 shows the modules of the X window server ant the logical extensions of this to the shared X server using our architectural building blocks. It shows that there is an addition of one coordination automaton to create the shared system.

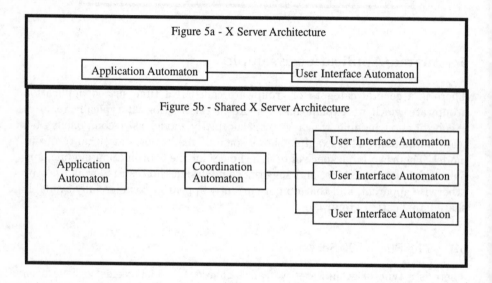

Figure 5a - X Server Architecture

Figure 5b - Shared X Server Architecture

There are some questionables and some drawbacks to the architecture of Figure 5b as opposed to the creation of "collaboration aware applications." Given this architecture, the application cannot distinguish between different users' inputs. Also, in some environments, the centralized nature of this architecture is a drawback. An alternative architecture was implemented in the GROVE document editor [9]. In this system, the architectural decision was made to have no centralized control, and no centralized data. Thus, the application (the document editor code) and the data (the shared document) were replicated at each users workstation, and decisions concerning concurrency control were implemented as fully distributed algorithms. There is no centralized coordinator or server in this system. This architecture is likely to be more prevalent in future systems since the amount of computing power and memory at a local workstation is becoming very large, and inexpensive.

Figure6 - GROVE Shared Editor Architecture

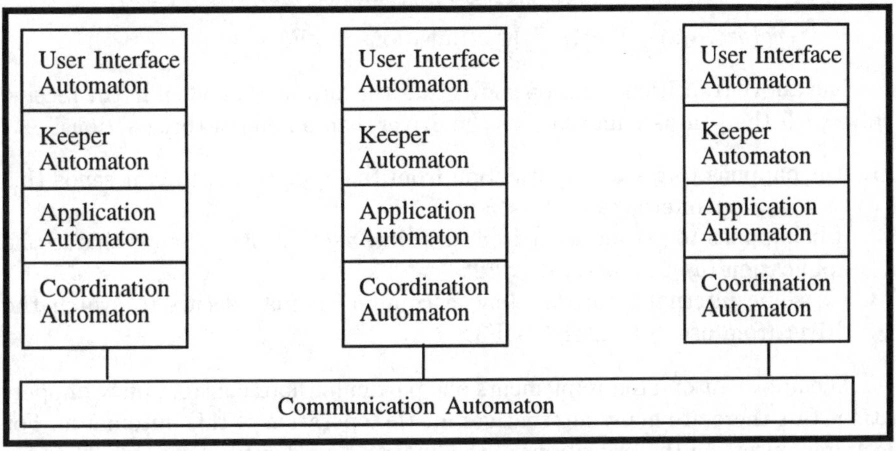

Figure 6 shows the architecture of the GROVE document editor system.An obvious question about the shared X server is what to do with asynchronous and sometimes simultaneous input from multiple users to the application. It is possible that two or more users may be concurrently typing into their keyboards. We explore this question by looking in detail at the automaton model specification of the coordinator module of Figure 5b. Many early shared X systems designated one user as the 'driver' of the application, and all others as 'spectators.' It is possible to have much better arrangements than this as we shall see presently.

5.2 The Shared Application Coordinator

The coordination module presented as an example in this section is driven by the architecture of Figure 5b. Thus it communicates with an application module and with some number, n, of user interface modules. We specify below an automaton which models a coordinator that implements two way communication. It communicates from the application which we denote ap, to and also from, user interface modules which we denote by ui^j . The superscript j ranges from 1 to n, and specifies which user interface we are addressing. A superscript of 0 denotes all user interfaces. The application and the user interface modules each have a set of valid operations that they can perform. For example, a document editor may include operations of insert, delete, etc. Subscripts on automaton symbols encode which one of the possible operations is being performed, as well as giving information about the semantic use of the element. For example, actions are tagged as either input or output, or internal.

$S = \{send^j_{i-ap}, send^j_{i-ui}, receive^j\} \; [j = 1 \cdots n] $ <states>

$A = \{a_{i-int}, ap_{i-in}, ap_{i-out}, ui^0_{i-out}, ui^j_{i-in}, ui^j_{i-out}\} \; [j = 1 \cdots n] $ <actions>

$F = \{(receive^j, ap_{i-in}, send^j_{i-iu}), (send^j_{i-ui}, ui^0_{i-out}, receive^j) $ <F1>

$$(receive^j, ui^j_{i-in}, send^j_{i-ap}), (send^j_{i-ap}, ap_{i-out}, receive^j) \quad \text{<F2>}$$

$$(receive^j, a_{i-int}, receive^k)\} \quad \text{<transitions>} \quad \text{<F3>}$$

The above transition function shows that the automaton, when in the receive state with the j-th user interface as the driver, can do one of three actions:

1. if it happens to get an input action from the application, then it sends this to ALL user interfaces (ui^0). <F1>
2. if it happens to get an input from user interface j, then it sends this to the application $(ap_{i-out}$ action). <F2>
3. via some internal algorithm (e.g. a counter) it may decide to switch the driver from user j to user k. <F3>

The above automaton implements one particular floor control policy of operation. But there are many alternatives for the operation of this automaton. For example, inserting the transitions of the line <F4> below implements a "free for all" floor control policy in which any user can send input to the application at any time. This notion of listening to everybody is denoted by the 0 superscript attached to the receive state. Under this policy we assume that social conventions will dictate that only one user does an action, and that they agree upon an informal protocol. For some groups, this is more appropriate than a policy dictated by the computers.

$$(receive^0, ui^j_{i-in}, send^0_{i-ap}), (send^0_{i-ap}, ap_{i-out}, receive^0) \quad \text{<F4>}$$

This automaton notation also makes it easy to specify round robin turn-taking for the role of driver. This is specified by the line below. Addition is (modulo n) + 1.

$$(receive^j, a_{i-int}, receive^{j+1}) \quad \text{<F5>}$$

The above specifications unambiguously capture the floor control policies of existing systems. However, it becomes clear that there are many alternative policies; for each action, it can be an input, output, or internal action. This opens up other categories of floor control. For example, if the change of driver function is caused by an external input, then either users can initiate the change by indicating "I want to be driver" or the application can initiate. Also, by adding rows to the transition function, we can implement mixed strategies. One useful strategy suggested by this automaton is to have more than one driver, but not all users. So one could have a floor control policy in which there is one rotating driver, and one unchanging "facilitator," both of whom are simultaneously enabled to send inputs to the application.

6   Summary and Conclusions

Groupware presents a need to integrate technical, social, and organizational concerns to produce systems which are truly beneficial. The author therefore believes that groupware modeling should encompass organizational goals and procedures, people (and groups) and their social structures and the tools and systems which can aid in the achievement of these goals. The author also believes that no one model will satisfy all needs and be good for all modeling purposes. In that spirit, this paper describes one of a number of models of interest, and does not represent the spectrum of our groupware concerns. The model is novel and useful in the domain of analysis of groupware architectural structures. It models keepers, coordinators, communicators, and specialized agents. It forms a framework for understanding the communication network, the application domain, and the information structures of groupware, but does not explicitly model the social or organizational aspects. This is a ripe area for future work.

7   Acknowledgments

The author would like to thank the members of CTRG, the Collaboration Technology Research Group at the University of Colorado, for fruitful and enjoyable discussions and debates. Particular gratitude is extended to Professors Jacques Wainer and Grzegorz Rozenberg for their significant contributions to the ideas presented in this document.

References

1. Baecker, R., (ed.) *Readings in Groupware and Computer Supported Cooperative Work*, Morgan Kaufmann Publishers, January 1993.
2. Bales, R. F., Cohen, S. P. (1979) *SYMLOG, A System for the Multiple Level Observation of Groups*. The Free Press.
3. Brauer, W., Reisig, W., and Rozenberg, G. "Petri Nets" in: Advances in Petri Nets. Lecture Notes in Computer Science, vol. 254, Springer Verlag, 1987.
4. Chandy, M., and Misra, J. *Parallel Program Design: A Foundation,* Addison Wesley, 1988.
5. *Computer Supported Cooperative Work (CSCW), An International Journal,* Kluwer Academic Publishers, Vol. 1, 1992.
6. Conklin, J., Begeman, M., (1988) gIBIS: A Hypertext Tool for Exploratory Policy Discussion. Proceedings of CSCW'88.
7. Coleman David, "Interview: Groupware and the Future of Organizations: A Conversation with Bob Johansen", Virtual Workgroups Magazine, May/June 1996.
8. Ellis, C., Gibbs, S. "Concurrency Control in Groupware Systems" in Proceedings of the ACM SIGMOD89 Conference on the Management of Data, May 1989.
9. Ellis, C., S.J. Gibbs, G. Rein "Design and Use of a Group Editor" in Engineering for Human Computer Interaction, G. Cockton, editor. North Holland, Amsterdam, 1990.
10. Ellis, C., Keddara, K. (1993) "Dynamic Change Within Workflow Systems". University of Colorado Technical Report
11. Ellis, C. A., S. J. Gibbs, and G. L. Rein, "Groupware: Some Issues and Experiences," Communications of the ACM, Vol. 34, No. 1 (January, 1991), pp. 38-58.
12. Ellis, C., and J. Wainer, "Goal Based Groupware Systems" in the International Journal of Collaborative Computing. 1,1, 1994, pp. 61-86.

13. Fischer, G, et. al. (1990) Using Critics to Empower Users. Proceedings of the ACM CHI'90 Conference on Human Factors in Computer Systems. Seattle, WA

14. Flores, F., Graves, M., Hartfield, B. and Winograd, T. (1988) Computer Systems and the Design of Organizational Interaction. ACM Trans. Office Information Systems, 6, 2, 153-172

15. Francez, N., and Forman, I. *Interaction Processes: A Multiparty Approach to Coordinated Distributed Programming.* Addison Wesley, 1991.

16. Forman, I. "Design by Decomposition of Multiparty Interactions in RADDLE" in Proc. of the 5th Workshop on Software Specification, 1989.

17. Goodman, G., Abel, M. (1986) Collaboration Research in SCL. Proceedings of CSCW'86, Austin, Texas.

18. Ishii, H., Miyake, N. (1991) Toward an Open Shared Workspace. Communications of the ACM 34, 12.

19. Jablonski, S. and C. Bussler, Workflow Management Systems: Modeling, Architecture, and Implementation, 1996.

20. Johansen, R. (1988) Groupware: Computer Support for Business Teams.The Free Press

21. Johnson-Lenz, P., Johnson-Lenz, T., (1982) Groupware: The Process and Impact of Design Choices. In Kerr, E. B. (eds.),Computer Mediated Communication Systems. Academic Press.

22. Keesmaat, N. *Vector Controlled Concurrent Systems.* PhD Thesis, Leiden University, 1996.

23. Losada, M. and Markovitch, S. (1990) GroupAnalyzer: A System for Dynamic Analysis of Group Interaction. Proceeding of the 23rd Annual Hawaii International Conference on System Sciences.

24. Lynch, N. *Distributed Algorithms.* Morgan Kaufmann, 1996.

25. Malone, T., et. al., "Semistructured Messages are Surprisingly Useful for Computer Supported Coordination," ACM Transactions on Office Information Systems (5,2) April 1987.

26. McGrath, J. E. (1984) Groups: Interaction and Performance, Prentice Hall, Inc. NJ

27. Mintzberg, H. "Typology of Organizational Structure", In Miller/Friesen (Eds.), Organizations:A Quantum View, 1984, pp. 68-86.

28. Newman, W. "Office Models and Office Systems Design," In Naffah, N. Ed. Integrated Office Systems, Burotics North-Holland,1979, pp.3-10.

29. Nunamaker, J., et. al. (1989) Experiences at IBM with Group Support Systems. Decision Support Systems,5 ,2

30. Olson, G., and McGuffin, L. *ShrEdit: A Shared Electronic Workplace.* CSMIL Technical Report #45, University of Michigan, 1992.

31. Rodden, T., Blair, G. (1991) CSCW and Distributed Systems: The Problem of Control. Proceedings of the Second European Conference on Computer Supported Cooperative Work.

32. Smith, John, *Collective Intelligence in Computer Based Collaboration,* Erlbaum Associates, 1994.

33. Stilian, G. N., et. al. (1962) PERT, A Management Planning and Control Technique. American Management Association publication 74.

34. Winograd, T. and Flores, F. *Understanding Computers and Cognition: A New Foundation for Design,* Ablex Publishing Co., NY, 1986.

Practical Experiences and Requirements on Workflow

Kwang-Hoon Kim and Su-Ki Paik

[1] Department of Computer Science
University of Colorado at Boulder
Boulder, Colorado 80309-0430
kwang@cs.colorado.edu
[2] Department of Computer Science
Kyonggi University
Suwon-Si, Kyonggi-Do, South Korea
skpaik@kucs.kyonggi.ac.kr

Abstract. The purposes of this paper are to describe practical experiences on a business process(Hiring Process) automation by a workflow automation approach, and to point out the limitations of current business process automation from the workflow application developer's point of view. The limitations may be caused from the lack of human coordination, collaboration, group-decision, interoperability, scalability, correctness/reliability of workflow applications, exception handling, and a dynamic reflex of the organizational changes in current workflow modeling methodologies and workflow management systems.[1]
By pointing out the insufficiencies through the practical experiences, we derive some requirements for workflow modeling methodologies and workflow management systems. We believe that those requirements are key infrastructures and research issues to successfully implement business process automation.
Finally, workflow application developers should carefully consider the business process modeling methodology as well as the workflow management system when they automate their corporate processes to avoid mismatches.

1 Introduction

Contemporary organizations employ a vast array of computing technology to support their information processing needs. An interesting class of tools that are "organizationally aware" are workflow systems. In fact, workflow systems are suddenly one of the hottest technologies going. According to recent reports [2], it was predicted for companies to spend $1 billion on workflow automation and technology to improve customer services, to reduce costs, and to increase benefits. Additionally, the number of companies using workflow technology totaled 514,000 in 1994, and could reach 5.8 million in the world by 1998. The reason

---

[1] This research was supported by the academic funds of the Kyonggi university.

why workflow is so hot is that it helps large organizations improve the way they operate.

Workflow systems are designed to assist groups of people in carrying out work procedures, and contain organizational knowledge. According to [10], workflow and its management system are defined as "systems that help organizations to specify, execute, monitor, and coordinate the flow of work items within a distributed office environment." That is, the workflow is the automation and management of business processes which must be done to achieve a business goal. In terms of terminology, it is critical to distinguish the 'workflow automation' from the 'task automation'. The emphasis in workflow management is on using computers to help manage business processes that may be comprised of many individual tasks, not on using computers to automate the individual tasks. The latter may be applied selectively to some tasks, but such task automation is not a prerequisite for using and benefiting from workflow.

As stated in [4], [13], and [19], the workflow system consists of two basic components: the first component is the workflow modeling module, which enables administrators and analysts to define procedures and activities, analyze and simulate them, and assign them to people. Many workflow products have no formal model, so this component is sometimes called the "specification module or build time module"; usage of this module is typically completed before the flow of work tasks actually begins.

The second component is the workflow execution module (the workflow system) containing the execution interface seen by end users and the execution environment which assists in coordinating and performing the procedures and activities. It enables the units of work to flow from one user's workstation to another as the steps of a procedure are completed. Various databases and servers may be accessed in a programmed or ad hoc fashion during the processing of any work step. Sometimes, this component is called the "Enactment module or Run time module".

Our work as described in the paper is focusing on two aspects, practical implementation of a workflow application, and requirements that might not be easy to be dealt with, however the next generation workflow systems should cope with; the former is the result of an attempt to show that the workflow provides the right information to the right persons in the right time through automatic fashion. We model a hiring process with the ICN (Information Control Nets) workflow modeling mechanism, and enact it through the FlowMark workflow management system commercialized by IBM. The execution of the hiring process is tested on a network environment set up for the hiring process management and automation.

The later is the description of the current practical implementation issues, that have been directly experienced during the workflow implementation, as well as the current research issues on workflow technology. The description consist of three aspects, the experienced problems, from which the requirements are able to be driven, the workflow system's extensions with respect to the modeling module part and the execution module part, and the organizational aspect of workflow systems.

The paper is organized as follows: In Section 2, we describe the approach for workflow automation established by defining the relationship between business process reengineering, workflows, and workflow management systems, and we introduce the business process reengineering methodologies and workflow management systems we explored for the project.

In Section 3, we describe the practical workflow implementation in detail, including the workflow model of the hiring process by information control nets, and the workflow execution of it by the FlowMark workflow management system. In Section 4, we discuss some difficulties on the workflow implementation found out through the practical experiences, some requirements for workflow management systems from workflow application developer's point of view, and some research topics on the workflow technology. Our conclusions and some perspectives on future expectations are presented in Section 5.

2 Workflow Automation Approach

According to [18], it is reasonable to establish and to maintain a direct relationship between business processes and workflows by enriching business process modeling with an implementation platform and by enriching workflow management with a powerful modeling environment. So, the approach for workflow automation should be established through the integration of a business process methodology and a workflow management system. But, what process to automate can be as important as what product to buy. Therefore, the approach we take consists of four phases, as shown in the Figure 1[20]; the first is to decide what process should be automated. The second is to redesign the process and to analyze it through a BPR methodology. The third is to model the process and to implement by a workflow management system. Finally, through the phase of performance evaluation, the process is evaluated.

To design a workflow process, it is important to define the details of the components of workflow, which are called the three Rs (Routes, Rules, Roles) and Ps (Processes, Policies, Practices) of workflow. One of the most effective ways to do this is by using a business process reengineering methodology. Such a methodology provides the structure and guidelines to help workflow developers identify all the elements of the process, and gives them models and methods that ensure they are providing the necessary depth of detail consistently for all components.

Marshak [24] introduced some guidelines to help workflow developers determine the most effective areas to implement BPR and workflow technology and some products that have been commercialized, so far. Typical BPR methodology tools are following: Action Technology's Workflow Analyst, Business Transformation Design's Business Management Transformation, Delphi Consulting Group's Workflow Factory, HOLOSOFX's Workflow-BPR (based on Windows platform), IBM's The Business Process Modeling Tool is based on OS/2 and

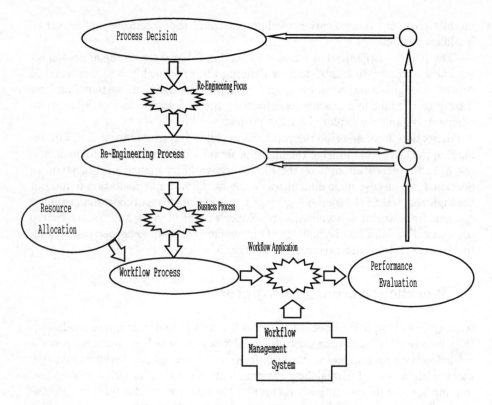

Fig. 1. Approach for Workflow Automation

Windows platform. IDS Prof. Scheer's ARIS (Client:Windows3.1 or Win95, Server: NT; Novell), Interfacing Technologies's FirstSTEP (based on Windows, Mac, UNIX), Knowledge Based System, Inc.'s ProSim (process modeling and simulation) and ProSim Workbench(process modeling, data modeling, function modeling with simulation)(based on Windows and Windows NT), and Meta Software's Workflow Analyzer(based on Windows, Mac, Sun).

The typical workflow management systems are following: Action technology's ActionProcess Builder, FileNet's Visual WorkFlo, IBM's FlowMark, BancTec's Plexus FloWare Family, Staffware's Staffware, ViewStar's ViewStar, Wang's OpenWorkflow, Workpoint's WorkPoint, Xsoft's InConcert, and Bull's Flow-Works.

For our workflow automation of the hiring process, we choose FlowMark of IBM as a workflow management system, because it's stable and available for the OS/2 environment our organization's information systems are based on.

3   Practical Experiences on Workflow

3.1   Modeling the Hiring Process

Before the hiring process is designed and implemented by the FlowMark [15, 13], it must be modeled and analyzed. The ICN (Information Control Nets) [9] is a graphical representation mechanism for modeling office and business processes. In this section, the basic ICN and the hiring process are described. That is, the hiring process is modeled by the ICN and analyzed by defining activities, staff on each activity, and roles of each staff. Based on the model, the hiring process will be designed and implemented by FlowMark in the next section.

ICN(Information Control Nets)   ICN is a mathematical formalism designed to model graphically office and business procedures. Unlike Petri Nets, ICN was specifically created and designed for business processes. ICN can be represented by ICNL(ICN Language), activity, procedure, actor, mechanism, policy and control flow graph.

ICNL is a collaboration language that allows administrators to dynamically define, describe, schedule, and modify their business processes, their interrelationships, and any organizational information associated with them. ICNL can be specified indirectly using ICN editor, like the one supplied by BULL corporation. It can also be generated indirectly by a computer agent, intelligent enough to initiate, for example, a change in the procedure.

An *activity* is a work step of a procedure. The activity can be either an elementary one or a compound one containing another procedure. A set of work steps will depend on many factors such as control, autonomy, cost and other organizational considerations.

A *procedure* is defined as a set of work steps and a partial ordering of these steps. A work step consists of a header (identification, precedence, etc.) and body (the actual work to be done).

An *actor* is a person or a computer program responsible for fulfilling a set of duties which is necessary for the procedure to continue execution.

A *mechanism* is a set of components used to implement a set of strategies. In the context of workflow systems, procedures and technology used in the office are considered to be mechanisms.

A *policy* is a particular strategy that dictates the way that a mechanism is used to achieve specific goals. It provides the necessary tools for explicit control. Policies are both restrictive and permissive at once. They spell out the limits to actions, but at the same time give freedom to act within the limits specified.

An ICN control flow graph is composed of a set of activities represented by large circles, OR control flow nodes represented by small-open circles, AND control flow nodes represented by small-filled circles, and edges to interconnect these nodes. An arc represents precedence among nodes: if activity A leads to activity B (i.e., (A, B) is an edge in the graph), then activity A must be applied to an individual transaction before activity B can be applied to it.

Fig. 2. (a) ICN OR-node Control Flow and (b) ICN AND-node Control Flow

Suppose we have activities A, B, and C. Let X be an OR-node with arcs (A, X), (B, X), and (X, C) in the graph (Figure 2 a); then the activity C can 'fire' after either activity A or B has been executed on a transaction. An AND-node uses conjunctive flow logic as opposed to the disjunctive logic of the OR-node; if Y is an AND-node and the graph (Figure 2 b) contains (A, Y), (B, Y), and (Y, C), then the activity C can only fire after both A and B have fired. If instead the graph contains (A, Y), (Y, B) and (Y, C), then both B and C can fire after A has fired.

Hiring Process Modeling by ICN The hiring process that we try to model consists of 18 activities having precedence through the control and data flow. There are 6 roles - applicant, hiring clerk, personnel clerk, security clerk, medical clerk, and hiring manager - that have the responsibilities to do the activities as shown the Figure 3.

3.2 Automating the Hiring Process

The FlowMark workflow management system consists of two parts: Build time and Run time. The build time part allows a model developer to define and maintain all the information necessary to eventually execute workflows. The workflows defined by the build time part are finally performed by the run time part of the workflow management system.

Infrastructure for Implementation In order to enact the ICN model of the hiring process, we need some infrastructures, such as application development environments which are used to implement programs on each activity in processes, and a workflow management system, which is used to control the flow of workcases and data in distributed computing environment. So, in this section, we introduce these infrastructures.

FlowMark: Workflow Management System: FlowMark is a typical server-client workflow management system developed and commercialized by IBM, it runs across different platforms such as AIX, OS/2 and Windows, and supports distribution of most of its components. It is based on a server-client architecture and uses a centralized database to store meta-information about workflows. An

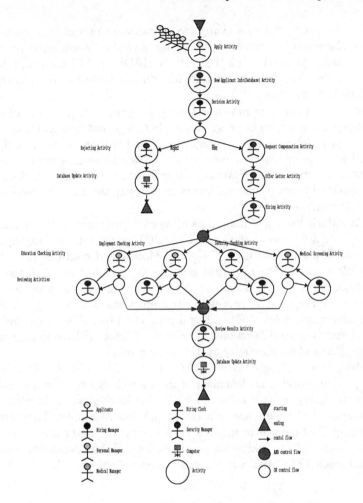

Fig. 3. Hiring Process Modeling by ICN

object-oriented database management system, ObjectStore, is used. In particular, the schema definition of a business process and all the runtime information related to active process instances(work cases) are stored in this database.

Besides the database server, FlowMark is organized into four other components: FlowMark Server, Runtime Client, Program Execution Client, and Buildtime Client.

- The FlowMark Server acts as the workflow engine,
- the Runtime Client acts as the worklist handler,
- the Program Execution Client acts as the application-agent, and
- the Buildtime Clients acts as the process-definition tool.

A single database usually acts as a repository to several workflow servers. The connections among the runtime components are shown in Figure 4. Workflow servers are connected to a centralized database. Connected to each workflow server, there can be several clients simultaneously. Communication among components takes place through TCP/IP, NetBIOS or APPC, except for the database and the workflow servers that function as ObjectStore client-servers and use their own internal protocol.

Vx-Rexx: Graphical User Interface Design Language: Watcom VX-Rexx [31] is an application development programming language and system for the OS/2 platform. It provides visual design and programming tools to create OS/2 applications having graphical user interfaces. The development system is used to create macro or script files for workflow applications. We used VX-Rexx, as a workflow application programming language, to design the user interfaces of each activity on the hiring process.

The FlowMark workflow management system provides workflow language APIs for C, REXX, Visual Basic, and COBOL programming language, and supports workflow client APIs for C++ and FlowMark Coalition. Through the APIs, workflow application programs are able to communicate with the FlowMark runtime part. The APIs consist of container functions such as GET and SET container variables, and process control functions such as Begin a process control session, start, delete, suspend, and resume a process instance, and other session and status control functions. We use the REXX APIs to implement the runtime programs of each activity of the hiring process.

FlowMark Server-Clients Distributed Computing Environment: The Figure 4 is showing the networking environment of the FlowMark workflow management system for the hiring process automation. A FlowMark server is located at the Suwon Cmapus, and clients are in a lab at the Seoul Campus. They are connected through T1 Line which supports 1.5 Mbps rate of data transmission. The network is controlled by Token-ring protocol. Two of the clients run buildtime and runtime clients of FlowMark, the other is only for the runtime.

Building the Hiring Process by FlowMark When the modeling of the ICN hiring process is done by the buildtime client, we have to define the following through the components of FlowMark workflow management system, before enacting(running) process instances through the Runtime FlowMark:

- Staff Definition: People, Roles, Organizations, Levels
- Program Definition: Programs used in each program activity must be registered.
- Data Structure Definition: Data structures used in the input and output data containers in each program activity, process activity, or block activity must be registered.
- Process Definition: We have to define the process that we develop, to link activities to staffs, to link activities to programs, to link input and output data containers of activities to data structures, and to set transition, start and exit conditions on activities.
- Server Definition

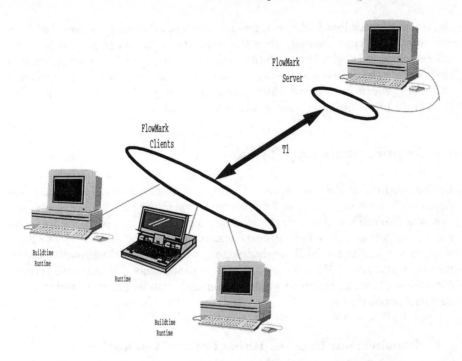

Fig. 4. FlowMark Server-Clients Networking for the Hiring Process

The ICN hiring process modeled by the Buildtime of FlowMark consists of 18 program activities and 4 block activities each of which has a resource and a sink data repository that are the input and output data container of the block activity, respectively. All activities have some precedence through control and data connectors including 5 transition conditions. And each block activity has an exit condition to break the end-less loop of internal activities. The programs and the user interfaces for each activity are implemented in VX-Rexx using the APIs provided by FlowMark.

Running the Hiring Process by FlowMark A Runtime process maintained in the Runtime folder of FlowMark consists of a hiring process and its instances(workcases). The instances have associated one of 5 states which are showing the status of the Runtime process. A hiring process and its instances are represented by 6 different process icons: Model used to instantiate a process, Ready displayed for an instance of the model which has not yet been started, Running displayed for an instance that is currently in execution, Suspended shown for an instance that has been interrupted, teminated shown for an instance that has been canceled, and finished shown for an instance that has completed normally.

An activity under control of the Runtime Client (Work Lists on each people's account) of FlowMark has a state associated with it. The state is identified in the Runtime work lists folder by different shapes of activity icons: ready when it can start to execute, running when the associated program or process instance is executing, finished when execution has completed and the exit condition is satisfied, disabled when it has been started by another user, and suspended when the process instance to which it belongs is suspended.

The Runtime hiring process is now fully operational.

4   Requirements on Workflow

In this section, we describe some difficulties, in terms of workflow application developer's point of view, that were perceived when the hiring process automation was implemented through the workflow automation approach and based on the FlowMark workflow management system. From these difficulties, we draw some requirements for BPR methodologies, workflow modeling, and workflow management systems. We also predict other requirements that take into account extensions of the hiring process automation and possible future workflow management applications.

4.1   Requirements from the Hiring Process Automation

Streamlining from Modeling to Workflow Implementation The concept of streamlining in workflow was at first introduced by [9], "Office Streamlining". The basic concept is related with to information flow within offices. The streamlining technique performs a number of useful transformations and optimizations of office flow diagrams, and derives a normal form description of any office flow in certain well-defined ways.

The concept of the streamlining should be applied to the workflow automation approach described in Section 2. That is, in order to accomplish efficient workflow application automation, from the business process decision step to the workflow application step in the workflow automation approach must be consistently done through certain well-defined ways. We show why streamlining in workflow automation is important; our hiring process automation experience may serve as an example: We used the ICN mechanism to model and to analyze the hiring process, and used the FlowMark workflow management system to enact the process. There is not any streamlining concept between ICN and FlowMark.

The difficulty with which we were faced was on here; The ICN model allows cyclic control flows, but FlowMark's buildtime doesn't allow any cyclic control flows. So, we had to spend some amount of time to transform the ICN model of the hiring process to the FlowMark's buildtime model, which is a difficult task.

The Figure 5 (a) is a part of the ICN hiring model which shows a cyclic control flow between Activity 1 and Activity 2. The difficulty is that there is no way for the ICN model to be automatically transformed to the FlowMark's buildtime model. So, we, as workflow application developers, transformed it, the

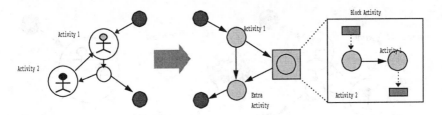

Fig. 5. (a) ICN Model Figure and (b) FlowMark's Buildtime Model

result is shown in Figure 5 (b). Here, the linkage of the business process model and the workflow management systems is so critical.

Fortunately, there is a good evidence showing that this becomes a crucial requirement for the workflow application automation. Recently, IBM has announced LOVEM, the ProModeler: Business Process Modeler [22], and The Business Process Modeling Tool [23]. LOVEM stands for Line Of Visibility Engineering Methodology(or Enterprise Modeling). The ProModeler and the Business Process Modeling Tool (BMT) are based on the LOVEM business process analysis methodology. ProModeler and BMT are not a workflow automation tools in itself, but they generate code for FlowMark. In other words, there is the concept of streamlining between LOVEM, the BMT/ProModeler, and Flow-Mark. The combination of the products is able to support a full business process solution, the streamlining from the business process modeling to the workflow implementation.

Merging Workflow and Groupware Groupware has been defined as "technology based systems that support groups of participants working on a common task or goal, and help provide a shared environment" [6]. It naturally includes technologies such as electronic mail, video conferencing, and shared document editors. The original motivation of this requirement is this [10]; Groupware typically does not contain any knowledge or representation of the goals or processes of the group, and thus cannot explicitly help to forward the group.

We say that these systems are not organizationally aware. On the other hand, workflow systems are typically organizationally aware because they contain an explicit representation of organizational processes. That is, groupware has been criticized because it is not organizationally aware, workflow has been criticized because of its typically inflexible and dictatorial nature compared to the way that office workers really accomplish tasks [17]. Therefore, features of workflow and groupware should be merged to produce a flexible collaboration management systems which is organizationally aware.

In the hiring process automation, we found that the merged features of workflow and groupware are needed, as shown in the Figure 6. We are faced with the difficulty that comes from the iterative conversations between managers and clerks. The programs supporting the conversations maintain and record the his-

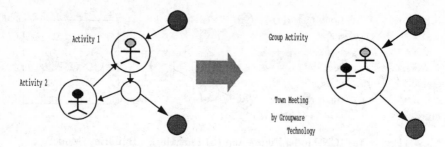

Fig. 6. Merging Workflow and Groupware in the Hiring Process

tory of conversations. At the same time, the control and data flows are back and forth, repeatedly, as shown in the left-side picture of the Figure 6.

The difficulty and complexity should be easily and effectively handled through the merged features, just like in the right-side picture of the Figure 6. Most of current commercial workflow management systems provide three kinds of activities, such as program, block, and process activity. By adding a new feature which may be called "Group activity", workflow management systems could provide the novel feature. Another example that requires the merged features is to merge the group decision support feature on a joining point of AND-nodes in ICN models.

Chautauqua project [10] ongoing on the collaboration technology research group in the University of Colorado at boulder is a good example for the efforts undertaken to merge workflow and groupware.

Integrating Workflow and Application: Transactional Workflow The motivation of this requirement [5] is the aim to ensure correctness and reliability of applications implementing business or information processes. That is, when multiple objects such as databases, files, documents, devices are accessed by a workflow execution, data consistency problems can arise either from concurrency, application failures, system failures, or network failures. These introduce the need for concurrency control, recovery, and transaction coordination. Most commercial workflow management systems provide limited capabilities to deal with these problems.

In many situations, concurrency control is essential when two or more users (or computer systems) can access the same data object. In the hiring process, all activities are associated with a application program programmed by VX-Rexx graphical user interface design language. These programs share a file which contains the information of an applicant. But, in the part of AND-node, as shown in the Figure 7, there are file access conflicts caused by the parallel activities. However, there is no resolution mechanism which is under control of the workflow management system. As a result, there are no parallel runtime executions in the real situation, because the file will be locked by the file system after one of four activity programs opens it.

We solved this problem through separated subfiles for each activity. However, this exposes another difficulty and inefficiency in programming the workflow process that should be handled by the workflow management system.

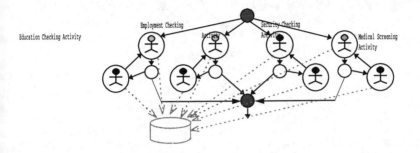

Fig. 7. Concurrency Control Among Programs in the Hiring Process

Some workflow management systems support the concurrency control through a form of check-in and check-out, human intervention after allowing multiple users to retrieve the same data object concurrently, or a pass-by-reference/pass-by-value approach. But, these may not ensure workflow consistency.

Workflow recovery involves how to undo completed or partially completed tasks that cannot be completed due to a failure, and how to undo a canceled workflow. In the hiring process automation, we have not been able to support those recovery mechanisms.

Handling Exceptions: Dynamic Change Dealing with exceptions is difficult; they tend to have no structure and typically occur in dynamic environments, such as offices. [27] reviewed and defined a set of concepts related to exceptions. According to his observations, groupware systems, and especially, office systems face many kinds of exceptions. Exceptions form an essential part of the behavior of offices. They are a major component of office work. So, exceptions are something that has to be managed through collaboration. It seems that the success of an OIS (Office Information System) implementation really depends more on the organizational culture and IS infrastructure than on the specific form and functions of the OIS.

The workflow management system is an efficient office information system, but, at the same time, a most fragile system if it is not equipped by robust exception handing mechanisms, because it manages and controls the flow of works in office where several kinds of exceptions are very likely to happen.

Figure 8 shows an exception that may happen in the hiring process. That is, for some applicants, a hiring manager would perform at first the background checking and medical before the decision. How can it be handled? Based on the current workflow management systems, the hiring process has to be redesigned.

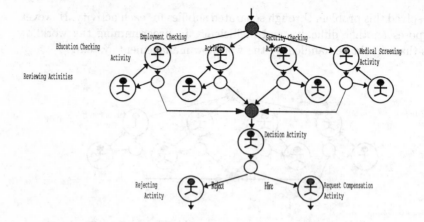

Fig. 8. A Serious Exception in the Hiring Process

But it is not the solution. At the same time, how can those workcases (applicants), which are already in process, be handled? The answer is to integrate the build time with the run time. Flexible process definitions and graceful handling of exception situations are necessary. Those workflow application developers who have engaged in the application domains should be eager to get the workflow management systems supporting dynamic changes.

4.2   Requirements from the Future Workflow Applications

Internet/Intranet Accessibility This is a crucial feature for customer-based workflow applications and intranet-based organizations. For example, in the hiring process, applicants access the process through the outside of the organization. So, this Internet accessibility is the right way to support the application for employment.

Scalability Workflow architecture is an execution infrastructure for workflows which is deeply related with performance issues such as reliability, scalability, extensibility, and robustness. Most of commercial workflow management systems have a server-client architecture. Finally, the server might become a bottleneck of the performance in larger scale application domains. We experienced in the hiring process enactment that the workflow sometimes didn't work correctly as the network traffic or the server's load fluctuate. We need some advanced architectures for workflow management systems.

Merging Build Time and Run Time The requirement of integrating build time and run time in workflow management systems is associated with the organizational structures which affect the way work is internally carried out in organizations. That is, the organizational structure is dynamically and continuously changing, e.g. exceptional cases. Most of the current commercial workflow management systems are static, because of the separation of build time and run time. So, it is hard to completely implement the organizational requirements and needs (Dynamic) through conventional workflow management systems(Static) without integrating those two parts.

5   Conclusions

We felt frequently during the implementation period that workflow application developers have to do too much work until the process is ready to enact through the run time part - the analysis and definition of workflow models, and the development of programs including graphical user interfaces for activities.

So, workflow management systems should reflect the needs of workflow application areas, and evolve and expand to enable successful workflow implementation. At the same time, to reduce the amount of work and effort of developers, and to increase the correctness and the completeness of workflow applications, it is necessary for workflow applications to be standardized through workflow application packages or libraries.

The workflow of the hiring process is quite operational, right now. But it needs to be extended to support the business situation. The most urgent extension should be internet (or intranet) accessibility. And in order for the workflow of the hiring process to provide enterprise-wide support, it should be waiting for the arrival of the workflow modeling methodology and the workflow management system that provide the features needed and satisfy the requirements perceived.

References

1. Kenneth R. Abbott and Sunil K. Sarin, "Experience with Workflow Management: Issues for the next Generation", Proceedings of ACM 1994 Conference on CSCW, pp.113 120, Oct. 1994
2. Doug Barrholomev, "Workflow Software: A Better Way to Work", Cover Story of Information Week, Sept. 1995
3. Nina Burns, "Ebb and Flow", LAN Magazine, May. 1993
4. Bull L.P.M., "FlowWorks: The BULL Workflow Product - Architectural Design and Functional Specification", Revision C, 1992
5. Diimitrios Georgakopoulos, Mark Hornick, "An Overview of Workflow Management: From Process Modeling to Workflow Automation Infrastructure", Distributed and Parallel Databases, 3, pp. 115-153, 1995
6. Clarence A. Ellis, J. Gibbs, and G.L. Rein, "Groupware: Some issues and Experiences", Communication of the ACM, Vol. 34, No. 1, Jan. 1991
7. Clarance A. Ellis, "Workflow Technology", Tutorial Notes, 1995
8. Clarance A. Ellis, "Formal and Informal Models of Office Activity", Information Processing 83, IFIP, Paris, 1983
9. Clarence A. Ellis, Robert Gibbons and Peter Morris, "Office Streamlining", In N. Naffah (ed.) Integrated Office Systems - Burotics, North Holland, Amsterdam, 1980

10. Clarence A. Ellis, Carlos Maltzahn, "The Chautauqua Workflow System, 30th Hawaii International Conference on System Sciences, Information System Track, Wailea, Maui, Hawai'i, January 7-10, 1997
11. Clarence A. Ellis and Gary J. Nutt, "Workflow: The Process Spectrum", Proceedings of NSF Workshop on Workflow and Process Automation in Information Systems: State-of-the-Art and Future Directions, May 1996
12. Clarence A. Ellis, Gary J. Nutt, "The Modeling and Analysis of Coordination Systems", University of Colorado/Dept. of Computer Science Technical Report, CU-CS-639-93, Jan. 1993
13. "Managing Your Workflow", IBM FlowMark, Version 2 Release 2, 1996
14. "Modeling Workflow", IBM FlowMark, Version 2.1, 1996
15. "Programming Guide", IBM FlowMark, Version 2.1, 1995
16. "The Business Imperative for Workflow & Business Process Reengineering", A Special Advertising Section, Fortune, Feb. 1996
17. Jonathan Grudin, "Groupware and Social Dynamics: Eight Challenges for Developers", Communications of the ACM, Vol. 37, No. 1, January 1994
18. Stefan Jablonski, "On the Complementarity of Workflow Management and Business Process Modeling", SIGOIS Bulletin, Vol. 16, No. 1, Aug. 1995
19. Stefan Jablonski, "MOBILE: A Modular Workflow Model and Architecture", Informatik: Database Support for Open Workflow Management Systems, Band 29, No. 5, May 1996
20. Dimitris Karagiannis, "Special Issue on Business Process Reengineering", ACM SIGOIS Bulletin, Vol. 16, No. 1, Aug.
21. Kwang-Hoon Kim, "Groupware", University of Colorado at Boulder, Computer Science Master's Thesis, 1994
22. "IBM LOVEM/Business Process Modeler (ProModeler)", Tutorial Notes for The Basic Course, 1996
23. Ronni T. Marshak, "IBM's Business Modeling Tool: BPR Methodology from the Customer Point of View", Workgroup Computing Report, Vol. 18, No. 6, Jun. 1995
24. Ronni T. Markshak, "Buyer's Guide: Taking the Mystery Out of Workflow Automation", Virtual Workgroups Magazine, May/June 1996
25. Gary J. Nutt, "Using Workflow in Contemporary IS Applications", University of Colorado/Dept. of Computer Science Technical Report, CU-CS-663-93, Aug. 1993
26. Christine Perey, "Stop Communicating and Start Collaborating!", Virtual Work-Group Magazine, Sept./Oct. 1996
27. Heikki Saastamoinen, "Exceptions: Three Views and a Taxonomy", Proceedings of COOCS, 1995
28. Amit Sheth, "Workflow Automation: Applications, Technology and Research", Tutorial Notes, SIGMOD Conference, May 1995
29. Kelly Trammell, "Work Flow Without Fear", BYTE, April 1996
30. Venkatraman, "IT-Enabled Business Transformation: From Automation to Business Scope Redefinition", Sloan Management Review, Winter 1994
31. "VX-Rexx Programmer's Guide", Watcom International Corp., Version 1, 1996

Coordination Science: Challenges and Directions

Mark Klein

Center for Coordination Science (CCS)
MIT Sloan School of Management
Cambridge MA 02139, USA

Abstract. Several distinct kinds of "coordination technology" have evolved to support effective coordination in cooperative work. This paper reviews some of the major weaknesses with current coordination technology and suggests several technical directions for addressing these weaknesses. These directions include developing semi-structured process representations that explicitly capture cooperative work inter-dependencies, exploiting advanced product and software design technologies for process design, and integrating coordination technologies to synergistically combine their strengths and avoid their individual weaknesses.

1 Why We Need Coordination Technology

Increasingly, cooperative work is being achieved by large-scale processes distributed across time, participants and functional perspectives. The design of a commercial jet, for example, requires the integrated contribution of thousands of individuals spread over several continents and a span of decades. Effective coordination is critical to the success of such cooperative processes since the distributed activities are typically highly interdependent e.g. due to shared resources, input-output relationships and so on. The sheer complexity of these inter-dependencies, however, has come to overwhelm traditional manual organizational schemes and paper-based coordination techniques, resulting in huge unnecessary rework costs, slowed schedules and reduced product quality. As a result, while individual productivity may be high, failures of existing coordination support practices and technologies have severe impacts on the bottom line. But what actually do we mean by coordination? Support for coordination can be viewed as being divided into three layers, each built on top of the ones beneath it (Figure 1):

Communication: allowing participants in the decision process to share information (this involves networking infrastructures)
Collaboration: allowing participants to collaboratively update some shared set of decisions (this involves support for tele-conferencing etc.)
Coordination: ensuring the collaborative actions of the individuals working on a shared set of decisions are coordinated to achieve the desired result efficiently

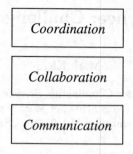

Fig. 1. Layers of Support for Cooperative Work.

This paper focuses on the topmost layer, with the understanding the significant challenges exist in providing mature effective technology for the supporting layers. In the conclusion to this paper the requirements that integrated coordination technology presents for the underlying collaboration and communication layers is discussed.

Coordination is only required, of course, when distributed activities are interdependent. Dependencies can be distributed in three ways (Figure 2), which has led to the emergence of three distinct types of coordination support technology:

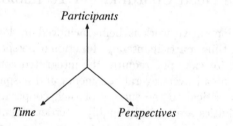

Fig. 2. Types of Distribution in Cooperative Work.

Distribution across participants requires support for the sequencing of tasks and flow of information among participants; this is addressed by process management (i.e. process modelling, workflow, simulation, planning/scheduling) technologies.

Distribution across perspectives arises because the participants involved work on different interacting aspects of the decisions and/or have different often-incompatible goals; consistency among their actions can be maintained with the support of conflict management (i.e. constraint or conflict management) technologies.

Distribution across time arises because the nature and rationale for decisions made at an earlier stage often need to be available later on, for example to support product design changes or retrieve solutions with similar requirements; this is addressed by memory management (i.e. rationale capture, organizational memory) technologies.

Each of these technologies face different challenges that have limited their effectiveness in different ways. This paper will review the state of the art of existing coordination technologies, identify their current limitations and identify some promising directions being pursued by the author and others to meet these limitations.

2   Current Coordination Support Technology

For each class of coordination technology we will consider in this section the coordination problem addressed, the current state of the art as well as key open technical challenges.

2.1   Process Management

The distribution of cooperative work across multiple participants requires that we be able to control the flow of tasks and information among them, i.e. be able to define, optimize and actually enact effective cooperative work *processes*. We can identify the full range of process management functions by considering the process "lifecycle" (Figure 3: ovals represents functions, while "dog-eared" rectangles represent data sets):

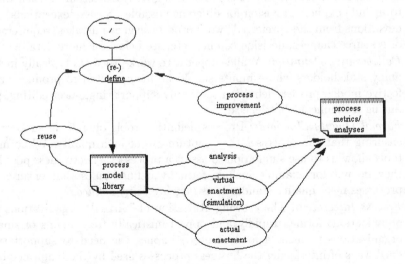

Fig. 3. The Lifecycle for Processes.

Process models once defined (or "modelled") must be stored (in some kind of process model library) using a representational formalism. They can then be analyzed to derive summary attributes (e.g. the cost or quality), simulated (e.g. to provide training or an alternate source of summary attributes), or used to guide actual process enactment. All of these can produce metrics reflecting the performance of the process models that can then be used to help improve them. Pre-existing process models can be re-used as examples or building blocks to define new process models that address similar challenges.

We review the technologies for addressing each of these functions in the paragraphs below.

Process Definition: A wide variety of commercial tools, ranging from simple flowcharters to high-end integrated process modelling and simulation tools, have emerged to support process definition. They typically allow one to graphically edit a visual representation of the tasks involved in a process, as well as the resources needed to perform these tasks and the (often conditional) sequencing among them. The tools differ mainly in the underlying representation they use (discussed in the next section) and in the services (e.g. simulation) that are included in the process definition tool.

Current process definition tools have several important limitations:

- *Scalability:* They can be overwhelmed by the sheer scale of cooperative work processes. Even a moderate business process can include hundreds or thousands of tasks. While the use of hierarchical process decomposition can help, it is easy to lose track of where one is, whether all important tasks have been captured, and so on. This problem is greatly exacerbated when we try to include explicit provision for different possible process "exceptions" (i.e. deviations from the "preferred" work process such as mistakes, requirements or resource changes, decision conflicts etc; see below for more detail).
- *Collaborative Definition:* While cooperative work processes typically involve many stakeholders whose inputs should be incorporated to produce an effective model, process definition tools only support single-user editing, producing a significant bottleneck.
- *Formal Quality Standards:* Process definition tools offer little support for ensuring that the processes they capture are of high quality. While many tools allow us to use simulation to assess a processes' effectiveness post hoc, they do not for example include formally defined rules that ensure that processes meet quality standards *as they are being defined.*
- *Process Integration:* The growing utilization of "virtual" organizations (i.e. organizations formed rapidly and opportunistically from teams of smaller organizations to meet a focused need) implies the need to support standard ways of interfacing the business processes used by the team members. Current technology does not yet provide such interfaces. Current EDI transaction sets, for example, support mainly such "arms-length" interactions as bidding and electronic funds transfer.
- *Rationale:* Process definition tools typically do not capture the *rationale* for a process having a particular structure. This can make it difficult for people

to understand the current process definition, or to modify it intelligently to adapt it to their own, perhaps differing requirements.

- *Integrating Process and Organizational Design:* Current tools do not integrate process and organizational design. Most process modellers capture little, if anything, about the organization for which the process is designed. No process modellers support co-design of the business process and the organizations that will enact them.

Process Model Library: There are two major classes of process representations: *IPO* (input-process-output) and *speech-act based.* IPO representations describe a process as a series of tasks that take several inputs (representing both control and data) and (typically using resources such as people or machinery) produce one or more outputs that are then routed to other tasks (Figure 4):

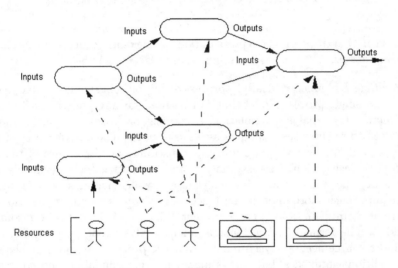

Fig. 4. IPO Process Models Capture Tasks, I/O and Resource Needs.

Examples of IPO representations include IDEF [3], CIMOSA [2], Petri Nets [26] and Finite State Automata [27].

Speech-act representations [33, 1] take the alternative approach of modelling cooperative work as being built up of prototypical loops of requesting, accepting, completing and accepting delivery of tasks (Figure 5: each loop represents a task, with the customer on the left and the performer on the right):

This representation encourages a useful mental discipline when defining processes in that one is always forced to identify the customer and supplier for every deliverable as well as explicitly consider such steps as customer acceptance of the final deliverable. This does come at the cost however of producing models that can be more complex than IPO representations.

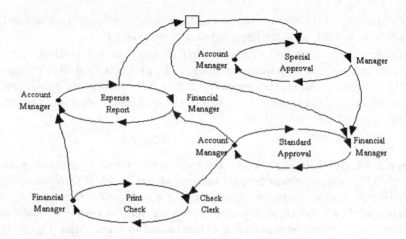

Fig. 5. Speech Act Models Capture Processes as Task Loops.

Both IPO and speech act representations as currently conceived face significant limitations:

- *Multiple-Use Models:* Ideally, a process definition tool should be able to capture a single process model that can be used for any process management function (i.e. analysis, simulation, enactment or reuse) - if not we may be forced to re-enter the same process several times. The different uses of process models, however, place different constraints on the nature of the process representation. Process analysis and simulation tools need only task resource need and sequencing information, while enactment tools typically require much more information (such as hooks to legacy systems and electronic form definitions). The representational needs can also be incompatible. Some forms of project management analysis tools (e.g. critical path and resource need analysis) require that the process description include no conditional branches, but this is inadequate for simulation and enactment uses.
- *Rigidity/Laxness:* Current process representations make it difficult to balance the need to prescribe a consistent process against the importance of allowing people to use their own judgement and initiative. One can either prescribe in detail the alternative ways a task can be performed (using a sub-process model), or else leave it entirely up to the performer. A model can thus end up either excessively rigid or excessively lax (the temptation is often towards excessive rigidity because it is "safer"); both can be counterproductive. Ideally a process representation should allow us to capture constraints (e.g. use no more than amount X of resource Y) and other guidelines without forcing us to prescribe the detailed procedure, but this is not supported by current representations.
- *Fragility:* Models defined using current process representations can be "fragile" in the sense that they risk becoming irrelevant, misleading or even harm-

ful when unforseen changes occur in the realities motivating the original process. These realities include those shown in Figure 6.

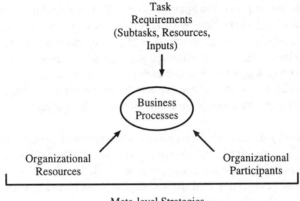

Fig. 6. The Factors That Shape Processes

Collaborative processes arise when a given task is too large to be performed effectively by a single individual, and thus must be decomposed (often recursively) into subtasks that taken together achieve the top-level goal. These tasks have interdependencies that may require some serialization in task execution. Some tasks for example may require as input the outputs produced by other tasks. Tasks that both use some limited organizational resource (e.g. a piece of equipment) may be serialized to avoid contention for that resource. Tasks can be merged if it turns out that one task, perhaps expanded slightly in scope, can achieve the requirements for two or more tasks more efficiently. Finally, tasks will be assigned to individuals or groups based on how skills and responsibilities are distributed throughout the organization. Since there are often many different alternatives available for how we do any of these things, processes are shaped by (implicit or explicit) meta-level control strategies that determine which options will be selected. An example of a meta-level policy for task assignment is "support cross-training by routing tasks to people who need experience with that kind of task" or "maximize throughput by routing tasks to acknowledged experts".

A given process model thus represents a frozen picture of what the "ideal" approach was for a set of constraints that applied at some time in the past. It has been widely recognized, however, that formal process models, to be effective, must also capture what should be done when constraints change, i.e. when an "exception" occurs [30, 12, 25, 14]. We can consider an exception to be any departure from a process that perfectly utilizes the current organizational resources, satisfies all extant policies and encounters no problems during process execution. Exceptions can thus include any significant change in resources, organizational structure, company policy, task requirements or task priority. They can also include incorrectly performed tasks, missed due dates, resource contentions between two or more distinct processes, unexpected opportunities to merge or eliminate tasks, conflicts between actions taken in different process steps and so on. Process models typically include conditional branches to deal with common anticipated exceptions. If unanticipated exceptions occur, however, which they do frequently, we are faced with "patching" the process model without any computer support to ensure that the changes address the new situation without violating other unchanged constraints. Including explicit branches for exceptions also greatly complicates process models and can obscure the outlines of the preferred process.

– *Poor Support for Ad Hoc Interactions:* Conventional process models are ill-suited to capture highly interleaved and ad-hoc interactions such as those typical of multi-functional design teams. Such interactions are difficult to formalize because strong and unpredictable dependencies among the participants' tasks arise frequently.

Analysis: Process analysis tools provide a way of assessing important process attributes without having to simulate or actually enact them. Examples of such analysis include critical path analysis, resource needs forecasting, concurrency opportunity detection [8] and "controllability" assessment [27]. A key weakness of current process analysis technology, as noted above, is that it typically places severe limits (e.g. no conditionals) on the expressiveness of the process representations it can work with.

Simulation: Simulation tools represent a highly robust and effective technology. One must take great care, however, to use realistic process models, to design the "experiments" (simulation runs) to adequately address the key questions, and to correctly map the masses of low-level statistics typically produced by simulation tools into high-level intuitions about how to improve the process.

Actual Enactment: A wide range of process enactment technologies have become available. These technologies can be placed on a continuum according to the extent to which they impose limits on how the process can be enacted (Figure 7).

Ad-hoc systems, typically based on shared databases or electronic mail, depend on process participants to decide to whom a work package should go next but ensure that the work package is routed correctly once this decision is made. They also typically provide some degree of tracking. Structured conversation systems such as those based on the contract-net [28] or speech act approaches provide a system-imposed protocol that structures how tasks can be distributed. These typically allow one to track entire "conversations" (series of task assignment negotiations and progress updates) as a unit, but do not constrain what

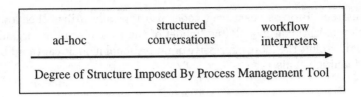

Fig. 7. Types of Process Management Systems.

tasks are created or to whom they are assigned. Workflow systems interpret a detailed process model of either the IPO or speech-act type. Participants in a given process simply perform their individual tasks and rely on the workflow system to understand the process and ensure it is followed and tracked correctly.

Many of the limitations faced by current process enactment systems are inherited from the process representations they use. Enactment tools can be, for example, excessively rigid and fragile because, as we noted above, traditional process models typically are as well. Enactment tools in general use idiosyncratic process representations and can not import/enact models defined by process definition tools. They tend as a result to include organizational models more rudimentary than those captured by many process definition tools, which limits the expressiveness of their languages for describing how tasks should be assigned to agents in the organization. Finally, current process enactment tools, with the exception of small number of high-end systems, do not incorporate the "self-awareness" (e.g. late task detection) and "mutability" (i.e. ability to modify a process while it is executing) features needed to support effective exception handling.

Process Improvement: To date little technology has been developed to provide substantive guidance for re-designing processes to better meet user needs. This is still largely an area where human experience reigns supreme. This kind of expertise is relatively rare and can be difficult to access, however.

Reuse: While it is clearly possible to collect "flat" libraries of process models that can act as examples for the design of new processes, current technology provides limited support for this function. The lack of a widely accepted process representation standard, of course, is one major problem. Other gaps include representational schemes that allow one to quickly find processes relevant to one's problem, as well as tools to help ensure that one does not unknowingly violate any process requirements when customizing a template to fit one's particular needs.

Overall Issues: One problem that cuts across all currently available process management technologies is their lack of integration. Process models defined by a process definition tool, for example, are typically not executable by a process enactment tool. Process enactment tools also typically utilize their own rudimentary organizational models (i.e. model of the resources in an organization) rather than exploit the more expressive organizational models captured by many process definition tools.

2.2   Conflict Management

Cooperative work is typically distributed across multiple functional perspectives addressing inter-related aspects of a single set of decisions. Maintaining consistency (i.e. avoiding conflicts) among these distributed activities becomes a significant challenge with major potential impacts on cost, quality and timeliness.

Current conflict management approaches are almost entirely manual, relying on coordination memos, cross-functional team meetings and the like. Such approaches have become increasingly costly and ineffective, however, as the sheer scale of cooperative activities have grown. Conflict management technology is emerging to address these issues by providing computer support for detecting [29, 23] and resolving [31, 10, 7, 4, 22, 11, 13, 32, 18] conflicts. This technology relies in general on the fact that there are relatively few abstract classes of conflict and associated general strategies for resolving them. Conflict resolution can then be achieved by heuristically classifying the conflict [5] and instantiating an associated strategy to generate a suggested resolution approach [15]. Determining the cross-perspective impact of decisions require representation standards capable of representing decision semantics throughout the life cycle. Existing standards do not in most domains provide adequate coverage or expressiveness yet. Another key challenge is improving the scalability of the decision impact assessment process; untrammeled dependency propagation can quickly become computationally intractable and overwhelm agents with floods of information on the impact of multitudes of changes made elsewhere. Abstract or qualitative representations of decisions and dependencies are needed to allow meaningful if approximate assessments of decision impacts at significantly reduced computational cost. We also need to be able to specify context-sensitive policies concerning what kind of dependency impact detection should be done when. Finally, better support needs to be provided for computer-supported conflict resolution. The first step in resolving a conflict is typically to understand how it occurred and why. Current conflict management technology records what other decisions impinged on this one but doesn't keep track of the intent or history (e.g. rejected options) behind the decisions. We need to be able to access a rich representation of the rationale behind conflicting decisions. In addition, the resolution of a conflict is typically reached through a multi-step process (e.g. negotiation over resource assignments) involving the people who produced the conflicting decisions. These processes need to be integrated into a general and robust process management approach.

2.3   Memory Management

The distribution of cooperative work across time implies the need to remember the reasoning underlying decisions made throughout the life cycle. When a set of decisions is made the typical output is made up of documents describing the final result of a long series of deliberations and tradeoffs. The underlying history, intent and logical support (i.e. the rationale) for the decisions captured therein, however, is usually lost, or is represented at best as a scattered collection of paper documents, project and personal notebook entries as well as individual's recollections. This rationale information can be very difficult to access by humans and is represented such that computers can provide little support for managing and utilizing it.

Many decision rationale capture approaches have been developed (e.g. [19, 34, 24, 20, 9]). Shortcomings with existing approaches include limited expressiveness and therefore limited computational usefulness due to lack of integration with decision capture technologies. They have for example the potential for inconsistency between the rationale and decision descriptions, spotty capture of rationale and the tendency to waste time on issues that later prove unimportant [9]. Existing rationale language technology has been used mainly to capture the pros and cons of alternative solutions for a given problem, but not intent, the relationships between decisions or their history, all of which, of course, can be extremely important. Rationale capture can be burdensome, especially given that the person who benefits is generally different than the person required to describe it. This is exacerbated by the fact that it is often unclear where and in how much detail rationale should be described, since the person who enters the rationale is unlikely to know how it will be used or even by whom. We should be able to describe preferred rationale capture processes to delimit what and how detailed rationale should be captured. If possible, these preferred processes should provide default rationale templates that can be quickly customized to describe the rationale for a given decision.

3   Promising Directions

Integrate Coordination Technologies

Many of the weaknesses of current coordination technologies derive from the fact that they evolved separately and are not as a result functionally integrated. Truly effective coordination, however, requires an integrated approach wherein dependencies across all the dimensions of cooperative work distribution are modelled and managed in a single computational framework [16]. Figure 8 summarizes some of the ways in which this integration can synergistically combine the strengths and avoid the weaknesses of the component coordination technologies.

Rationale capture technology provides argumentation and intent information for process (and product) decisions. This can be used to support process redesign (e.g. allowing us to avoid process changes that violate important goals). Rationale capture derives increased expressiveness from the notions of process

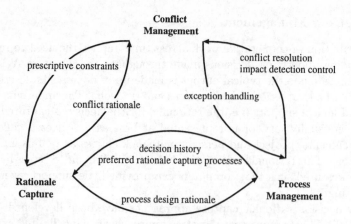

Fig. 8. Synergism Among iDCSS Component Technologies.

execution history and prescriptive constraints. We can also use process templates to delimit what and how much rationale information needs to be captured for given decisions (e.g. by specifying for which sub-goals we need to justify the way the goal was achieved), helping to reduce the potential rationale capture burden. Process management technology benefits from the exception handling capabilities made possible by generalizing conflict management technology. The beginnings of an approach to integrating coordination technologies is described in [16].

Beyond Traditional Process Representations

As we have seen, process management plays a pivotal role in the area of coordination technology. Many of the problems with current process management tools stem from two properties of traditional process representations:

- Process models are "compiled" responses to highly fluid work inter-dependencies. Changing a process model to account for new contingencies is akin to changing a computer program by patching the executable - a difficult and error-prone undertaking.
- Process models can be too highly prescriptive. In many cases it is appropriate to give process performers significant discretion in the steps they perform subject to general constraints such as total allowable resource usage. Current representations are designed to capture only task decomposition/sequencing constraints.

The fundamental problem is that while process templates represent a good way of capturing some kinds of procedures they are the wrong level of abstraction to fully capture coordination expertise. Rather than tweaking process models we should be identifying the kinds of underlying work inter-dependencies that exist in our work environments and uncovering/inventing the coordination mechanisms (including e.g. traditional process models, speech act approaches, asynchronous messaging or multi-functional teams) that work for these kinds of dependency structures [21]. Computer systems can then help us opportunistically identify and apply the appropriate coordination mechanism as needed. When the underlying work dependencies change, "exception handling" tools [17] can detect this and help us decide whether to incrementally modify the current coordination mechanism (e.g. by "patching" a process model) or select an entirely different one. In a design context, for example, unexpectedly severe impacts of design innovations on manufacturability could motivate us to replace a serial design process with multi-functional design teams for a particular product. For this to work, of course, we need to address the issues of how we can represent and maintain explicit models of organizational goals and constraints as well as work inter-dependencies.

	Traditional Process Models	Flexible Coordination Approach
Representational depth	"Compiled" process descriptions only.	Explicit representation of organizational goals, constraints and dependencies, along with the coordination mechanisms used.
When coordination mechanisms are selected	Processes are fully defined ahead of time.	Coordination mechanisms are opportunistically selected given current coordination requirements.
Prescriptiveness of coordination mechanism	Highly detailed prescriptive models.	Semi-structured (possibly proscriptive) models.
Adaptability of coordination mechanism to exceptions	Processes are adhered to as rigidly and consistently as possible. Exception handling if any is pre-defined.	Coordination mechanisms are sensitive to exceptions and adapt themselves appropriately.

We also need to invent a wider range of approaches for specifying coordination, including some that are "semi-structured" (i.e. only partially prescriptive).

One promising approach is to use "proscriptive" rather than "prescriptive" constraints. Such constraints describe the limits on the desired result (e.g. don't conflict with decision Z) and the process used to achieve it (e.g. don't use more than amount X of resource Y) rather than how the decision should be made.

We can summarize the differences between traditional process models and the flexible coordination approach proposed here as shown in the table above.

Note that this is not suggesting that traditional process models be abandoned, but rather that they be incorporated into a broader more flexible approach. In some cases (e.g. most kinds of manufacturing) it is important to maintain consistent high-level processes to achieve consistent product quality. It should be noted, however, that even highly formalized work environments can be surprisingly exception prone.

Exploit Product & Software Design Technologies

Many of the challenges faced by current process management technology have been addressed by research on physical artifact and software system design. Tools for requirements specification, rationale capture, cooperative design, case-based design and exception handling have been developed in these contexts, and are likely to provide important insights into how analogous problems can be dealt with in the process world. While some initial work has been performed, e.g. in applying case-based [21] and collaborative design [6] approaches to process definition, this direction is worthy of more investigation.

References

1. The Action Workflow Approach to Workflow Management Technology. In Proceedings of CSCW '92, 1992
2. Kosanke, K. CIMOSA: Open System Architecture for CIM, Springer Verlag (1993)
3. Bravoco, R.R. and Yadav, S.B. Requirements Definition Architecture - An Overview. Computers in Industry 6(1985), 237-251
4. Brown, D.C. Failure Handling In A Design Expert System, Butterworth and Co. (November 1985)
5. Clancey, W.J. Classification Problem Solving. AAAI (1984), 49-55
6. Dean, D.L.D., Lee, J.D.L., Orwig, R.E.O., and Vogel, D.R.V. Technological Support for Group Process Modelling. Journal of Information Management Systems 11, 3 (Winter 1994-95)
7. Descotte, Y. and Latombe, J.C. Making Compromises Among Antagonist Constraints In A Planner. Artificial Intelligence 27(1985), 183-217
8. Eppinger, S.D., Whitney, D.E.W., Smith, R.P.S., and Gebala, D.A.G. A Model-Based Method for Organizing Tasks in Product Development. Tech. Report 3569-93-MS, Working Paper, MIT Sloan School of Management, May 1993
9. Fischer, G., Lemke, A.C., McCall, R., and Morch, A.I. Making Argumentation Serve Design. Journal of Human Computer Interaction 6, 3-4 (1991), 393-419
10. Fox, M.S. and Smith, S.F. ISIS - A Knowledge-Based System For Factory Scheduling. Expert Systems (July 1984)
11. Goldstein, I. Bargaining Between Goals. In .IJCAI, 1975, 175-180

12. Grudin, J. Groupware and Social Dynamics: Eight Challenges for Developers. Communications of the ACM 37, 1 (January 1994), 93-105

13. Hewitt, C. Offices Are Open Systems. ACM Transactions on Office Information Systems 4, 3 (July 1986), 271-287

14. Karbe, B.H. and Ramsberger, N.G. Influence of Exception Handling on the Support of Cooperative Office Work. In Multi-User Interfaces and Applications. Elsevier Science Publishers, Gibbs, S. and Verrijin-Stuart, A.A., 355-370, 1990

15. Klein, M. Supporting Conflict Resolution in Cooperative Design Systems. IEEE Systems Man and Cybernetics 21, 6 (December 1991)

16. Klein, M. iDCSS: Integrating Workflow, Conflict and Rationale-Based Concurrent Engineering Coordination Technologies. Concurrent Engineering Research and Applications 3, 1 (January 1995).

17. Klein, M. Conflict Management as Part of an Integrated Exception Handling Approach. AI in Engineering Design Analysis and Manufacturing (AI EDAM) (1995)

18. Lander, S. and Lesser, V.R. Negotiation To Resolve Conflicts Among Design Experts. Tech. Report Dept of Computer and Information Science, August 1988

19. Lee, J. and Lai, K.Y. What's In Design Rationale?. Human-Computer Interaction 6, 3-4 (1991), 251-280

20. MacLean, A., Young, R., Bellotti, V., and Moran, T. Questions, Options and Criteria: Elements of a Design Rationale for User Interfaces. Journal of Human Computer Interaction: Special Issue on Design Rationale 6, 3-4 (1991), 201-250

21. Malone, T. and Crowston, K. Towards an Interdisciplinary Theory of Coordination. Tech. Report 120, Technical report, MIT Center for Coordination Science, 1991

22. Marcus, S., Stout, J., and McDermott, J. VT: An Expert Elevator Designer. Artificial Intelligence Magazine 8, 4 (Winter 1987), 39-58

23. Mark, W. and Dukes-Schlossberg, J. Cosmos: A System for Supporting Engineering Negotiation. Concurrent Engineering Research and Applications: Special Issue on Conflict Management in Concurrent Engineering II, 3 (September 1994), 173-182

24. McCall, R. PHIBIS: Procedurally Hierarchical Issue-Based Information Systems. In Proceedings of the Conference on Planning and Design in Architecture, ASME, Boston MA, 1987

25. Mi, P.W. and Scacchi, W. Modelling Articulation Work in Software Engineering Processes. In Proceedings of the First International Conference on the Software Process, IEEE, IEEE Computer Society Press, 1991, 188-201

26. Murata, T. Petri Nets: Properties, Analysis and Applications. Proceedings of the IEEE 77, 4 (.apr 1989), 541-580

27. Peluso, E., Goldstine, J., Phoha, S., Sircar, S., Yukish, M., Licari, J., and Mayk, I. Hierarchical Supervision for the Command and Control of Interacting Automata. In Proceedings of the Symposium on Command and Control Research, June 21-23 1994

28. Smith, R.G. The Contract Net Protocol: High-Level Communication And Control In A Distributed Problem Solver. IEEE Transactions on Computers C-29, 12 (December 1980), 1104-1113

29. Stefik, M.J. Planning With Constraints (Molgen: Part 1 & 2). Artificial Intelligence 16, 2 (1981), 111-170

30. Suchman, L.A. Office Procedures as Practical Action: Models of Work and System Design. ACM Transactions on Office Information Systems 1, 4 (October 1983), 320-328

31. Sussman, G.J. and Steele, G.L. Constraints - A Language For Expressing Almost-Hierarchical Descriptions. Artificial Intelligence 14(1980), 1-40

32. Wilensky, R. Planning And Understanding, Addison-Wesley (1983)
33. Winograd, T. A Language/Action Perspective on the Design of Cooperative Work. In Proceedings of CSCW '86, 1986
34. Yakemovic, K.C.B. and Conklin, E.J. Report on a Development Project Use of an Issue-Based Information System. In CSCW 90 Proceedings, 1990, 105-118

Supporting Autonomous Work and Reintegration in Collaborative Systems

Michael Berger[1], Alexander Schill[2], and Gerd Völksen[1]

[1] Siemens AG, Corporate Technology, D-81730 Munich, Germany,
Email: {Michael.Berger | Gerd.Voelksen}@mchp.siemens.de
[2] Dresden University of Technology, Department of Computer Science,
D-01062 Dresden, Germany,
Email: Schill@ibch10.inf.tu-dresden.de

Abstract. Collaborative systems supporting coupled work scenarios by audio/video conferencing, application sharing, or electronic mail have found their acceptance in many domains. Going beyond these systems, user groups require cooperation support also for decoupled work in environments with mobile and location-independent sites. Support of different modifications made to replicated common data on each decoupled site is necessary to guarantee flexible and unrestricted decoupled work. This mostly implies inconsistencies and hence different versions of replicated data which must be unified during a reintegration phase. This paper defines requirements for an efficient and flexible reintegration, and it compares existing reintegration mechanisms with these requirements. In its central part, the paper presents a generic Merge And Resolve Conflicts (MARC) component which provides history based automatic conflict detection and semi-automatic resolution on object nets. An implementation of this component extends the CoNus CSCW system by Siemens Corporate Technology with functionality supporting autonomous work and subsequent reintegration.

1 Introduction

To improve business processes, administrative work, and many other activities in the industry and service sector, groupware and computer supported cooperative work (CSCW) have been recognized as highly useful strategies [1]. However, CSCW systems must integrate both, the computer based information management and the communication and cooperation support. They are only flexible and efficiently applicable for comprehensive team work if a lot of collaboration scenarios and easy transitions between different work phases are supported.

Existing CSCW systems support *coupled work phases* (see Figure 1). Coupled work of two or more sites means that all messages sent from one site are deliverable to all group sites. Additionally, during *synchronous* coupled collaboration all messages are sent in real-time. If the messages do not need real-time delivery, the two sites are working in an *asynchronous* coupled collaboration. Synchronous collaboration includes desktop audio/video conferencing and data and application sharing while asynchronous collaboration includes electronic mail or distributed calendar tools, to name just a few. For more details see [2] and [3].

Today, more and more working environments consist of mobile and location independent computing equipment, which needs to be independent from temporary intended or unintended disconnections of group members. Such working environments require support of *autonomous collaboration* during *decoupled work phases* (see Figure 1). Two sites are working in a *decoupled* phase if any site can neither send messages to nor receive messages from any other site.

Autonomous collaboration enables decoupled work within and among organizations in case of temporarily high data transfer cost, high network load, connection breakdowns, or when using mobile components. Examples of such working environments can be found in distributed development teams using home-teleworking, or in outdoor and service teams. While decoupling because of high network load or cost is *intended*, a connection breakdown implies an *unintended* decoupling.

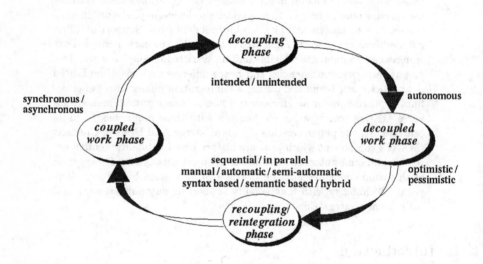

Fig. 1. Collaborative work and transition phases

The *replication of common data* and applications is the prerequisite for spontaneously initiated and *immediate transitions* from coupled to decoupled work phase without any delay and allows users also to work in cases of connection failures.

During decoupled work, only an *optimistic approach* guarantees the effectiveness of continuous work by allowing unlimited, concurrent and therefore efficient work for group members by supporting different modifications of replicated common data on each decoupled site. All data operations are allowed during autonomous collaboration as they are during coupled work without any restrictions on the creativity of the users.

Decoupled work under this optimistic strategy results in several different and inconsistent versions of replicated data. During the transition from decoupled to coupled work – also named as *recoupling/reintegration phase* (see Figure 1) – these versions must be transformed into one integrated version (see Section 3). Current collaborative systems usually do not support an efficient merge of such different versions. A detection, presentation, and resolution of conflicts needs new mechanisms of reintegration with consistency restoration.

Section 2 defines requirements for a reintegration component in collaborative systems. Section 3 describes existing reintegration mechanisms and conflict resolution approaches and compares them to the defined requirements. Section 4 describes the implemented Merge and Resolve Conflict (MARC) component. Finally, in Section 5 and 6, implementational aspects are given, the evaluation environment will be described, and conclusions for future work are given.

2 Reintegration After Optimistic Decoupled Work

2.1 Requirements for Reintegration

Any of the existing mechanisms such as those in database or file systems [10, 15–17] support optimistic autonomous collaboration. Decoupled work phases supported by these systems are expected to be short and inconsistencies are simple and occur rarely [4]. In contrast, CSCW systems should support intentionally long decoupled work phases. *Inconsistencies are to be expected* and occur very often [5, 6]. Under these circumstances, a main requirement for a reintegration tool in CSCW systems is that the efficiency gained by autonomous work must not be compensated by an inefficient reintegration.

To increase the *efficiency of a reintegration* the following parameters will be considered for optimization and will be discussed in the subsequent sections:

- the mechanism of detecting inconsistencies
- the definition and granularity of conflicts,
- the intuitivity of conflict presentations,
- the order of conflict resolution,
- the granularity of conflict resolutions, and
- the automation of conflict resolutions.

The requirement to support optimistic autonomous work and reintegration for all or at least most collaborative systems leads to the idea of creating a generic CSCW middleware component. The mechanisms should be application and platform independent and should be placed between the operating system and the CSCW applications.

Therefore, the component to be developed is based on *syntactic mechanisms*, but should be also extendable by application (*semantics*) dependent conflict presentations and resolutions. Syntactic mechanisms are based on the information structure or update operation syntax while semantic based mechanisms involve the real world representation of the inconsistent information or update operations.

The reintegration mechanisms should also be *scalable*: a *sequential reintegration* of two integrating sites, *parallel reintegrations* of more than two users at the same time, as well as *immediate and lazy* reintegrations should be supported. An immediate reintegration resolves all conflicts during reintegration time. In contrast, a lazy reintegration subdivides between essential and insignificant conflicts and only essential ones are resolved during reintegration time due to time pressure or even high network costs and load. The insignificant conflicts are resolved later during coupled work pauses, when accessing inconsistent data, or during time intervals where network load or costs are low [18, 27].

2.2 Detection of Inconsistencies

The *detection of inconsistencies* may be performed, first, by a *complete comparison of the information replicas* or, second, by a *comparison of history lists* containing all operations executed on both sites during decoupled work. A history based reintegration, named as *history merge*, has many advantages. History lists permit a more efficient inconsistency detection by comparing executed operations and autonomous changes rather than comparing the whole replica on both sites [8, 18]. This is more efficient if the size of a data replica is large compared to the list of changes. In contrast to the approach of a history merge, a *data merge* is based on the complete comparison of the data replicas. Furthermore, if a data object exists on one site only, either a create operation was executed on this site or a delete operation was executed on the other site. This may be easily detected by merely comparing history operations. Additionally, in case of a data merge a comparison with the last consistent replica state is needed. Finally, timestamps or additional semantic information may be assigned to the operations in the history and may be used for reintegration. The additional administration overhead and resource requirements are minor disadvantages of maintaining and comparing history lists.

The inconsistencies to be detected by a history based reintegration have their origin in single operations or pairs of history operations, named as *inconsistency generating operations* where each part of a pair was generated at a different site. In order to optimize the detection of inconsistency generating operations, histories can be reduced in length by removing overwritten and redundant operations before merging. This process will be called as *history shortening*.

The consistency of two partitioned data replicas can be defined in analogy to object-oriented data bases: Two replicas are consistent if and only if they contain the same objects which have identical associations and attributes. The consistency of data replicas using a history based reintegration can be defined by the equivalence of history lists (see Figure 2): Two histories (HA and HB, containing an equal or different number of operations) are equivalent if and only if applying them to consistent replicas (A0, B0) results in consistent replicas (A2, B2). That means, if the two replicas are consistent at decoupling time (A0, B0), and non-equivalent sequences SA1 and SB1 generate different and inconsistent replica versions A1 and B1, a reintegration mechanism has to generate and to execute two different *replay sequences* SA2 and SB2, one for each replica, to restore the equivalence of both histories (HA, HB) and to reach the consistent state of the replicas A and B. These replay sequences will be generated by a history merge algorithm.

Other history based reintegration mechanisms, such as in the *GINA* system [28], use the approach of appending one sequence at the end of the other. They perform an undo of all autonomous changes on a site A (sequence SA1) and reexecute the operations from site B on site A (sequence SB1). After that, the operations in the undone sequence SA1, but not all of them, are reexecuted on both sites. Conflicting operations between the sequence SA1 and SB1 are selectively undone and deleted in sequence SB1 and will not be reexecuted. This mechanisms does not allow a flexible reintegration, because one of both sequences (SA1 or SB1) will be overtaken automatically and only changes from one site may be undone. In contrast, the generation of replay sequences does not limit the generation of the consistent version.

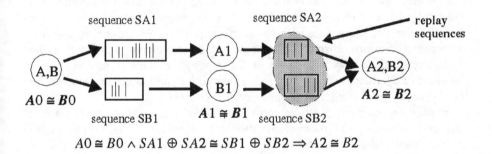

$$AO \cong BO \wedge SA1 \oplus SA2 \cong SB1 \oplus SB2 \Rightarrow A2 \cong B2$$

Fig. 2. Generating consistent replicas by equivalent operation histories

2.3   Definition and Granularity of Conflicts

As said above, the inconsistencies to be detected by a history based reintegration have their origin in single or pairs of history operations, named as *inconsistency generating operations*. These inconsistency generating operations form conflicts whereas each conflict must be detected at once and resolved by a single decision during reintegration. In this paper, only data operations and their conflicts are considered, based on concurrent write activities on the replicated data. Read/write conflicts and external conflicts involving the real world, for example printing a letter or booking a ticket by an email, are not considered.

The *granularity of conflicts*, defined by the granularity of history operations, is an essential parameter for an efficient history based reintegration. Fine grained operations generate exactly one data inconsistency while coarse grained operations generate more than one inconsistency at once and the reintegration mechanism must resolve these inconsistencies together as one conflict. For example, a single character represents the finest grained entity in a texteditor. A differently changed character is an inconsistency in the text file. Based on a fine grained operation which changes only one character, this inconsistency may be detected and resolved as one conflicting change. A mechanism which stores only change operations on word, line or text file base, allows only to resolve such coarse grained conflicts. The more coarse grained conflicts are, the less flexible is a resolution which cannot fully correspond to the user's reintegration wishes. For this reason, a reintegration approach must support most possible fine grained operations and conflicts.

2.4   Presentation and Resolution of Conflicts

During reintegration conflicts will be resolved by manual decisions. For manual resolutions, the user has or users have to resolve conflicts by *democratic* or *authoritarian decisions*. In case of democratic decisions, it should be noted that merging is a cooperative process of negotiations between the users. Therefore, users would interact with other users by a text or gesture based communication and finally by an audio/video conference. For managing the reintegration process, the user has to interact with the reintegration tool by answering questions or changing interface objects, e.g. by moving a document into a new folder. The conflict resolution, however, is part of the application. This is only possible, if the effect of operations can be generally reversed for consistency restoration. The inconsistency generating operations must be *reversible*.

Supporting user decisions, an *intuitive conflict presentation* as well as user-user and user-computer *interactions* should be supplied. A merge tool should provide both a *descriptive textual* and a *graphical* presentation of conflicts set upon the last consistent state. The textual presentation includes the description of what has changed, which operations were used for the change, and who performed the change. A graphical presentation may display differences of the replicated data by highlighting or marking, using for example different colors and textstyles, or by animating the actions leading to conflicts, for example moving a file between directories.

2.5   Order, Granularity, and Automation of Conflict Resolutions

Another possibility to influence the efficiency of reintegration is to define an *efficient order of conflict resolutions*. This becomes more important when the amount of conflicts increases and histories become longer. A useful order of resolutions has to *avoid undoing earlier decisions*. Also, in case of an interactive reintegration, it is decisive for the user to *keep an overview* of the reintegration process. Additionally to the reintegration main goal of reconstructing consistency, especially for a history based reintegration, the *serializability of operations* in the replay sequences and equivalent histories is a second main goal. The reason is, that a newcomer to a group would see a correct history, in which for example an object will not be changed before it was created.

The *granularity of conflict resolutions* is also a parameter influencing the reintegration efficiency. The granularity of a conflict resolution may be defined by the amount of conflicting operations resolved by one decision only (compared to the granularity of conflicts). In case of a history merge, the resolution granularity corresponds to the amount of involved conflict operations. The more coarse grained resolutions are, the less decisions are needed and the reintegration time may be strongly reduced. Therefore, *coarser grained resolutions* should be supported.

As a final requirement, *automatic resolutions* must be supported on the syntax and the semantic level. Automatic resolutions being almost correct is a main goal. However, automatic resolutions may be predefined by an application programmer or by end users before the reintegration.

The following chapter discusses how existing systems fullfil the requirements defined above and support reintegration after optimistic decoupled work.

3   Related Work

Considering existing systems supporting autonomous work it will be noticed that most of them support only a pessimistic strategy during decoupled work by avoiding concurrent changes on different copies of the same data. Nevertheless, the optimistic work strategy during decoupled work is used in some systems and a number of merge tools already exist. These will be presented and discussed briefly. Also, systems supporting decoupled work with partly optimistic and partly pessimistic strategies have been developed [8] but are not considered in detail in this paper. Existing approaches can be subdivided into reintegration tools for database systems (*Data Patch* [10], *Optimistic Protocol* [9] and *Log Transformation* [11]); operating and file systems (*Version Vectors* [12], *Fcomp* [13], *Unix Diff* [14], *Application Specific Resolver* [15], *Conflict Resolvers* [16], *Disconnected Operation for AFS* [17] and *Coda* [18], *File Merge* [19], and collaborative systems. Within collaborative systems three specific application domains may be distinguished: text editing systems (*Flexible Diff* [20], *Object Merging* [21], *FrameMaker* [22]); software development (*Rcsmerge* [23], *Fileresolve* [24], *FileMerge* [25], *Integrate* [26], *Code Inspection* [5], *Lazy Consistency* [27]), and framework systems (*COCOON* [5], *GINA* [28], *Lotus Notes* [29], *Liveware* [30]). Less comprehensive classifications with different point of emphasis are given in [8] and [21].

3.1   Detection of Inconsistencies, Definition and Granularity of Conflicts

The detection of inconsistencies in existing reintegration tools is based on both different application-specific history operations and on the data structures and conflicts are of different granularities.

All existing systems and tools support syntax based write/write conflict detection. But only approximately half of them provide a history based detection, partly detecting read/write conflicts (*Optimistic Protocol, Log Transformation mechanism, Disconnected Operation* mechanism for AFS). External effects are not considered in any system.

History and data comparisons detect conflicts based on creations and deletions of directories, files, database entities and relations, objects and links, as well as creations of annotations per line in a program file. Furthermore, they detect changes to directories, files, object attributes, to database entities and relations. Additionally, only data comparisons detect conflicts based on creations and deletions of lines in text files and changes of program statements and expressions.

To reduce the expenditure of a conflict detection the *Log Transformation* mechanism, the *Disconnected Operation* mechanism in Coda, and the *File Merge* mechanism provide a history shortening to reduce the history length.

3.2   Conflict Resolution and Conflict Resolution Granularity

With the *Version Vectors* mechanism, the *Fcomp* mechanism, the Unix *Diff* tool, the *Flexible Diff* tool, and most existing single user text editors such as *FrameMaker*, mechanisms exist just for detecting conflicts based on a data comparison which does not provide any conflict resolutions. All other systems provide conflict detection and automatic, semi-automatic or manual resolution in different ways.

Collaborative systems usually support syntax based semi-automatic conflict resolutions. All automatic resolutions are predefined by the application. The *Optimistic Protocol* mechanism resolves all conflicts automatically using a syntax based generated and transformed dependency graph to achieve the serializability of read/write transactions and therefore consistency of replicas. The *File Merge* mechanism integrates changed parts of files in an application independent way by using the definition of operation priorities to resolve conflicts automatically. Other mechanisms (*Lotus Notes*) use timestamps to define the resolution.

In contrast to the syntax based approaches, semantic based resolutions use the role of users, as well as the specific semantics of data objects such as database entities, directories, files, text objects, and program code statements.There are also syntax/semantic combined mechanisms provided by the *GINA* system.

The reintegration tools support different granularity levels of resolutions:

- *fine grained resolutions* by supporting one decision for each *single* conflict operation or for each *single* changed data entity of different granularity,
- *medium grained resolutions* by allowing one decision for a *set* of conflict operations, for example for all non-overlapping text line changes (*Rcsmerge*, Sun's NSE *Fileresolve, FileMerge* tool), all operations to a file, to a directory, to an object, or for a *set* of changed data entities, and
- *coarse grained resolutions* by supporting one decision for *all* conflict operations or for *all* changed data entities on one site (*COCOON*).

Considering a specific data entity, non-overlapping changes are changes to the entity on one site only. Overlapping changes occur if an entity was updated in different ways on both sites. For example, a data entity has been deleted on one site while on the other site the data entity has changed.

Additionally, there are collaborative systems supporting flexible combinations of resolution granularity levels (*GINA* system, Sun's NSE *Fileresolve*, and *FileMerge* tool).

3.3 Conflict Presentation and Resolution Order

A lot of systems support manual or semi-automatic resolutions but not all of them provide intuitive conflict presentations. Most of the reintegration mechanisms in operating and file systems use e-mail based syntactic notification about the conflicting file or directory changes (*Application Specific Resolver*, *Conflict Resolvers* tool, *Disconnected Operation* mechanism for AFS and Coda). Syntax based presentations in the *Fcomp* mechanism and the Unix *Diff* tool produce an edit script which presents the differences by the minimal set of inserted and deleted lines in a text file. When applied this script to one of the files, will produce a consistent file combining changes from both. Additionally, the *Flexible Diff* tool focuses on an intuitive and semantic based graphical presentation of different text parts and provides several filters and levels for presenting text differences. *FrameMaker* generates a file describing the changes textually. The *GINA* system and the *Data Patch* tool describe the cause of a single conflict textually and show the conflicting operations or data entities.

Most history based reintegration tools, such as the *Optimistic Protocol*, *Disconnected Operation* mechanism for AFS and Coda, the *Code Inspection* tool, the *COCOON* system and the *GINA* system, support a syntax based order of conflict resolutions. They detect and resolve conflicts chronologically, defined by the top down order of operations in the history. Additionally, the *Log Transformation* mechanism and *Lotus Notes* resolve conflicting transactions chronologically, ordered by timestamps. Other merge tools, such as the *File Merge* mechanism, the *Rcsmerge* operation and the algorithm *Integrate* resolve conflicts from the beginning to the end of a file. Only the *Data Patch* tool and the *Lazy Consistency* mechanism define a resolution order based on the semantics of changed database entities and software development steps. Sun's NSE *Fileresolve* and *FileMerge* tool support a resolution order defined manually by the user, while all other approaches use a predefined resolution order.

The *Application Specific Resolver* and the *Disconnected Operation* mechanism in Coda provide lazy reintegration. They send the user mails describing conflicts which can not be resolved automatically. These conflicts must be resolved later by the user, when he or she has time left or server load is low.

3.4 Conclusions

Related work shows that the new dimension of decoupled work in CSCW environments becomes important and that tools already exist to support optimistic decoupled work strategy and reintegration. But the requirement of a general-purpose reintegration support in CSCW systems is not fulfilled.

Existing reintegration tools lack in an efficient sequence of resolutions. All systems except the *Coda* system do not provide delayed reintegration and parallel reintegrations with several sites are not supported. There is no system supporting reintegration based on general syntactic operations extended by semantic information. The existing reintegration tools, except the *Flexible Diff* tool, pay no attention to an intuitive presentation of conflicts. No reintegration tool provides democratic decisions or communication between users during reintegration, for example by audio. Additionally, there is no concept for defining automatic resolutions by the end user itself. Concerning the decoupling process, most systems do not support continuous work after unintended decoupling.

Thus, an efficient and flexible reintegration tool is still needed. MARC, a reintegration tool corresponding to most of the requirements above was build for the CoNus CSCW system [6] developed at Siemens Corporate Technology. This tool provides an efficient syntactic history based merge algorithm to detect, present, and resolve conflicts in object nets as well as semantic based extensions. It helps users to (semi-)automatically integrate their work after finishing decoupled work phases in collaborative environments.

4   MARC – A Merge And Resolve Conflicts Component

4.1   Overview

MARC was developed as an object-oriented CSCW middleware component to support optimistic autonomous work and history based reintegration in collaborative systems. In this section the information model, communication model, and synchronization model will be presented. The information model describes how data in collaborative systems is organized. The communication model describes the implicit communication between users and how they can manipulate the shared database. At last, the synchronization model describes the history based reintegration mechanism for consistency restauration after decoupled work.

4.2   Information Model

Information used in a CSCW system may be subdivided into private information, accessible only by its owner, shared information, accessible by a certain group of users, and public information, accessible by all users. Based on ideas from [30] the notions of *private information unit (PRIU)*, *shared information unit (SIU)* and *public information unit (PIU)* are used. Data which a single user has access rights to are replicated to the user's local machine. Therefore, the PIUs and SIUs are replicated to the sites of each user or concerned group member while the user's PRIU is only on his or her local machine. The instance managing all existing information units (IUs) at one site will be named as *unit manager (UM)*. MARC employs an object-oriented information model. Based on an entity-relationship model, an *object* represents a real world information entity. *Attributes* hold the entities contents and *links* represent relations between objects. Links in an object net are classified as follows: *Hierarchy links* represent subpart-superpart or aggregation relations between objects. Non-hierarchy links between objects are logical relations, named as *semantic links*. An object net restricted to hierarchy links forms a tree. Objects which may have one or more subpart object are named *container objects*, other objects are *atomic objects*. The object net is related to the IUs and users manipulate the object net through applications which access parts of the object net. An example net is shown in Figure 3.

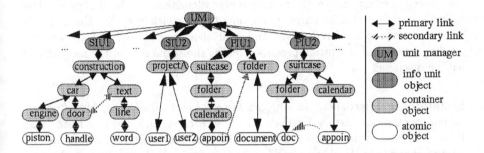

Fig. 3. An example object net

4.3   Communication Model

User interactions cause events processed by the application on different sites. A central serialization and multicasting service distributes corresponding operations to the involved members of the IUs according to consistency and ordering guarantees (see [5]). Each IU reacts on incoming update operations by adjusting its information structure and by informing the involved applications.

There are five *fine grained* and *reversible operations* for manipulating the network part of common, replicated objects belonging to one IU:

- *createObj(OID, ClassName)*, *deleteObj(OID)*,
- *createLink(OID, OID1, LinkName)*, *deleteLink(OID, OID1, LinkName)*,
- *changeAttr(OID, AttributeName, NewValue, OldValue)*.

An OID is a system wide unique object identifier. For an unambiguous detection of hierarchy and secondary link changes, the atomic link operations must be extended by a *LinkType* parameter.

In addition, a bracket construct is used to define composed operations containing several fine grained operations between brackets. Brackets are needed to compute a sequence of atomic operations as one complex operation without interruption. These bracket constructs are also useful to postpone the visualization after the execution of several operations. For example, a single createObj(...) operation cannot be displayed on the user interface, because there is neither a super hierarchy link to a defined object nor is the position on the user interface correct. General move operation containing deleteLink(...), createLink(...) and attribute operations between the brackets are also composed. Composed operations are sent as a left and right bracket message with a sequence of fine grained operations and a special *updateVis*(...) operation in between.

4.4   Synchronization Model

In this subsection the mechanism to maintain and manage history lists and the generic mechanism for the history merge algorithm will be described. This includes the detection of autonomous operations which generate the inconsist state, the reduction of redundant and equivalent operations, and the ordered conflict search and resolution process. Finally, the scalability of the mechanisms will be discussed.

Maintaining Histories. To support *history-based integration*, MARC maintains a continuous history for each IU on each client site and one history per IUM. The history maintained by the IUM contains all create, delete and attribute changes of IU objects itself. A history for each IU will be used because the history list should contain only operations according to the access rights of users. Furthermore, it is faster to detect conflicting operations in short histories for some IUs during reintegration than in one long common history for all IUs. A history for each atomic or container object is not useful because the reintegration mechanism is based only on operations and such a storage needs information about the object net structure.

The histories contain a chronologically ordered list of operations performed by a group of users working in a coupled mode or by an autonomous user. The history will only store implicit operations. Others like cursor positions, video sequences, etc. will not be held in the history because the focus of the histories is to reintegrate inconsistent data versions.

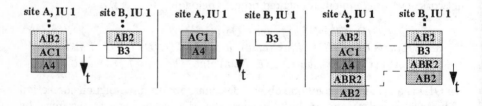

Fig. 4. a) history sequences on site A and B for information unit 1,
b) relevant sequences for detecting inconsistency generating operations,
c) histories on site A and B after reintegration

Operations in the history are attached to *sequences* which receive system wide unique names (see Figure 4a). A new sequence is started after each coupling or decoupling action to the IU. This helps to findout which users were participating in which sequence and subsequently, who is involved in a reintegration process. Other approaches, such as described in [5] use a special operation stored in the history when a user couples or decouples. The decoupling operation of one or more user are more difficult to detect the longer the history becomes.

Generic History Merge Algorithm. As described in Section 2, the aim of reintegration is to generate two equivalent histories for both recoupling sites. At this place, we assume that coupled work and decoupling do not generate inconsistencies. Using one history for each IU replica, the related object nets are consistent if the histories for the specific IU are equivalent. Therefore, after decoupled work the reintegration mechanism has to generate and to execute two replay sequences for each shared and public IU, one for each replica (see Figure 2), to gain equivalence of the histories and to reach the consistent state of the object nets and a consistency of the IUs.

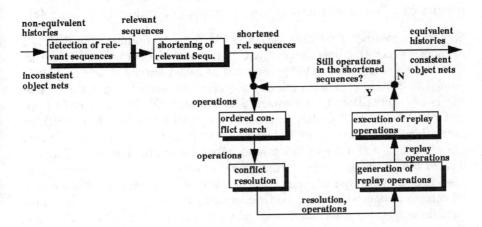

Fig. 5. History merge process

Our approach is presented in Figure 5. It gives an overview of all necessary steps of reintegration. All these steps will be described in detail on the next pages. Formally, the algorithm within each IU looks as follows:

```
(relevantSequA, relevantSequB) :=
  detectRelSequ(aUnitHistoryA, aUnitHistoryB);
(shortSequA, shortSequB) :=
  shortSequences(relevantSequA, relevantSequB);
while (notEmpty(shortSequA, shortSequB)) do
  (affectedOpsA, affectedOpsB) :=
    orderedConflictOpsSearch(shortSequA, shortSequB);
  (decision, newOps) :=
```

```
  resolveConflict(affectedOpsA, affectedOpsB);
  (replayOpsA, replayOpsB) :=
    generateReplay(decision, newOps, affectedOpsA, affectedOpsB);
  execute(siteA, replayOpsA); execute(siteB, replayOpsB);
  removeAffectedOps(affectedOpsA, shortSequA);
  removeAffectedOps(affectedOpsB, shortSequB)
done
```

Step 1: Detection of relevant sequences. In a first step MARC detects all relevant sequences for a reintegration containing inconsistency generating operations. Only those updates made since the disconnection (during the decoupled work) must be considered because only these – but not necessary all of them – may be a reason for conflicts. The last common sequence in both histories represents the last equivalent state of the histories and the last consistent state of the IU. All sequences after these sequences are generally relevant for a reintegration. In the example in Figure 4a the sequence AB2 is the last common sequence. All following sequences (AC1 and A4 on site A and B3 on site B) are generally relevant for a detection of inconsistency generating operations (see Figure 4b).

Step 2: Shortening of relevant sequences. In order to optimize the detection of conflict generating operations, MARC reduces the length of the relevant sequences in a second step. This process will be called *history or sequence shortening* (see Section 2). Within relevant sequences on each site, operations whose effects are overwritten by subsequent ones are removed. This includes all createObj(OID)/deleteObj(OID) pairs and all operations to the object OID between them, all createLink/deleteLink and deleteLink/createLink pairs with the same linkname and different link targets, all operations to an object before it is deleted and all changes to an attribute except the last one. Visualization update operations and brackets of composed operations are also removed. Additionally, all equivalent operations detected by comparing the relevant sequences of both sites do not generate inconsistencies and are also removed. After both steps, the remaining *shortened relevant sequences* only contain operations generating inconsistencies directly. After shortening the sequences only four conflicting operation combinations can occur:

1. site A executed any operation with object OID:
   createObj(OID, ClassName); *deleteObj(OID)*;
   createLink(OID, OID1, LinkName); *deleteLink(OID, OID1, LinkName)*;
   createLink(OID1, OID, LinkName); *deleteLink(OID1, OID, LinkName)*;
   changeAttr(OID, AttrName, NewValue, OldValue);
   while there is no operation with the object OID in the shortened relevant history on site B
2. site A executed any link and attribute operation with object denoted by OID
   createLink(OID, OID1, LinkName); *deleteLink(OID, OID1, LinkName)*;
   createLink(OID1, OID, LinkName); *deleteLink(OID1, OID, LinkName)*;
   changeAttr(OID, AttrName, NewValue, OldValue);
   while site B performed a *deleteObj(OID)* operation

3. both sites created a link with the same name *LinkName* to different target objects. {siteA: *createLink(OID, OID1, LinkName)*; siteB: *createLink(OID, OID2, LinkName)*}, and

4. both sites set the same attribute of an object to a different value {*changeAttr(OID, AttrName, NewValue1, OldValue)*; *changeAttr(OID, AttrName, NewValue2, OldValue)*}

Step 3: Ordered conflict search. To avoid undoing earlier decisions and to guarantee the *serialization of replay operations*, MARC uses the syntax of operations to define a general order in which inconsistencies are resolved. The serializiability depends on operations which are not commutable, that means on operations which must be executed in a special order. Delete operations commute with delete operations, create operations with create operations and changes with changes. They are not critical. But all link and attribute changes are related to createObj and deleteObj operations. For example an attribute change can be executed only after the creation of the object or a link can be created after the creation of source and target object. Based on this, a resolution order can be defined in which the resolution of deleteObj() operations precede createObj() operations, link operations and attribute change operations. This order guarantees that after deciding which objects are currently in the system (create or delete objects), the position in the object net structure (create or delete links) and finally their attributes are considered. So we generate the object-, link- and attribute consistency step by step.

Additionally, to support the users by providing an *overview of the reintegration process*, the resolution order based on the operation-syntax may be combined with different definitions of which createObj() or deleteObj() operations, which link changes or which changeAttr() operations should be considered first. The order and time stamps of operations in the histories may be used. Therefore, MARC provides forward and backward search through the histories and time stamp based search of operations. For example, based on a forward selection of operations in the history, the user can follow the development steps and may have a better understanding on how a change was generated. In contrast, newly created and changed objects may be selected first because these changes are still in mind of the users. Currently, the correct resolution order must be defined by the application programmer.

Furthermore, the resolution order based on the operation syntax may be extended by different resolution strategies depending on the data structure. MARC focuses on conflict detection and resolution in applications using tree structured information, as in file systems, text and graphic editors, document standards (OpenDoc see [31]) and in general object-oriented systems. As described in the information model, links in tree structured object nets may be subdivided in hierarchy and semantic links and objects may be containers or atomic objects. The general resolution order can be enhanced by this knowledge. Considering the link operations during reintegration, first the hierarchy links must be resolved and the position of an object in the hierarchy is defined before decisions about all other semantic links are taken.

MARC supports a top-down and bottom-up procedure according to the tree. Using a top-down procedure, the goal is to resolve conflicts on the highest hierarchy level first. Hierarchy levels are defined according to the node depth in the tree structure (root = level1). For example, a container object (see Figure 3), deleted on level2 on site A, will be considered before an object in level3 as subpart of the container on site B. Using the bottom-up method, first the atomic objects will be associated with containers and after that the container hierarchy will be defined. To support a structure based reintegration order, the operations are extended by a level description on which the object was changed. Before the reintegration, the level information in all operations must be transformed into the last and final state.

Step 4: Conflict resolution. The detection algorithm does not take the responsibility from the user for resolving conflicts. Users still have to decide which changes apply and which do not. Therefore, in this step, MARC presents automatically the detected conflict operations. The presentation of conflicting operations uses template based syntactic textual descriptions while the concerned object visualizations are blinking. For example, both users are asked: "Should the object with OID, deleted by user1 and changed by user2, really be deleted?" (see Figure 6a). Supported by an audio connection, both users decide between "Yes" or "No". Only one user has the possibility to accept the common decision. In case of change operations both changes are described and the users can decide between both changes clicking on a specific Button. As in the create/delete decision, only one user has the right to accept.

Not all conflicts are easy to resolve by this mechanism. Special link decisions, for example, cause problems. Assume a target object of a created or moved link not exists on the other site, because the users removed that object. To reestablish the link as it was in the last consistent version is not possible. Therefore, only the resolution can be recreating a new target object. MARC presents this case to the users. The users can decide between the old target (if the old target object is still existing), they can define a new target or they decide the definitive deletion of the link. This case may occur if the users want to undo a deleteObj and to reinstall the links or to overtake a createObj and the created links. Currently, the users can decide between the old target and the final deletion of the link. Another link problem occurs, when there are two objects (OID1 and OID2) in a hierarchy relation: on site A object OID1 is the superpart of object OID2 and on the site B object OID2 is the superpart of object OID1. In this case the decision for OID1 as superpart from OID2 makes it impossible to take over OID2 as superpart from OID1. MARC handles both links at the same time to ensure the right decision without withdrawing it later.

A problem occurs also after overtaking a delete operation. There may be new subparts or related objects on the site replaying and executing the delete operation. If there are subparts the users are asked if these objects and links should also be deleted or if the links should be changed.

Step 5: Automatic generation of replay operations. Based on the conflict resolutions, MARC automatically constructs two special replay sequences, one for each IU. MARC provides a resolution for each conflict by taking over one of both sites or by reset both changes to the last consistent state. Depending on the conflict operation combinations defined in step 2 and the decision wether site A or B is right, the replay operations are generated as decribed in Table 1 below. If A is right, then no operations are to replay on the site A. In all other cases replay operations need to be constructed.

operations on site A	operations on site B	replay operations on site B (A is right)	replay operations on site A (B is right)
any operation(OID,...)	no operation(OID)	any operation(OID,....)	"undo" any operation(OID,...)
any createLink(OID,...) any deleteLink(OID,...) any changeAttr(OID,...)	deleteObj(OID)	"undo" deleteObj(OID) any createLink(...) any deleteLink(...) any changeAttr(...)	deleteObj(OID)
changeAttr(OID, AttrName, newVal1,..)	changeAttr(OID, AttrName, newVal2,..)	changeAttr(OID, AttrName, newVal1,..)	changeAttr(OID, AttrName, newVal2,..)
createLink(OID, OID1,LinkName)	createLink(OID, OID2,LinkName)	deleteLink(OID, OID2,LinkName) createLink(OID, OID1,LinkName)	deleteLink(OID, OID1,LinkName) createLink(OID, OID2,LinkName)

Table 1. Automatic generation of replay operations

Conflict combination (1) (first row): In case A is right, the operations from site A are replayed automatically to site B in the order they occur in the shortened sequences of site A. In case B is right, the inverted operations from site A must be replayed reverse on site A. The inverse operation of a *changeAttr(OID, AttrName, NewValue, OldValue)* is a *changeAttr(OID, AttrName, OldValue, NewValue)*; a *createLink(OID1, OID, LinkName)* operation is undone by a *deleteLink(OID1, OID, LinkName)* operation and vice versa. A *deleteObj(OID)* operation is undone by a search and replay of all operations concerning the object OID from the beginning of the history until the end of last common sequence (see detection of relevant sequences). The execution of these operations, including the *createObj(OID, ...)*, any *createLink(OID, ...)*, *createLink(OID, OIDn,...)*, and *changeAttr(OID, ...)* generates the last consistent state of the object. A *createObj(OID, ClassName)* operation is inverted by searching all link operations for the object OID from the beginning of the history until the end of the last sequence, their reverse execution followed by a single *deleteObj(OID)*.

Conflict combination (2) (second row): In case A is right, the *deleteObj(OID)* operation must be inversed by recreating the last consistent state of the object (see above) and replaying it on site B, followed by all link and attribute conflict operations concerning the object OID on site A. In case that site B is right, the *deleteObj(OID)* operation must be replayed on site A.

Conflict combination (3) (third row): In case A is right, the *changeAttr(OID, AttrName, NewVal1, OldValue)* is easily replayed on site B. Otherwise, in case that B is right, the *changeAttr(OID, AttrName, NewVal2, OldValue)* is easily replayed on site A. In both cases the OldValue comprises the attribute value of the last consistent state.

Conflict combination (4) (fourth row): In case A is right, the *createLink(OID, OID2, LinkName)* operation from site B must be inverted by replaying a *delete-Link(OID, OID2, LinkName)* operation on site B, followed by a *createLink(OID, OID1, LinkName)* operation from site A. In case that B is right, first the createLink operation on site A must be reversed by a deleteLink operation and second the createLink operation from site B will be replayed on site A.

Step 6: Execution of replay operations. After the creation of the replay operations for each conflict, these operations are replayed to the according sites. Additionally, all operations in the shortened sequences on site A and B concerning the conflict are removed. If the shortened sequences are empty, the reintegration process has finished. Otherwise, the merge process beginning with step 3 must be executed again.

5   Scalability

The described mechanism is also applicable for more than two users in more than two participating sites in a reintegration. In order to achieve, the conflicting operations combinations must be extended, so that more than one user may be assigned to a site which has not changed the object, deleted the object, changed the object, changed a special link or changed an attribute. For the presentation of conflicts MARC extends the template based conflict description for cases where users have to decide between more than two changes. The automatic generation of replay operations is also flexible enough to generate replay operations for more than two users.

For a faster resolution process, MARC provides coarse grained resolutions with one decision to more than one conflict. Using the data structure a user may decide, for example, that all remaining attribute changes to one object may be overtaken according to the first attribute decision or if a container was deleted/created all subparts (objects) may be deleted/created on the other site, too. These questions are asked automatically by MARC during the reintegration process.

Automatic resolutions can be predefined by each user for a specific reintegration or by the system administrator for all reintegration processes. Automatic conflict resolutions may follow, for example, the "one site is right" or the "don't lose any changes" strategy. The first strategy resolves all conflicts by taking over all changes from one site and non-overlapping changes from the other site. The second takes over all non-overlapping changes and the remaining conflicts must be discussed. Automatic resolutions include also, for example, an undo of all deletes and the automatic acceptance of all newly created objects. The user can make these predefinitions at the beginning of the reintegration process.

The use of the semantics of operations (timestamps, user names, role, ...) makes the presentation of conflicts easier to understand and is useful for a more efficient reintegration. MARC allows semantics based extensions. Each class may generate object descriptions such as "folder", "notice", or "document" and a description for each operation may be generated, for example "moved" or "deleted". Using templates, this information enables MARC, for example, to ask the users: "The blinking document was moved by user jarczyk to the right wall and by user berger to the left wall. On which position do you want it to be?" (see Figure 6b).

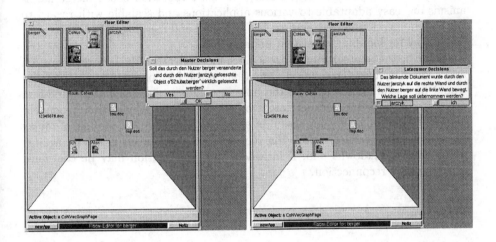

Fig. 6. a) Syntactic conflict presentation   b) Semantic conflict presentation

6   Implementation and Evaluation

The MARC component is implemented in Smalltalk. For the reintegration process a hand-shaking protocol between the reintegration participants is implemented. The master site, which coordinates the reintegration, will be detected automatically.

In order to validate the MARC approach we integrated the component in the CoNus CSCW system (see [6]). CoNus (**Co**operative **N**etworking for Gro**u**ps) is a groupware system for small groups where the interaction control mainly relies on social protocols. The system is intended for users who are distributed locally within the range of a LAN or for global distribution via ISDN/ATM. To express the new power of cooperative work, CoNus visualizes workspaces as three-dimensional virtual rooms. A virtual room is related to one IU and may contain equipment such as overhead projectors, documents, folders, blackboards, briefcases, schedulers, etc. and enables actions such as invitations, navigation in other rooms, managing documents and folders, file transfer, messaging, data hiding by locking doors, document sharing, etc.

7 Conclusion and Future Work

The application of our mechanism shows that consistency may be established after optimistic autonomous work and users may integrate their work efficiently. Furthermore, the realization shows that the detection and resolution of conflicts based on operations has many advantages compared to a data merge. The basic reintegration mechanism is application and platform independent and useful for all collaborative systems. Additionally, the used operation based merge mechanisms are easy adaptable to various applications and scalable with regard to the communication infrastructure. The handling and merging of histories opens a new way for handling persistent informations.

To make the reintegration process much more effective, the lazy reintegration and semantics based resolution definitions must be possible. A functionality would be useful, which enables the user to create an intermediate state of an attribute or to define another target object for a link. Application dependent conflict resolution orders are useful in any cases. Based on the storage of replay operations after each decision, the reintegration mechanism is robust against unintended breakdowns and, if intended, the reintegration may be continued after the next reconnection.

References

1. Schill, A.: Cooperative Office Systems. Prentice Hall International (UK), London, 1995.
2. Malm, P.S.: The unofficial yellow pages of CSCW. University of Tromso, April, 1994. (http://tft.tele.no/cscw/)
3. Jarczyk, A., Löffler, P., Völksen, G.: Computer Supported Cooperative Work (CSCW) - State of the Art and Suggestions for Future Work. Internal Report, Version 1.0, Siemens AG, Corporate Research, 1992.
4. Kottmann, D. A.: Support for Data Management in Mobile Systems. (in German) GI/ITG Workshop: Development and Management of Distributed Systems. J. W. Goethe Universität Frankfurt, October 1993.
5. Kolland, M., Jarczyk, A., Löffler, P.: Information Sharing in Collaborative Environments. Proceedings of the IEEE Third Workshop on Enabling Technologies: Infrastructure for Collaborative Enterprises. Morgantown, WV, April 17-19, 1994, pp. 140-154.
6. Berger, M.: CoNus - a CSCW system supporting synchronous, asynchronous, and autonomous collaborative work. Schill, Spaniol, Mittasch, Popien (eds.): (industrial) Proceedings of the ICDP'96, Dresden, Germany, February 1996, pp. 27-39.
7. Kolland M., Berger M.: An Application Framework to Support Information Sharing in Collaborative work. In: Proceedings of the IFIP'96 World Conference - Advanced IT Tools. Canberra, Australia, September 1996, pp. 331-339.
8. Davidson, S. B., Garcia-Molina, H., Skeen, D.: Consistency in Partitioned Networks. Computing Surveys, Vol. 17, No. 3, September 1985, pp. 341-370.
9. Davidson, S. B.: Optimism and Consistency in Partitioned Distributed Database Systems. ACM Transactions on Database Systems, Vol. 9, No. 3, September 1984, pp. 456-381.

10. Garcia-Molina, H., Allen, T., Blaustein, B., Chilenskas, R. M., Reis, D. R.: Data-Patch: Integrating Inconsistent Copies of a Database after a Partition. Proceedings of the 3rd IEEE Symposium on Reliability in Distributed Software and Database Systems, October 1983, N.Y., pp. 38-48.
11. Blaustein, B. T. et al.: Maintaining Replicated Databases even in the Presence of Network Partitions. Proceedings of the 16th Electrical and Aerospace Systems Conference, Washington D.C., September 1983, N.Y., pp. 353-360.
12. Parker, D. S. et al.: Detection of Mutual Inconsistency in Distributed Systems. IEEE Transactions on Software Engineering, Vol. SE-9, No. 3, May 1983, pp. 240-246.
13. Miller, W., Myers, E. W.: A File Comparision Program. Software - Practice and Experience, Vol. 15, No. 11, November 1985, pp. 1025-1040.
14. Hunt, J. W., McIlroy, M. D.: An Algorithm for Differential File Comparison. Computing Science Technical Report No. 41, Bell Labs, N.J., June 1976.
15. Kumar, P., Satyanarayanan, M.: Supporting Application-Specific Resolution in an Optimistically Replicated File System. Proceedings of the 4th IEEE Workshop on Workstation Operating System. Napa, CA, October 1993, pp. 66-70.
16. Reiher, P., Heidemann, J., Ratner, D., Skinner, G., Popek, G.: Resolving File Conflicts in the Ficus File System. Technical Report CSD-940017, University of California, Department of Computer Science, L.A., April 1994.
17. Huston, L. B., Honeyman, P.: Disconnected Operation for AFS. Proceedings of the 1993 USENIX Symposium on Mobile and Location-Independent Computing, Cambridge, MA, August 1993.
18. Kumar, P., Satyanarayanan, M.: Log-Based Directory Resolution in the Coda File System. Proceedings of the 2nd Int. Conf. on Parallel and Distributed Information Systems, San Diego, CA, January 1993, pp. 202-213.
19. Hild, S. G., Robinson, P.: Disconnected Operation for Wireless Nodes. Proceedings of ECOOP'95 - Workshop on Mobility and Replication, Aarhus, Denmark, August 1995.
20. Neuwirth, Ch. M. et al.: Flexible Diff-ing in a Collaborative Writing System. Proceedings of the 1992 ACM Conference on CSCW, November 1992, Toronto, pp. 147-154.
21. Munson, J. P., Dewan, P.: A Flexible Object Merging Framework. Proceedings of the 1994 ACM Conference on CSCW, Chapel Hill, NC, October 1994, pp. 231-242.
22. Frame Technology Corporation: Using FrameMaker 4, San Jose, California, 1993.
23. Tichy, W. F.: RCS - A System for Version Control. Software - Practice and Experience, Vol. 15, No. 7, July 1985, pp. 637-654.
24. Adams, E. W., Honda, M., Miller, T. C.: Object Management in a CASE Environment. Proceedings of the 11th International Conf. on Software Engineering, May 1989, pp. 154-163.
25. SunPro: Merging Source Files. CodeManager User's Guide, Sun Microsystems, Inc., Mountain View, CA, January 1993.
26. Horwitz, S., Prins, J., Reps, T.: Integrating Noninterfering Versions of Programs. ACM Transactions on Programming Languages and Systems, Vol. 11, No. 3, July 1989, pp. 345-387.
27. Narayanaswamy, K., Goldman, N.: "Lazy" Consistency: A Basis for Cooperative Software Development. Proceedings of the 1992 ACM Conference on CSCW, November 1992, Toronto, pp. 257-264.
28. Berlage, T., Genau, A.: A Framework for Shared Applications with a Replicated Architecture. Proceedings of the ACM Symp. on User Interface Software and Technology, Atlanta, November 3-5, 1993, pp. 249-257.

198   Berger et al.

29. Lotus Development Corporation: Lotus Notes Version 4 - User's Guide, Lotus Park, UK, 1995.
30. Whitten, I. H., Thimbleby, H. W., Coulouris, G., Greenberg, S.: Liveware - A new Approach to Social Networks. S. Greenberg (eds.): Computer-supported Cooperative Work and Groupware, University Press, Cambridge, UK, 1991, pp.211-222.
31. ISO/DIS 8613: Information Processing - Text and Office Systems - Open Document Architecture, Parts 1 - 8. International Organization for Standardization, 1988.

Workspace Awareness for Distributed Teams

Johann Schlichter, Michael Koch, and Martin Bürger

Technische Universität München, Institut für Informatik,
D-80290 München, Germany

Abstract. Research in distributed problem solving in the last years focused on distributed applications which cooperate to accomplish a task. Another level of distributed problem solving is that of human teams which are distributed in space and cooperate in solving a problem. In this paper we will introduce distributed problem solving from the 'human level', briefly present the accompanying research area of Computer-Supported Cooperative Work (CSCW) and the different basic mechanisms of computer support for workgroup computing, and then focus on the awareness information that is of special importance for supporting coordinated cooperation of groups with unstructured tasks.

1 Introduction

The emergence of high-speed local area computer networks at the beginning of the 1970s resulted in distributed systems becoming an important topic in computer science. As a sub-discipline of distributed systems, distributed problem solving (DPS) emerged by combining the ideas of distributed systems and those of artificial intelligence.

Distributed problem solving can be defined as the cooperative activity of several decentralized and loosely coupled problem-solvers that act in separated environments. Hence, one generally assumes a number of instances, the problem-solvers, that are distributed in space and collaborate in completing a common task.

Most approaches assume that the cooperating instances are software components, programs or agents. Important issues at this 'application level' are group communication, RPC, concurrency control, replication, and distributed objects (see [8, 29] for more details).

The increasing network availability in the last decade has not only been an enabling factor for building distributed systems with cooperating applications, it also has been a major breakthrough enabling distributed group work using computer and network technologies. Hence, the scenario of distributed applications trying to solve a given task is only one possible viewpoint of distributed problem solving. Another very important viewpoint is to investigate distributed human teams that collaborate to achieve a common goal using computers connected through a communication network.

This viewpoint is very important because nowadays the members of human teams are often spread among several departments or companies. Computer technology and increased network availability has enabled and improved distributed group work. The coordination of the contributions of the team members is an important task in supporting distributed group work.

The collaborating teams often use distributed applications for their work. Coordination tasks in particular are carried out through the distributed software system (application level). Figure 1 shows this relationship of human level cooperation and application level cooperation. In this paper we will focus on the human level.

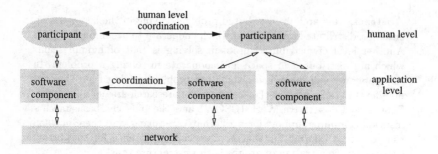

Fig. 1. Different levels of distributed problem solving in teams.

The rest of this paper is organized as follows: In Section 2 we will give a brief overview of the basics in collaboration among people and in the research area that focuses on providing computer support for collaboration. Then we will summarize the basic support mechanisms from the human level view (Section 3). Thereby, we will also touch upon the application level details that are needed for providing support at the human level. In Section 4 we will focus on one basic mechanism for supporting coordination in collaborative work on unstructured tasks: group awareness. The basic concepts listed in Section 4 will be highlighted in the context of providing support for distributed teams collaborating on writing documents in Section 5. In this section we will present the mechanisms the group editor environment IRIS provides for supporting workspace awareness as an example.

2   Collaboration and Computer Support for Collaborative Work

2.1   Collaboration at the 'Human Level'

The terms 'cooperation' or 'collaboration' are used to refer to a set of participants working together to produce a product or service [3, p.362]. Collaboration requires two or more participants who contribute to a common task. A crucial point for successful collaboration is the manner in which individual work is related to the group as a whole. Co-workers make autonomous decisions when working alone, under changing and unpredictable conditions, which the group cannot foresee or plan for. To enable a separated group of co-workers to collaborate, they need to coordinate themselves [27]. The importance of coordination can be seen in the need to bring the efforts of all co-workers together in order to produce a product or service. Examples of the need for coordination in collaborative work is the need to ensure the completion of all work, the lack of redundant work (e.g. avoid conflicting actions) and the timely completion of the work.

Communication mechanisms are critical to coordination and thus essentially needed for collaborative work. To perform communication participants typically use two fundamental human skills [4]:

- direct communication with other participants and
- manipulation of shared artifacts.

Typically, manipulation of shared artifacts can be observed by other participants, thus constituting a form of indirect communication. These skills are often used in combination. For example, when communicating directly participants often use references to shared artifacts as an easy way of establishing referential identity [7]. Similarly, when working with shared artifacts, participants often communicate directly with each other.

Figure 2 shows the different communication and coordination channels among the participants considering that in most cases the participants are working on shared artifacts and some of the communication and coordination is done via manipulation of the shared artifacts.

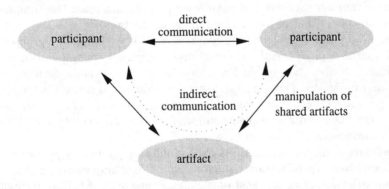

Fig. 2. Cooperation with shared artifact (adapted from [28]).

2.2   CSCW and Groupware

Computers and the emerging networks can be used to support collaboration. The research area that is concerned with computer support for collaborating teams is called "Computer-Supported Cooperative Work" (CSCW). The term

CSCW was coined by Irene Greif (Massachusetts Inst. of Technology) and Paul Cashman (Digital Equipment Corporation) to explain the scope of a small workshop with attendants from different fields [2, 19]. CSCW is not a self-contained research area with its own technology but an interdisciplinary area of study within which the main issues are to understand collaboration and to integrate different technologies in order to support collaborating teams. Wilson defines CSCW in [36] in the following way:

> *"CSCW is a generic term which combines the understanding of the way people work in groups with the enabling technologies of computer networking and associated hardware, software and techniques."*

While CSCW is the name for the research area, the term *groupware* stands for the systems that support group work. In practice this means that groupware is software and/or hardware which implement the theoretical foundation of CSCW activities. Johansen writes [20]:

> *"Groupware is a generic term for specialized computer aids that are designed for the user of collaborative work groups. Typically, these groups are small project-oriented teams that have important tasks and tight deadlines. Groupware can involve software, hardware, services and/or group process support."*

A major issue in CSCW is to understand the way in which computer systems can be instrumental in reducing the complexity of coordinating cooperative activities. Groupware reflects a change in emphasis from using the computer to solve problems to that of facilitating human interaction [13].

Groupware can be designed to support a face-to-face group or a group that is distributed over many locations. Furthermore, a groupware system can be built to enhance collaboration within a real-time interaction, or an asynchronous, non real-time interaction. These time and space considerations suggest the separation of the groupware domain into four quadrants based on whether users are working at the same place or different places and whether they are working synchronously or asynchronously, as shown in Figure 3[1].

As listed in the examples in Figure 3 groupware provides support for many functional areas. There are now numerous examples of both commercial products and research prototypes for most of the major categories of CSCW technologies (the unOfficial Yellow Pages of CSCW lists 340 commercial or experimental groupware systems [26]). For example there are media spaces for real-time communication, email systems for asynchronous communication, groupware tools for cooperative development of documents, drawings, software for meeting facilitation, and tools for workflow management (see [6, 9, 13, 26] etc. for references to concrete systems).

---

[1] The figure is called 'Any-Time Any-Place' matrix because it shows that groupware may bridge space and time constraints and enable collaboration at any time from any place.

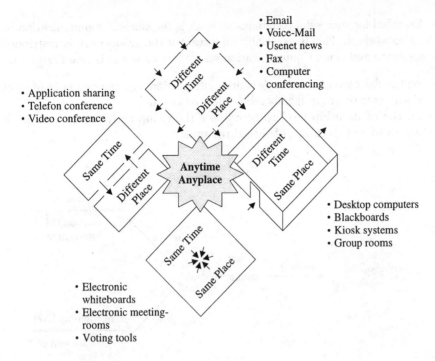

Fig. 3. Any-Time Any-Place Matrix (adapted from [21]).

Numerous groupware products are now in use in many commercial environments, for example, Lotus Notes, Microsoft Exchange, IBM's WorkGroup, Novell's GroupWise, Collabra Share, etc. These systems typically integrate a number of tools for communication, workflow, database-sharing, contact management, and group scheduling, and operate across a variety of environments.

3 Support Mechanisms for Collaborative Work

The cooperation of people who engage in a common task requires the coordination of the task-related activities as well as the coordination of the resources used during the execution of these activities. As already mentioned above the coordination at the human level is often implemented by a distributed software system. The components of this system negotiate with each other at the application level to achieve the desired coordination behavior at the human level. In this section we first discuss the main mechanism to support coordination from the human perspective and second, how this mechanism may be implemented at the application level. Thus, from the mechanism required at the human level we derive the desired application level support.

Essential for successful collaborative work is the efficient communication between co-workers. This is especially important if the group work is distributed
across space and time. Communication serves two main needs (see Figure 4):

- on the data level to exchange shared information, e.g. the exchange of group
  documents or group membership information, and
- on the relationship level to coordinate the group activities as well as the
  access to and the usage of shared resources.

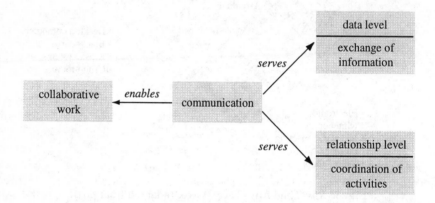

Fig. 4. Support of collaborative work on the human level.

The exchange of information may be achieved by direct or indirect communication (see Figure 2 in Section 2). In the first case a direct communication link between the involved group members is established; the information is
exchanged along this link either asynchronously (e.g. email) or synchronously
(e.g. video conferencing). Indirect communication assumes a shared information
space which may be used to exchange and propagate information. Information
stored in the shared information space may be accessed and retrieved by other
group members. A typical example of this communication type is a bulletin
board system where the communication link between the cooperating partners
is achieved via the shared information space. Indirect communication is only
suitable for situations where co-workers cooperate loosely.

For both direct and indirect communication the coordination dependencies
among co-workers are not explicitly defined. The coordination task is fuzzy and
it can only be supported by exchanging sufficient information to get a mutual
understanding of the progress and the current situation of the group work.

The second aspect of communication at the human level refers to explicit
coordination. In this case, the dependencies among co-workers are well-defined
and explicitly specified. Communication in this context intends to initiate transitions within group work states. Examples are the notification of co-workers
after documents have been modified or the hand-over of a circulation folder to

another co-worker. Notifications might inform another co-worker that a group document has reached a certain state in which he can start working on it.

These two communication aspects at the human level can be supported by the following technical mechanisms at the application level (see Figure 5) :

1. direct communication,
2. indirect communication.

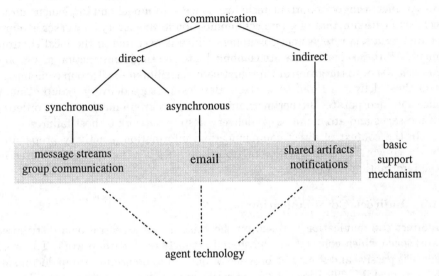

Fig. 5. Support of collaborative work on the application level.

3.1   Direct Communication

From the technical viewpoint direct communication handles the propagation and management of message streams between the involved co-workers. Services include the creation, transfer, synchronization and filtering of message streams. The direct communication can occur either synchronously or asynchronously. In the synchronous mode a real-time communication link is established and the information is exchanged in real-time between the involved co-workers. The video conferencing scenario in particular requires the synchronization of multiple message streams, such as audio, video and data. The data component itself may consist of multiple streams; for example one data stream contains the shared group document while other data streams may specify telepointer coordinates of the different group members. The communication has to be adapted to the available network bandwidth and to the quality of service requirements as well as to the characteristics of the coordination tasks. Examples of the latter case are the urgency of the coordination or the relationship between the group members, e.g. does there already exist a trusted relationship between them because they cooperated successfully in the past? A trusted relationship requires a much smaller communication channel because there is already a mutual understanding between the involved partners. Thus, it is not necessary to specify explicitly all coordination goals and requirements.

Asynchronous communication is typically based on email, i.e. there is no real-time interaction between the involved co-workers. Thus, the requirements for the necessary communication infrastructure are less stringent than for the synchronous communication.

An increasingly important technical concept to model and implement direct communication is that of group communication [8, 35]. Every co-worker is represented by a separate system component which is executed in the local environment. All these components are combined into the single abstraction of a group. Messages sent to the group are automatically distributed to all group components and thus, delivered to all co-workers. Besides message delivery, group communication incorporates further mechanisms, such as group management, ordering of messages and atomic message delivery despite network or host failures.

In the context of direct communication, information is actively propagated to the co-workers. Coordination of group activities is based on events caused by the information flow.

3.2   Indirect Communication

Indirect communication is based on the existence of a central or a distributed workspace which contains all the shared artifacts of the group work. The work space is passive and it may be browsed or queried to determine group documents for retrieval. Modifications of shared artifacts may cause notifications which are propagated to interested co-workers.

Shared Artifacts Inherent with group work is the existence of a shared context which consists of a shared environment as well as a multiuser interface to this environment. The environment incorporates a variety of shared artifacts which are managed and manipulated by the whole group. A simple example of a shared artifact is the group document which is jointly authored by a group of authors. Besides different views of the same object, shared artifacts must also allow a wide variety of working modes ranging from individual to collective work. A CSCW system must support a seamless transition between these working modes as well as between different activities operating on these artifacts.

The application level provides functionality to manage and to handle the access to the shared artifacts. Two important functions are concurrency control and replication management. Both functions must be supported transparently at the human level. Concurrency control handles the concurrent access of multiple users to shared information in order to preserve information consistency. Concurrency control mechanisms may be categorized into pessimistic and optimistic approaches.

Pessimistic approaches attempt to keep the documents consistent at all situations even in the case of network partitionings. Well known examples of these approaches are access locks and transactions. Past CSCW-systems favored the pessimistic approach, but recently optimistic approaches gained more interest in the CSCW community, especially when mobile workers are included in the shared environment. In the latter case, it is not possible to assume a permanent network connection between all involved co-workers. Optimistic approaches assume that the cooperating co-workers are less likely to get into conflict while manipulating the shared information. Additionally, people use social protocols to avoid any conflicting actions, e.g. a person announces via audio link to his co-workers that he will manipulate a certain paragraph. Pessimistic approaches apply technical protocols in order to avoid conflicts while the optimistic protocols prefer social protocols to ensure information consistency. Social protocols are less restrictive and offer group members more freedom to adjust the concurrency control to the characteristics of the group and its current state. Social protocols need a high degree of group awareness in order to be effective.

Closely related with concurrency control and the distributed environment is the replication of information. Replication improves the access times as well as the availability despite network or machine failures. Besides the internal consistency of a single copy this requires additionally the mutual consistency of the copies. The concurrency control mechanism must be extended to handle multiple copy consistency.

Notifications Notifications are an essential means of improving group awareness. They are based on messages which are generated automatically through user interaction with the workspace. For example, the modification of a paragraph by one co-worker might generate a notification which is then sent via multicast to all other co-workers. The notification mechanism and its relationship to the coupling mode of the co-workers will be discussed in more detail in later sections.

At this point we can summarize by stating that communication at the human level which is required in order to achieve group coordination is implemented at the application level by direct and indirect communication.

3.3   Agent Technology

For the design and implementation of the application level mechanisms we can apply agent technology. Thus, the distributed system consists of a number of agents which operate autonomously and cooperate with each other to perform the global task. The knowledge and strategies needed to solve the global task are distributed across the individual agents. Basic agent functions are the execution of assigned subtasks and the communication with other agents. The latter function corresponds to the communication at the human level.

Besides the well-known general usage of agents in distributed systems, agents may be applied to handle some specific coordination tasks in the context of CSCW. One important usage is the filtering of messages [24]. This can be done at the sender's side according to his privacy needs, at the receiver's side according to his interests, or at the organizational level according to basic company policies.

The second potential usage of the agent technology refers to the implementation of concurrency policies depending on the desired quality of service and the currently available network infrastructure. Agents continuously monitor the current network traffic and the type of interaction between co-workers. For example, in the case of network partitionings agents switch from pessimistic to optimistic concurrency models to enable work progress despite interrupted message traffic. The policies may also change according to the coupling modes of the co-workers. In the case of loose coupling the system might prefer technical protocols while in situations of tight coupling the system might switch to social protocols.

Another important aspect where agents may be applied is the delegation of tasks. Agents interact and negotiate with each other to determine a suitable contracting agent. The contract net model [34] provides a suitable general protocol to design and implement this negotiation process. If agents are representatives of users then the negotiation process at the agent level may result in the delegation of activities at the human level.

4   Awareness for Supporting Collaboration

4.1   Coordinating Unstructured Work

There are two different extreme types of tasks which should be considered when talking of computer support for distributed teams (see Figure 6). On the one hand there are tasks which are done according to a standard procedure, such as that for approving business trips or processing bank credit applications. For these tasks one often can provide a detailed model that clearly describes the steps that are necessary to complete the task. On the other hand, there are tasks that are never done in the same fashion because they are inherently chaotic. Examples are creative work such as writing a paper for a conference or work that is subject to external influences, such as brokering shares. In contrast to the first task type there is no obvious structure. Single steps inside the task can only be described in a very high-level manner. In this paper we will address tasks that show a fine granular structure as *structured tasks* and tasks that do not show such a structure as *unstructured tasks*.[2]

Because these task types are so different, different mechanisms are needed to effectively support their coordination. A suitable mechanism for structured work is *explicit coordination*. The term 'explicit coordination' is chosen because the coordination is handled by actions explicitly initiated for coordinating the task. The initiator can be a software component that reacts upon a given task model by initiating some coordination actions. In the real world, this leads to the class of workflow systems, where the standard procedure is described by a model of the task.

For unstructured tasks, however, there is no abstract model of work that describes the steps that are necessary to complete a task. Instead, the system

---

[2] Practical tasks usually incorporate aspects of both, the structured and unstructured task models, and they are classified according to the dominating part.

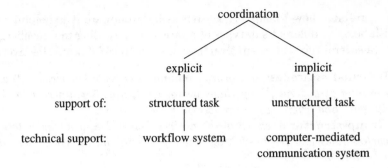

Fig. 6. Coordination for different types of tasks.

must offer as much freedom as possible to the co-workers so that they can do whatever they think is necessary to reach a particular goal. In this scenario, no automatic coordination is possible, because there is no predefined flow of work but coordination has to be adapted dynamically to the actual situation. This can not be done by an automatic system, but it must be done by the people themselves. This requires a high degree of group awareness where co-workers are aware of each other's past, current and possibly future activities within the shared environment. The awareness information needed can be exchanged by direct communication or by indirect communication (see Section 3) with the help of the system (computer-mediated communication). This whole process is called *implicit coordination.*

To summarize, one can say that awareness *"is part of the "glue" that allows groups to be more effective than individuals"* [18]. In the next subsection we will present an overview of the research results on awareness and their importance for coordination in group work.

4.2   Awareness Basics

The emphasis of much of recent research within CSCW has been to provide awareness-oriented collaboration systems where users coordinate their work based on the knowledge of what the members of the collaborating group are doing or have done. *Group awareness* can be defined as *"an understanding of the activities of others, which provides a context for your own activity"* [11]. An increase of awareness within a collaborating group has several advantages:

- It encourages informal spontaneous communication (e.g. via video conferences, phone calls, etc.), since people are more likely to use direct contact to others when they know their partner is not too busy and can be interrupted without interfering too much with the ongoing work (see for example Portholes [11] and Peepholes [17]).
- Awareness is important to keep group members up-to-date with important events and therefore contributes to their ability to make conscious decisions.

To determine how to support awareness by groupware it is helpful to distinguish between different sub-types of awareness. According to Greenberg [18], there are several types of group awareness needed to collaborate effectively:

- **"Informal awareness** *of a work community is basic knowledge about who is around in general (but perhaps out of site), who is physically in a room with you, and where people are located relative to you."*
- **"Group-structural awareness** *involves knowledge about such things as people's roles and responsibilities, their positions on an issue, their status, and group processes."*
- **"Social awareness** *is the information that a person maintains about others in a social or conversational context: things like whether another person is paying attention, their emotional state, or their level of interest."* Other information can be the special skills a co-worker has.
- **Workspace awareness** is *"the up-to-the minute knowledge a person requires about another group member's interaction with a shared workspace if they are to collaborate effectively".*

It is rather simple for a groupware system to retrieve *a lot* of information about the interactions of the users with the workspace. But it is necessary to present this information in an adapted way to avoid swamping the users with useless information. So we will focus in the next subsection on models of workspace awareness that can be exploited in real systems to reduce the amount of information that is presented to the users.

4.3   Orientation Models for Workspace Awareness

There has been research on orientation models in collaborative processes. This is important to find new ways to present awareness information to the users (and to select which information is presented). One particular example is the GROUPDESK project [1, 15, 16]. One result of this research was the discovery of the four modes of awareness [16]. These modes can be described by two orthogonal classifications:

- *Coupling:* There is the coupled awareness (participants have the same focus of work, e.g. they work on the same shared artifact and are aware of each other) and uncoupled awareness (*"information independent of the user's current focus of work"*).
- *Synchrony:* Participants may either be aware synchronously (knowledge about events that happen currently) or asynchronously (knowledge about events in the past).

Together, these classifications result in the aforementioned modes of awareness which can be described by typical questions (see Figure 7).

When designing a real system, these modes must be treated differently. For example, uncoupled awareness information may be treated in a less obtrusive way at the user interface than coupled awareness information, which may be of

	synchronous	asynchronous
coupled	What is currently happening in the actual scope of the work?	What has changed in the actual scope of the work since last access?
uncoupled	Things of importance which occur currently anywhere else?	Has anything of interest happened recently somewhere else?

Fig. 7. Modes of awareness (adapted from [16]).

a greater interest to the collaborating person. Coupled awareness information may be presented by a pop-up message (which can be very intrusive), while uncoupled awareness information can be presented by changing the color of an icon or by printing a short message in a status bar. The same applies to synchronous vs. asynchronous awareness, where it would be desirable to have some sort of summary about past events, so that one can catch up quickly to the current state of things without wading through too many details.

Another more sophisticated awareness model was presented by Rodden [32, 33]. This model describes the interactions of users with a shared workspace in terms of a spatial metaphor (like in a virtual reality meeting place). The most important terms here are *nimbus* and *focus*:

- *Nimbus* describes the location(s) that a user is occupying in the workspace.
- *Focus* describes the location at which the user is looking (may be several places at the same time).

The nimbus and focus of users in a workspace can then be used to describe how (and if) two users are aware of each other. The strength of awareness user A has of another user B can be described by the amount of overlap between A's nimbus/focus and B's nimbus/focus. Some simple examples in a two-dimensional space can be seen in Figure 8.

Is is easy to see that these different situations should result in a different strength of awareness of the two users of each other. These strengths could then be used in an implementation to select how (and if) actions of B should be presented to A and vice versa.

4.4 Filtering Awareness Information

There are some reasons why the groupware system should filter the awareness information before it is brought to the user's attention:

- Avoidance of information overflow by adapted presentation as described above by the orientation models.
- Privacy issues, which will be described next.

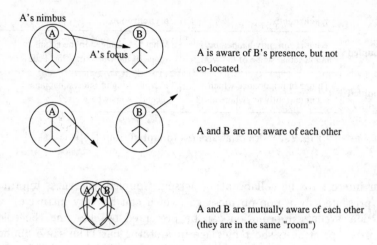

Fig. 8. Overlap of nimbus and focus.

There is one trap for an unwary designer of groupware systems with awareness mechanisms: the issue of privacy may arise (see [5, 37] for more). This can lead to acceptance problems of the system, because people may not want the system to look over their shoulder and distribute everything it sees to other people. These problems are not likely to occur in a small group of socially equal persons (like in joint editing of a conference paper), but this can be a very serious issue for larger systems spanning several departments within a big company.

Mechanisms to reduce the probability of rejection by the users can be:

– Show users what others see of them.
– Give users control about information that is sent to others by means of an outgoing filter that filters all information that is broadcast to the other co-workers.

In the next part we will present group editors as an application area for group awareness and discuss the application of workspace awareness for supporting coordination in collaborative writing groups.

5   Awareness Information for Supporting Coordination in Collaborative Writing

5.1   Collaborative Writing

One of the most common type of tasks undertaken by groups is the collaborative editing of documents. Additionally, this task is probably the most suitable for CSCW applications because computer systems are already adept at document manipulation.

Collaborative writing is defined in [25] as a '*process in which authors* [e.g. editors, graphics experts, users, reviewers] *with differing expertise and responsibilities interact during the invention and revision of a common document*'. Regarding the types of cooperative tasks introduced at the beginning of Section 4 collaborative writing in general is an unstructured task. One cannot rely on a fine granular work plan that shows all interaction needed for coordination.

Different writing strategies can be identified in writing groups (see [31] for some examples). The strategy most commonly identified with collaborative writing is the 'separate writers strategy': Work begins with a division of work and responsibilities. Then the co-authors produce their parts of the document separately. This asynchronous phase can last a long time and is usually interrupted by several synchronous coordination meetings. Finally, the parts are distributed for annotating and for assembling into the final document. Sometimes the co-authors work very closely together (start-up meeting, regular coordination meetings, spontaneous conferences) but most of the time the authors work on their own.

Software applications supporting collaborative writing are called *group editors*. Many tools have already been proposed to support collaborative writing for different media. Examples for such group editors are QUILT [14], GROVE [12] and PREP [30].[3]

5.2   Awareness Information in Group Editors

As for all unstructured tasks, information and awareness are very important for successful collaboration in group writing. Therefore, support for achieving awareness has been an issue in many group editor projects[4]. A brief introduction in the usage of awareness information in several group editors can be found in [10].

In a group editor we have one major shared artifact, the common document with additional information such as annotations. The co-authors usually work asynchronously on parts of the document. The interaction of the authors with the common workspace can be used to construct different awareness information. One can distinguish events and status information:

- *Events* hold information on a particular action that has happened. Events are distributed to users and filtered on demand (see Section 4.4). Examples of events are notifications about a document change or about the login of a user.
- *Status attributes* are gained by combining events to form some kind of longer-lived information. A status might be a list of active users, a list of working areas or the reachability of certain hosts on the network.

---

[3] See [22] and [23] for more examples of commercial and academic group editors.
[4] Most of the other issues were not related to human level coordination but to application level coordination like concurrency control with replicated document data.

In addition to events and status attributes one has to mention the history (a log of changes to the document) as a source of awareness.

To investigate the notions of awareness, we have developed a group editor environment called IRIS [22, 23]. In the following subsection we will briefly present the method of implementation of support for group awareness in IRIS.

5.3   Awareness Information in IRIS

The core of the IRIS system consists of several replicated components that communicate with each other to ensure document consistency and to calculate and distribute awareness information. This core service is called 'storage and awareness service'.

The service provides access to the document itself and to a history of document changes. Additionally, notification event are generated from the interaction of the user applications with the document data, and status attributes are distributed. A status attribute consists of a name and a value. The awareness service stores attributes for every document, for every user and for every host participating in the editing process.

Most of the status attributes are set automatically by the awareness service according to the user actions. The following listing describes the standard attributes for documents and users as defined in IRIS. (For more information on the attributes and on the implementation of the storage and awareness service of IRIS see [23].)

- *Document information*: Automatically generated standard attributes for documents are lists of read- and write-work areas[5], a list of the hosts that store replicas of the document and a list of the users who accessed the document. In addition to the main information all these lists store the time of the last change.
- *User information*: For every user that is or has been working with documents the system maintains a status attribute (possible values are 'active-in-groupware-application', 'idle-in-groupware-application', 'active-on-host', 'idle-on-host', 'inactive', 'no-info'). Other attributes calculated by the system are a list of hosts and of the documents the user has been working on (the last-changed time of the list elements provides information on when the user has last worked on the document/host).

In addition to the information calculated from the interaction of the users with the workspace, the user applications may set additional status attributes. This is important for information that is valuable to the group process but which cannot be determined from the interaction with the workspace. User-defined standard attributes are a document status attribute, and a list of reservations[6].

---

[5] The 'work areas' store information on document positions that different users have been working in within a configurable period of time.

[6] A 'reservation' can be seen as an optimistic lock. Reservations can be set for parts of a document and are displayed by the editing applications.

User defined user attributes are a name attribute, a list of roles the user has for different documents, and an additional status value (e.g. 'on leave', 'do not disturb', 'in meeting'). This additional status value supersedes the automatically calculated user status when defined. The user may also provide a validity time and a comment for the user defined status value.

Changes in the document information or in the status attributes are distributed as events. The events are automatically generated from the interaction of the users with the shared document data. At present there are no means for filtering events at the event source or at the event receivers.

5.4   Awareness Information at the User Interface

User interface applications use the storage service to access the document and to access the awareness information.

At present the user interface applications offer special support for displaying the status attributes only. Events are just listed in extra windows[7].

Figure 9 shows a screenshot of the structure editor, a tool for displaying the structure of a document. This tool displays the document structure and provides functionality for editing the structure, for requesting information on (sub-)documents and for launching editor applications for (sub-)documents.

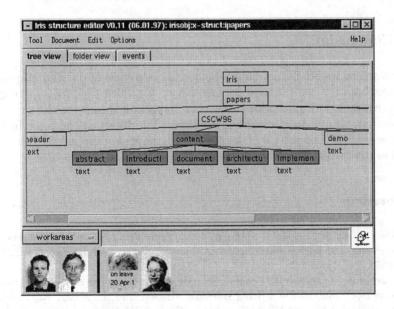

Fig. 9. IRIS document structure editor.

---

[7] A service for a configurable adapted display of events as mentioned in the previous section is in progress.

In the structure display the value of status attributes which are related to sub-structures of the document is visualized. It is possible to display different types of work areas and reservations in the tree display. The nodes are colored according to their status (e.g. reservation set, no reservation set). By selecting the nodes more information is displayed (owner of the reservation, time until the reservation is valid). In another display mode the nodes are colored according to the date of the last history entry. By selecting the node, the appropriate history information is displayed.

In addition to the possibility of displaying sub-document related awareness information the structure editor provides features for displaying document related information. In the first prototype we included a user list display. Here the pictures of all users working on the document are displayed. The status of the users is indicated by placing them on the left or on the right side of a bar (active - inactive). The more detailed status values are displayed by overlaying the user pictures with the extra information (e.g. a note that the user is on leave until a given date).

In the applications for editing (sub-)documents awareness information is also displayed. We provide possibilities to display the work area and reservation information for the edited document parts. Additionally, one can access history information for the edited (sub-)document. For more information one can use parallel running navigation tools and awareness tools.

For further information about IRIS see [22] or the IRIS-Web pages[8].

6   Conclusion

In this article we briefly presented the human level view of distributed problem solving. From the coordination perspective we identified the provision of group awareness and workspace awareness as an important means for the support of cooperation within distributed human teams. We discussed the topic in detail and presented an application of the concepts in the area of support for distributed collaborative writing.

References

1. Agostini A., de Michelis G., Grasso M. A., Prinz W., and Syri A. Contexts, work processes, and workspaces. *Computer Supported Cooperative Work*, 5(2-3):223–250, 1996.
2. Baecker R. M., Nastos D., Posner I. R., and Mawby K. L. The user-centred iterative design of collaborative writing software. In Ashlund S., Mullet K., Henderson A., Hollnagel E., and White T., editors, *Proc. ACM Conf. on Human Factors in Computing Systems (INTERCHI'93)*, SIGCHI, pages 399–405. ACM Press, New York, NY, Apr. 1993.

---

[8] http://www11.informatik.tu-muenchen.de/proj/iris/

3. Bannon L. J. and Schmidt K. Cscw: Four characters in search of a context. In *Proc. 1st European Conf. on Comp. Supported Cooperative Work*, pages 358–372. Computer Sciences House, Sloug, UK, Sep. 1989.

4. Beaudouin-Lafon M. Beyond the workstation: Mediaspaces and augmented reality. In Cockton G., Draper S. W., and Weir G. R. S., editors, *Proc. HCI'94*, pages 9–18. Cambridge University Press, 1994.

5. Bellotti V. M. E. and Sellen A. Design for privacy in ubiquitous computing environments. In de Michelis G., Simone C., and Schmidt K., editors, *Proc. 3rd European Conf. on Comp. Supported Cooperative Work*, pages 77–92. Kluwer Academic Publishers, Dordrecht, Sep. 1993.

6. Borghoff U. M. and Schlichter J. H. *Rechnergestützte Gruppenarbeit — Eine Einführung in Verteilte Anwendungen.* Springer Lehrbuch. Springer Verlag, Berlin, 1995.

7. Clark H. H. and Brennan S. E. *Grounding in Communication,* In Resnick L. B., Levine J. M., and Behrend S. D., editors, *Perspectives on Socially Shared Cognition,* pages 127–149. Washington, DC: American Psychological Association, 1991.

8. Coulouris G., Dollimore J., and Kindberg T. *Distributed Systems, Concepts and Design.* Addison-Wesley, Reading, Mass. and London, 1994.

9. Crowe M. K., editor. *Cooperative Work with Multimedia,* volume 1 of *Research Reports ESPRIT, Project 6310 - MMTCA.* Springer Verlag, Berlin, 1994.

10. Dourish P. and Bellotti V. Awareness and coordination in shared workspaces. In Turner J. and Kraut R. E., editors, *Proc. Intl Conf. on Comp. Supported Cooperative Work*, pages 107–114. ACM Press, New York, NY, Oct. 1992.

11. Dourish P. and Bly S. Portholes: Supporting awareness in a distributed work group. In Bauersfeld P., Bennett J., and Lynch G., editors, *Proc. ACM Conf. on Human Factors in Computing Systems (INTERCHI'92)*, SIGCHI, pages 541–547. ACM Press, New York, NY, May 1992.

12. Ellis C. A. and Gibbs S. J. Concurrency control in groupware systems. In Clifford J., Lindsay B., and Maier D., editors, *Proc. ACM SIGMOD Intl Conf. on Management of Data*, volume 18, pages 399–407. ACM Press, New York, NY, June 1989.

13. Ellis C. A., Gibbs S. J., and Rein G. L. Groupware – some issues and experiences. *Communications of the ACM*, 34(1):38–58, Jan. 1991.

14. Fish R. S., Kraut R. E., and Leland M. D. P. Quilt: A collaborative tool for cooperative writing. In Allen R. B., editor, *Proc. ACM SIGOIS/IEEE TC-OA Conf. on Office Information Systems*, volume 9, pages 30–37, Mar. 1988.

15. Fuchs L. *17: Interest in Work Situations: Awareness Support Revisited,* In Bullock A. and Mariani J., editors, *Assessment and refinement of models of interaction,* pages 337–356. Lancaster Univ., Aug. 1995.

16. Fuchs L., Pankoke-Babatz U., and Prinz W. Supporting cooperative awareness with local event mechanisms: The groupdesk system. In Marmolin H., Sundblad Y., and Schmidt K., editors, *Proc. 4th European Conf. on Comp. Supported Cooperative Work*, pages 247–262. Kluwer Academic Publishers, Dordrecht, Sep. 1995.

17. Greenberg S. Peepholes: Low cost awareness of one's community. In *Proc. ACM SIGCHI Conf. on Human Factors in Computing Systems, Companion Proceedings*, pages 206–207, Apr. 1996.

18. Greenberg S., Gutwin C., and Cockburn A. Using distortion-oriented displays to support workspace awareness. Technical report, Dept of Comp. Science, Univ. of Calgary, Canada, Jan. 1996.

19. Greif I., editor. *Computer-supported cooperative work: A book of readings.* Morgan Kaufmann Publ. Inc., Los Altos, CA, 1988.

20. Johansen R. *Groupware: Computer Support for Business Teams.* The Free Press, Macmillan Inc, NY, 1988.

21. Johansen R. Teams for tomorrow. In *Proc. 24th IEEE Hawaii Intl Conf. on System Sciencs*, pages 520–534. IEEE Comp. Soc. Press, Los Alamitos, 1991.

22. Koch M. Design issues for a distributed multi-user editor. *Computer Supported Cooperative Work — An International Journal*, 3(3-4):359–378, 1995.

23. Koch M. *Unterstützung kooperativer Dokumentenbearbeitung in Weitverkehrsnetzen.* PhD thesis, Inst. für Informatik, Techn. Univ. München, Germany, 1997. (also available as: 'Kooperation bei der Dokumentenbearbeitung - Entwicklung einer Gruppeneditorumgebung für das Internet', DUV, Wiesbaden, 1997).

24. Lai K.-Y. and Malone T. W. Object lens: A "spreadsheet" for cooperative work. In *Proc. Intl Conf. on Comp. Supported Cooperative Work*, pages 115–124. ACM Press, New York, NY, Sep. 1988.

25. Lay M. M. and Karis W. M., editors. *Collaborative Writing in Industry: Investigations in Theory and Practice.* Baywood Publishing Company, Amityville, 1991.

26. Malm P. S. CSCW and Groupware, a classification of CSCW-systems in a technological perspective. Technical report, University of Tromsø, Apr. 1994. masters thesis, only available in Norwegian.

27. Malone T. W. and Crowston K. The interdisciplinary study of coordination. *ACM Computing Surveys*, 26(1):87–119, Mar. 1994.

28. Miles V. C., McCarthy J. C., Dix A. J., Harrison M. D., and Monk A. F. *Reviewing Designs for a Synchronous-Asynchronous Group Editing Environment*, In Sharples M., editor, *Computer Supported Collaborative Writing*, pages 137–160. Springer Verlag, London, 1993.

29. Mullender S., editor. *Distributed Systems.* Addison-Wesley, Reading, Mass. and London, 2nd edition edition, 1993.

30. Neuwirth C. M., Chandhok R., Kaufer D. S., Erion P., Morris J. H., and Miller D. Flexible diff-ing in a collaborative writing system. In Turner J. and Kraut R. E., editors, *Proc. Intl Conf. on Comp. Supported Cooperative Work*, pages 147–154. ACM Press, New York, NY, Oct. 1992.

31. Posner I. R. and Baecker R. M. *How people write together*, In Baecker R. M., editor, *Readings in groupware and computer- supported cooperative work, assisting human-human collaboration.* Morgan Kaufmann Publ. Inc., Los Altos, CA, 1993.

32. Rodden T. *17: Objects in Space, the Spatial Model and Shared Graphs*, In Benford S., Bullock A., Fuchs L., and Mariani J., editors, *Computable Models and Prototypes of Interaction*, pages 355–379. Lancaster Univ., Oct. 1994.

33. Rodden T. Population the application: A model of awareness for cooperative applications. In *Proc. Intl Conf. on Comp. Supported Cooperative Work*, pages 87–96, Nov. 1996.

34. Smith R. G. The contract net protocol: High-level communication and control in a distributed problem solver. *IEEE Trans. on Computers*, C-29(12):1104–1113, Dec. 1980.

35. Tanenbaum A. S. *Computer Networks - third edition.* Prentice Hall, Upper Saddle River, NJ, 1996.

36. Wilson P. *Computer Supported Cooperative Work.* Oxford, UK: Intellect Books, 1991.

37. Wulf V. and Hartmann A. *The Ambivalence of Network Visibility in an Organizational Context*, In Clement A., Kolm P., and Wagner I., editors, *NetWorking: Connecting Workers In and Between Organizations*, pages 143–152. North Holland, Amsterdam, 1994.

GeM and WeBUSE: Towards a WWW-Database Interface

Madhav Sivadas and George Fernandez

Department of Computer Science,
Royal Melbourne Institute of Technology,
Melbourne, Australia
(madhav,george)@cs.rmit.edu.au

Abstract. This paper describes a generic metadatabase model to enable efficient browsing of structured databases by remote users in the World Wide Web environment. Existing Web-database interfaces rely on the premise that users know the database schema, and that they posses enough knowledge of the context of a schema for the correct interpretation of database semantics and query results. We propose a framework consisting of data structures, mechanisms and tools for representing a more complete description of database schemata. The Generic Metadatabase (GeM) model is capable of storing, as metadata, information about databases designed using most of the popular data modelling techniques. WeBUSE (Web-Based Uniform Schema-browsing Environment) is a suite of tools which enable remote users to browse the augmented database schemata using conventional Web browsers.

1 Introduction

Databases are accessed by users and applications through a set of interfaces, such as SQL, QBE, and graphical interfaces. Regardless of the interface, users are required to know the database schema to issue appropriate queries and to be able to correctly interpret query results. Although database metadata describe the structure of the database, not all the required information for query and result interpretation is available. Also, metadata are usually represented in formats which are better utilised by database management systems rather than users. Users and applications must use implicit contextual information, which is not part of the currently available metadata, to properly interpret data retrievals and updates. For example, if the attribute salary is retrieved with a query, the necessary contextual information to precisely determine its value should include currency, periodicity of pay, whether it is based on an hourly, or daily rate, whether it is gross or after tax, etc. Since database metadata was originally directed to support the DBMS in the management of data, they do not support structures to consistently store the complete context of an attribute, and their interfaces do not provide browsing or querying mechanisms to explore this context information.

In traditional database situations, this is reasonable since the contextual knowledge is embedded in the applications run by the organisation that owns the schema, or is common knowledge among the users within the organisation. However, advances in communications are making possible a different type of access by remote users, who are not in possession of this knowledge. Casual access and database interoperation via the Internet and the WWW require the storage of a more complete description of a database schema and data semantics, as well as adequate mechanisms to support browsing of contextual information.

Semantic modelling of a database schema is the process of formally describing the structure of the data to produce the Conceptual Schema, typically using methods such as Extended Entity/Relationship (EE/R), NIAM, or OMT. These methods attempt to capture the structure of the universe of discourse by describing the *type* of the relevant entities and the relationships between them. Many of the characteristics of these entities and relationships are described in the model itself. However, the experience of researchers and practitioners working in database interoperation highlights the shortcomings of modelling techniques to completely specify database schemata which in turn impedes the integration of databases. Their requirements for mediation, integration or interoperation are much more extensive than the detail supported by standard modelling techniques. Although this research does not deal with multidatabase integration or interoperation, our central concern is the same: how to provide a more complete description of database schemata, how can this information be stored, and how to provide mechanisms to retrieve the contextual knowledge.

The remainder of this paper is divided as follows. A review of related research is presented in Section 2. In Section 3 we describe a generic specification of the kinds of information stored in database schemata. Section 4 discusses GeM, a structural model for storage of schema information. A complete example of how to use the model is discussed in Section 5. Section 6 describes an architecture for the deployment of this model on the World Wide Web. We conclude in Section 7 with a summary and suggestions for further research.

2   Related Work

Research in the area of multidatabase interoperability has provided considerable insight about the different types of conflicts (incompatibilities) which may occur between two or more database systems [1, 12, 8, 13, 3]. Interoperability requirements ultimately require agreements on the meaning of data, otherwise interoperability is not possible [9]. The aim therefore should be to make information about the database as explicit as possible. If semantics were made explicit in the metadata, it would be possible to detect mismatched assumptions and to create mappings to overcome them [6]. Although this is not an easy task, it has been suggested that repository technology is the best available technique for achieving the goal [6]. A substantial research effort has been devoted to detecting and classifying conflicts between multiple databases. Batini et al provided the first compilation of research in the area of interoperability and schema integration [1].

Two types of conflicts were detected: naming conflicts and structural conflicts. Kim and Seo [8] provide an excellent classification of conflicts between relational databases. Reddy et al also provide an exhaustive classification of incompatibilities [12]. Unlike [8], this classification is independent of the database model. The conflicts were classified under two major categories: semantic incompatibilities and quantitative data incompatibilities. All these incompatibilities are mainly due to incomplete information about the database as stored in the schema and data-dictionary. A new technique for interoperability was proposed in [3], involving the coupling of context along with other metadata. The paper also discusses another type of incompatibility called source-receiver heterogeneity, and shows that explicit representation of contextual knowledge provides a satisfactory solution to most conflicts including source-receiver conflicts.

At this stage, our research efforts have concentrated primarily on what kind of information is missing from, or implicit in, existing database schemata, and how can this information be presented in a uniform manner for a wide range of modelling techniques. We take the view that from both the casual user and the multidatabase interoperability perspectives the goal should be the provision of a uniform, augmented description of database schemata. A major problem to is the existence of several data models used for specifying a schema, since the models differ widely in their ability to express the complexity and semantics of the Universe of Discourse (UoD). Our objective was to build a framework to describe the structure of databases specified by a wide range of data models. This proposed model should store enough information about the schemata so that similarities and differences between data items can easily be detected. The solutions suggested in previous research efforts for solving this problem can be divided into two categories: proposal of a neutral model [14], and creation of a uniform information resource dictionary system (metadata repositories) [10,2, 11]. While neutral models provide an excellent technique for schema translation, their main drawback is that database administrators and users are forced to learn a new modelling technique and abandon the methodology with which they are familiar. Since the existing models have been used quite successfully in different application domains, we believe that any new methodology for establishing uniformity among data models must incorporate existing modelling techniques. Our proposed framework is therefore based on the concept of a metadata repository. The development and design of such a generic metadatabase is describe in the next two sections.

3   A Generic Specification of Database Schemata

In the last thirty years, the database community has witnessed a proliferation of data models for the specification of complex data structures. Database schema information is represented using a modelling technique in order to develop a machine-independent description of the database [5]. Information about a database can be classified into two major categories:

- Syntactic information: pertaining to the format and computer representation of elements in the database. It is computer-oriented information.
- Semantic information: describing the meaning and interrelationships between the syntactic elements in the Universe of Discourse. It is user-oriented information.

Syntactic information is easy to specify and translate, whereas semantic information is often quite subtle and implicit within the model. However, interoperability among database systems requires syntactic as well as semantic interoperability. In our context, semantic information is needed for accessing remote databases where the user is not aware of the details of the Universe of Discourse. These problems are intensified due to the lack of a clear definition of semantics, as well as fact that data models have varying capabilities for representing semantics.

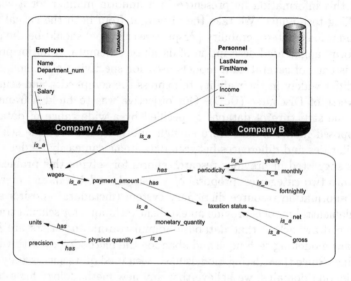

Fig. 1. Using Ontologies to Map Applications

We use the concept of ontologies in order to develop a generic specification of database schemata. An ontology is defined as a specification of a conceptualisation [4]. In simpler terms, ontology is a formal description of a specific domain. Ontologies can be constructed for different domains and consist of the terms in a domain and their relationships with other terms within the same domain and in other domains. Our interest in ontologies is due in their potential for exchanging information between remote applications. An ontology of a domain can be used to represent the link between a particular application and all the resources available in that domain [15]. Thus, an ontology attempts to establish an agreement on the terminology used by different applications. Figure 1 shows how an ontology can be used to map the terminology of one application to that of another. Company A uses the term salary in its employee database while Company B uses the term income in its personnel database. Both have similar meanings but differ in terminology and context of usage. For example salary in Company A may not be tax deducted whereas income in Company B may represent amounts after tax deduction. A common ontology establishes that both salary and income refer to payment amounts and hence are similar. Additional information such as tax status and currency are properties of payment amounts. Appropriate annotations can be made to the salary and income attributes to show this additional information. Thus, ontologies are a useful concept for developing a generic metadata model.

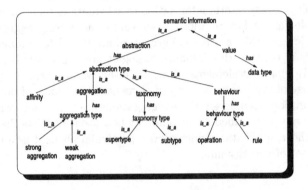

Fig. 2. Ontology For Semantic Information Represented By Database Schemata

In developing the generic metadata model we have analysed the features and capabilities of various existing data models and attempted to discover some underlying concepts on which all data models are based. It has already been acknowledged that all data models adhere to the *object-association* philosophy [5]. That is, at the very least every data model represents data objects and associations between them. In addition, database semantics include semantics of the domain of the database (Universe of Discourse), that is, the meaning of the values of database entities. Therefore, the types of semantic information found in a schema can be broadly categorised as a) semantics of the value of data elements, and b) semantics of the structure of the database. Schema elements can be classified into different semantic categories as shown in figure 2. A schema element can either depict abstraction or be simple valued. Semantics of value include information peculiar to the domain. Within the abstraction category, elements could depict taxonomy (inheritance), affinity (association), substance (aggregation), and behaviour semantics. Behaviour could be further classified as rules and operations, which imply that a schema element could represent some business rule or define some operation on other elements in the database.

The above range of information need not necessarily be available in any one modelling technique. For example, data models such as the relational model do not support the concept of taxonomy. The relational model also does not directly support affinity. It is possible to represent the Universe of Discourse in some higher semantic model and convert it to a semantically lower form of representation such as the relational model. In such cases some higher order semantic information is lost during the conversion. However, on closer inspection it is found that semantic information (such as taxonomy or affinity) has been transformed into other semantic forms (such as aggregation). It is therefore essential that aggregations in *semantically poor* models be properly dissected to reveal the actual semantic information about the objects in the aggregation. The Generic Metadatabase model described in section 4 is capable of representing semantic information in the above categories, and also maintain a separate record of semantic information for each element in an aggregation.

The ontology for semantic information of schemata is then linked to domain specific ontologies by has relations from value and strong aggregation. Only elements depicting value or strong aggregation are linked to domain specific ontologies. This is because the domain ontologies are constructed in such a way that they only represent elements which are either value-based or significant aggregations. Use of the latter category of elements in our form of domain specific ontologies is discouraged. Even when aggregations are used, their constituent elements should not be specified in the ontology because it restricts the usage of the ontology to those application which view a particular element as an aggregation of the given set of constituents.

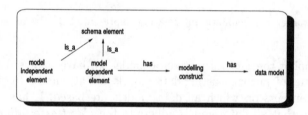

Fig. 3. Ontology For A Generic Model of Database Schemata

Next we develop an ontology for a generic model of database schemata (figure 3). The schema of a database can be viewed as a collection of schema elements. These elements describe the various objects and their interrelationships for a particular application. Most of the schema elements are model dependent elements. That is, they are defined using modelling techniques such as relational, object-oriented etc. Each model dependent element is based on a modelling construct (e.g. attribute, class, relation, association, method, rule etc.), and each construct belongs to a particular data modelling technique. For example *class* belongs to the *object-oriented* modelling technique, and *relation* belongs to the *relational* model. Confusion may arise due to the fact that *attribute* is a construct used in both *object-oriented* as well as *relational* models. This is solved by assuming that simply the name of a construct does not identify its data model and that every construct name must be explicitly associated with a data model name.

Model independent elements denote complex rules and operations which are not capable of being represented by the data model. In the past, such elements have been omitted from database specifications. As a result, users of databases are required to learn these by experience. The Generic Metadatabase model is capable of storing this information along with other model specific information.

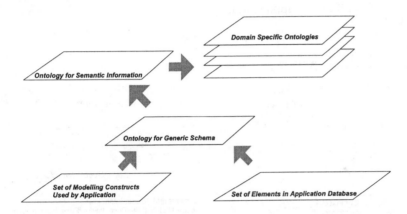

Fig. 4. Complete Scheme Of The GeM Approach

The complete scheme of our approach is shown in Figure 4. The ontology for generic database schemata is an attempt to view the contents of database's schema without the bias of the modelling technique. This enables us to develop a general format for the storage of metadata. The set of elements of a specific modelling technique is linked to the modelling construct and data model nodes by is_a links. Similarly, the set of elements in a specific database application are linked to the model-independent and model-dependent nodes of the ontology. Thus a database's components can be viewed with respect to the domain(s) of the application without the bias of a particular application or a modelling technique. In the next section, we describe a method and model for storing this information in a database.

4   The Generic Metadatabase (GeM) Model

A database management system needs metadata, data describing data conventionally stored in data dictionaries, to control the management and use of data [10]. This type of repository system can also play an important role as a passive kernel for information integration [HSU91]. However, a major problem to this use has been the inherent heterogeneity among different metadata repositories; since each type of repository is based on the information model used by the DBMS or CASE tool. In this paper we intend to provide a model-independent repository by dissociating metadata from existing modeling techniques.

The GeM approach advocates that all data models (schemata) should be broken down to their component elements and a minimum amount of information should be provided for each schema component in the form of metadata. We acknowledge the fact that existing models have been time-tested for their applicability and ease of use. Therefore, our metadata model is capable of being represented by the same data-model as the application and also developed on the same DBMS as the application.

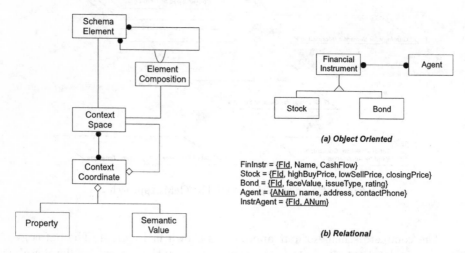

Fininstr = {<u>FId</u>, Name, CashFlow}
Stock = {<u>FId</u>, highBuyPrice, lowSellPrice, closingPrice}
Bond = {<u>FId</u>, faceValue, issueType, rating}
Agent = {<u>ANum</u>, name, address, contactPhone}
InstrAgent = {<u>FId, ANum</u>}

(a) Object Oriented

(b) Relational

Fig. 5. The Generic Metadatabase model in OMT notation

Fig. 6. An Example

Figure 5 shows an OMT version of the generic schema for metadata. The basic unit of storage is the **schema element**. Every schema element has a **name** and a **description**. Since *aggregation* is the most common and fundamental abstraction supported by all data models (to varying degrees), this information is stored in the **element composition** object. **Element composition** is an object which associates an element with another element of which it is a part. This object is also used for storing information about binary links (such as inheritance and associations etc.) between two elements, since a (binary) link can be considered as an aggregation of the two elements it connects. Associated with every schema element and element composition object is a **context space**, which stores most of the semantic information about the schema element. The context space of an element consists of several **context co-ordinates**. A context co-ordinate is a triple consisting of **property_list**, **property**, and **semantic_value**. Note that in the figure **property_list** is missing. This is because the list of properties can be constructed from the recursive definition of **context coordinate**, which could have its own context space as shown in the figure. The value for property is obtained from the set of ontologies. Details of selecting valid properties are explained in the next section.

5 An Example

In order to understand details of the generic metadata model, consider a simpli-
fied database in a financial trading application domain. As shown on Figure 6,
this database consists of information about financial instruments such as stocks
and bonds, as well as information about the agents who deal with these instruments. Figure 6(a) shows an object-oriented schema, and figure 6(b) shows the
relational schema of this database. Attributes of the classes in the object-oriented
schema are not shown in the diagram but could be considered to be the same as
in the relational model.

It can be seen that the object schema contains more semantic information
than the relational schema. The fact that stock is a kind of financial instrument
(as shown in the object model) is not reflected in the relational schema. The primary key FId in the Stock and Bond relations is an indication of the inheritance
of stock from financial instrument. However, this is not evident from the relational schema. In order to store information about these schemata in the generic
metadatabase, we break them into their constituent components. The object-
oriented schema can be broken into the following schema elements: Financial
Instrument, Stock, Bond, Trader, inherit_1, inherit_2, Name (financial instrument),
cashflow, highBuyPrice, lowSellPrice, closingPrice, faceValue, issueType , rating,
price, Name(agent), address, contactPhone. The element composition class cap-
tures the aggregation relations in the schema. For example, attributes of the
Financial Instrument class are linked to Financial Instrument by associations like:
(Financial Instrument, name), (Financial Instrument, cashflow). Similarly, inheritance and association relations are represented as aggregations of the two classes
connected by these relations. For example the inheritance relation between bond
and financial instrument (inherit_2) has the following entries in the element composition class: (inherit_2, Financial Instrument), (inherit_2, Bond). However, this
does not specify which object is the superclass and which is the subclass. Such
information will be stored in the context space of the element composition.

The context spaces of the elements and element compositions store most of
the relevant information about the semantics of the schema. The context space of
the stock class contains the following context coordinates: (modelling_construct,
class (data_model, object_oriented)), (semantic_information, abstraction (abstrac-
tion_type, aggregation (aggregation_type, strong_aggregation))). The inheritance
relation between Financial Instrument and Stock has the following context coordinates: (modelling_construct, inheritance(datamodel, object_oriented), (seman-
tic_information, abstraction (abstraction_type, taxonomy)). The schema element
inherit_1 itself does not specify the elements it connects. This is done by instances
of the element composition class. An instance of this class is a pair consisting of
the parent element and one child element. Thus, the fact that inherit_1 is an inheritance between Financial Instrument and Stock is represented by two instances
of the Element Composition class: (inherit_1, Financial Instrument), (inherit_1,
Stock). To find out the names of the two classes connected by an inheritance
relation, we can simply query the element composition class by specifying the
symbolic name of the inheritance relation (in this case inherit_1). All pairs with

inherit_1 as the first element will be retrieved. This however does not indicate which of the elements is the superclass and which is the subclass. The context space of each of the element composition relations stores this information. For example, the context space of the element composition (inherit_1, Financial Instrument) comprises of the following context coordinates: (semantic_information, abstraction (abstraction_type, taxonomy (taxonomy_type, supertype))). Note the additional information about the taxonomy type which states that the element composition between inherit_1 and Financial Instrument signifies a supertype relation. In other words, Financial Instrument is the supertype in the inheritance relationship defined by inherit_1.

Value based elements have domain specific context coordinates in addition to context coordinates which represent semantic information. For example, the attribute highBuyPrice in the relation Stock has the following standard context space: (modelling_construct, attribute (data_model, relational)) (semantic_information, value (data_type, float)), (units, australian_dollar) (precision, 999999.99).

Rules and operations are also incorporated into this metadatabase by storing a textual description of the rule or operation, as well as storing associations between the rules (or operations) and other schema elements on which they operate using the element composition class.

An advantage of the Generic Metadatabase is that it can be created using any of the popular database management systems which are available. A set of standard *canned queries* has been developed which enables retrieval of the complex semantic information. Since the Metadatabase is model-independent, the same set of queries can be used for schemata developed by different modelling techniques. The only impediment to achieving this is the heterogeneity in the querying languages. The next section describes the architecture of WeBUSE, a tool for browsing a metadatabase on the World-Wide-Web.

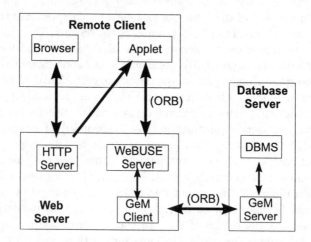

Fig. 7. Architecture of WEBUSE

6   Architecture of WeBUSE

In the previous sections we described the model which is used for storing and retrieving information about a database schema. The metadatabase created using the model would be of little use if it cannot be queried by remote users over a network. WeBUSE (Web-Based Uniform Schema browsing Environment) is a tool, currently being developed by the Distributed Computing Research Group, RMIT, to enable users to remotely connect to databases equipped with the Generic Metadatabases and to successfully query the metadatabase and elicit maximum information about the available schemata. As shown on figure 7, We-BUSE makes use of the Hypertext Transfer Protocol (HTTP) to send an executable code to a remote client. This code (or applet) is designed to establish an independent connection with the HTTP server using an Object Request Broker (ORB). An object request broker is used because we can specify standard queries understood by the metadatabase using a high-level-language. The client (applet) requests services from the server using the high level functions. These functions are in fact canned queries which can retrieve all the necessary information from the metadatabase. The WeBUSE server accepts the client's requests and sends an appropriate request to the metadatabase client which determines which database to send the query. The query is sent to the selected (remote) database where the GeM server understands and interprets the high level query to the native language of the local DBMS. This translation can be achieved using available technology such as Open Database Connectivity (ODBC) or Java Database Connectiviy (JDBC).

7   Conclusion and Future Work

Recent developments such as the WWW and the new generation of database interfaces present a challenge to researchers and developers: how to make database information interpretable to users who don't know the database schema. The existence of several data modelling techniques and the inherent complexity of database semantic information make the problem more acute. We are proposing here a generic metadata model to represent syntactic and semantic information, and a set of standard mechanisms to store and retrieve the required information. WebUSE includes standard 'canned queries' to be able to perform retrievals, and an adequate user interface. It will also have the ability to describe its own modelling constructs. Work is in progress on an architecture based on the Common Object Request Broker Architecture (CORBA) standard.

References

1. Batini, C., Lenzerini, M., Navathe, S.B. *A Comparitive Analysis of Methodologies for Database Integration.* ACM Computing Surveys, vol. 18, no. 4, Dec 1986.
2. Dolk, D.R., Kirsch II, R.A. *A Relational Information Resource Dictionary System.* Communications of the ACM, vol. 30, no. 7, January 1987.

3. Goh, C.H., Madnick, S.E., Siegel, M.D. *Ontologies, Contexts and Mediation: Representing and Reasoning.* about Semantic Conflicts in Heterogeneous and Autonomous Systems. Sloan School of Management, Working Paper #3848.

4. Gruber, T.R. *Toward Principles for the Design of Ontologies Used in Knowledge Sharing.* Formal Ontology in Conceptual Analysis and Knowledge Representation, Guarino, N., Poli, R., (eds), Kluwer Academic Publishers, 1993

5. Hainaut, J-L *A Generic Entity-Relationship Model.* IFIP TC8/WG8.1 WC on IS Concepts: An In-depth Analysis - Wepion 1989.

6. Heiler, S. *Semantic Interoperability.* ACM Computing Surveys, vol. 27, no. 2, June 1995.

7. Hsu, C., Bouziane, M., Rattner, L. *Information Resources Management in Heterogeneous, Distributed Environments: A Metadatabase Approach.* IEEE Transactions on Software Engineering, vol. 17, no. 6, June 1991.

8. Kim, W., Seo, J. *Classifying Schematic and Data Heterogeneity in Multidatabase Systems.* IEEE Computer, vol. 24, no. 30, December 1991.

9. Manola, F. *Interoperability Issues in Large-Scale Distributed Object Systems .* ACM Computing Surveys, vol. 27, no. 2, June 1995.

10. Mark, L., Roussopoulos, N. *Metadata Management.* IEEE Computer, December 1986.

11. Mark, L., Roussopoulos, N. *Information Interchange Between Self-Describing Databases.* Information Systems, vol. 15, no. 4, 1990.

12. Reddy, M.P., Prasad, P.G., Reddy, P.G., Gupta, A. *A Methodology for Integration of Heterogeneous Databases.* IEEE Transactions on Knowledge and Data Engineering, vol. 6, no. 6, December 1994.

13. Spaccapietra, S., Parent, C., Dupont, Y. *Model Independent Assertions for Integration of Heterogeneous Schemes.* VLDB Journal, vol. 1, no. 1, July 1992.

14. Su, S., Fang, S.C., Lam, H. *An Object Oriented Rule-based Approach to Data Model and Schema Translation.* Database Systems R&D Center, University of Florida, CIS Technical Report TR-92-015, May 1992.

15. Wiederhold, G. *An Algebra for Ontology Composition.* Proceedings of 1994 Workshop on Formal Methods, September 1994

Post-Client/Server Coordination Tools

eva Kühn and Georg Nozicka*

University of Technology Vienna
Institute of Computer Languages
Argentinierstraße 8, 1040 Vienna, Austria
{eva,nozicka}@complang.tuwien.ac.at

Abstract. The exploitation of new application possibilities, like collaboration and cooperation, offered by distributed systems requires advanced coordination support. Traditional tools are based on the message passing paradigm and lead to asymmetric client/server application architectures. The other – conceptually superior – paradigm uses a virtual shared memory. The development of distributed programs is easier in the latter model and leads to elegant solutions that meet well the new possibilities. We term software support that follows this second approach *post-client/server* tools. CoKe *(Coordination Kernel)* is a new middleware layer of this new generation. It particularly eases the development of fault-tolerant, distributed applications.

We discuss, why coordinative data structures (on *virtual shared objects*) provide more advantages than the traditional method invocation model (on *distributed objects*).

1 Introduction

Computer networks offer new application scenarios that cannot be realized on single workstations. Resources and services may be distributed because of political, organizational, etc. reasons which make a centralization impossible. The parallelism gained through the simultaneous processing of subtasks at distributed sites may lead to a better system throughput. Architectures comprising workstations connected to Intranets, distributed Intranets or the Internet offer a better price/performance behavior for coarse grained, commercial applications than parallel hardware. The market for the latter one being primarily massively parallel and highly scientific applications.

Each connected workstation contributes to the common *global distributed architecture*, which makes the hardware scale-up easy to plan and to manage. To participate in the pool of common hardware, one has simply to connect a new workstation or a network terminal.

New application domains offered by the distributed hardware are for example:

---

* Current address of the author: IBM Austria Ltd., Lassallestraße 1, 1020 Vienna, Austria, nozicka@vnet.ibm.com.

- **Electronical Supermarket.** Many components can be found in the network that need not be reinvented. This idea exceeds the traditional notion of software reuse, which basically refers to existing program libraries. In the network, data and services are offered that need not resp. cannot be transferred to the own site, but rather are to be used on the site where they are installed and maintained. Programming will move towards organization of distributed resources [16].
  Sophisticated accounting and security systems are needed for this supermarket, the implementation of which in turn requires advanced software tools to guarantee their reliability.
- **Workflow Management.** A workflow management system describes units of work and specifies the data and control flow between different activities, including constraints and dependencies. Workflow serves to reengineer business and information processes with the goal to reduce the cost of doing business [2].
  A workflow management system involves many distributed resources and users that contribute to the global task in several roles.
- **Multi Database Systems.** A multidatabase systems integrates several, distributed autonomous database systems, that are pre-existing (so-called legacy systems). The objective is to offer a unique and homogeneous view on the different data, models, and representations, while keeping local system's autonomy [1, 11].
  Besides the semantic integration issues, the heterogeneous transaction processing is a main aspect of a multi database system. Communication and site failures must not destroy the global transaction's semantics.
- **CSCW.** The cooperation of teams on larger tasks via electronic communication facilities adds more flexibility for employees, including the possibility of teleworking.
  However, computer supported cooperative work in the network requires complex transaction and synchronization mechanisms. For example, the early commit of subtransactions that allows intermediate results to become visible, before the global transaction commits, is a new requirement here. Advanced transaction models like the Flex Transaction Model [3] have been designed for these meets.

Alas, these issues pose a lot of new challenges on the application developer. Obviously, the new technical possibilities and requirements cause distributed applications to be more complex and difficult than software for a single computer; take only into consideration how difficult it is to verify the correctness of programs if deadlocks must be avoided, heterogeneity of the different systems, data types and models must be hidden, reliability of communication including message loss or duplication has to be considered, security and accounting has to be established to avoid unauthorized accesses, concurrent and parallel activities must be synchronized, etc.

Besides these extra burdens, however, distributed architectures allow for software improvement through exploitation of the distribution. As is known, replication of data and services can improve availability and reliability, and also improve performance. The possibilities to add **fault tolerance** and **high performance** to the software should in any case be exploited by the programmers. It is not sufficient just to implement an operational distributed system, but the real challenge is to *improve* the software by the possibilities offered through distribution.

For the management of these new tasks, the employment of high-level development tools is crucial. A heterogeneous environment is less static than one computer. Frequent changes must be anticipated. The scale-up mostly cannot be predicted a priori. This means that software solutions must be flexible, easy and if possible dynamically to tune and adapt. New requirements must not claim the redesign and rewriting of a huge amount of code lines. This will, however, be the case, if the used software tool cannot provide a high enough abstraction of the complexity imposed by distribution. The more it can hide from the programmer, the rather programs will turn towards *specifications*, concentrating at the problem at hand, and thus enable their adaptation to different requirements with a reasonable effort.

2 Software Support Through Middleware

Why do we need middleware?
What is middleware?

2.1 Application on a Single Computer

```
┌─────────────────────────┐
│                         │
│      Application        │
│                         │
├─────────────────────────┤
│                         │
│       Hardware          │
│                         │
└─────────────────────────┘
```

The development of applications for a single computer is directly based on the hardware[1] of this computer.

2.2 Application on Computers Distributed in a Network

The development of software on distributed sites reveals the heterogeneity of the underlying hardware. Without any further software support, the programmer is responsible to care for the heterogeneity; this includes the following issues [15]:

---

[1] In the figures "hardware" stands for "hardware plus the corresponding operating system".

Application		
Hardware 1	Hardware 2	Hardware 3

without middleware

Location. The addressing of resources on different sites requires different names there.

Migration. The movement of resources to other sites must be done explicitly and requires a solution for how to rename the resources there.

Replication. The administration of data copies at different sites, showing identical behavior, requires complex communication and replication protocols.

Access. The access to local data usually will be different than the access to data located on remote sites.

Transaction. Concurrent accesses to the distributed resources must be explicitly synchronized to guarantee data consistency. In addition, collaboration requires more complicated access patterns than the access to one single resource. This in turn will require the realization of more complicated transaction features. E.g., the manipulation of a set of data items or the booking of a set of services in one atomic step.

Failure. In distributed environments, single sites may fail individually (*partial failure*) which need not cause the stagnation of the entire computation. The substitution of a failing service through an alternative one should be provided by the developer to mask system and site failures (*function replication*).

Representation. Related data stored on different sites may have different representations there, e.g., different data modeling schemas, or different interface definition languages.

Scaling. The distributed computers will have different loads, so it is a challenge for the programmer to distribute the single tasks fairly to achieve an optimal throughput.

Persistency. If a site or network failure occurs, it is desirable that after the reestablishment of the failing component the computation can continue. This requires to store well defined checkpoints on disc from which both data and computations can be recovered. Best, if the failing component restarts automatically to continue its work.

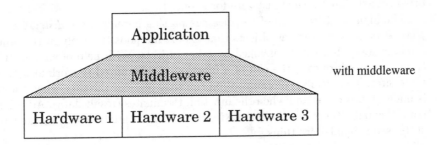

with middleware

Middleware is a software layer between the heterogeneous hardware and the application program that shall shield as many as possible of the above mentioned problems from the programmer. Its objective is to make distributed application development approximately as easy as for single workstations. Besides this ambitious goal, we have also to take into consideration the previous argument that a distributed application should exploit the new possibilities offered by distribution (primarily fault-tolerance and better performance).

3 Two Models for Distributed Systems

There exist two models for the communication and synchronization of distributed systems: message passing versus a virtual shared memory. The following discussion aims to make plausible why the former model necessarily leads to asymmetric, client/server based application architectures, whereras the latter one enables symmetric post-client/server application architectures.

The limitations and possibilities of middleware solutions are pointed out for both categories.

3.1 Message Passing

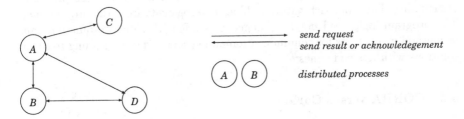

With message passing, the distributed, parallel executing processes communicate through the explicit sending and receiving of messages. Mostly, the synchronous mode is preferred, where both sender and receiver must be active at the same time (handshake). Asynchronous message passing requires more effort, as an intermediate storage for communicated data is required, and some kind of multi threading must be employed in the programs.

Message passing in its basic form implies a new dimension for the application programmer that he/she must care for explicitly.

The highest abstraction of the message passing paradigm are *distributed objects*. Processes are seen as objects that export methods (possibly in the object oriented way) that can be invoked by other objects. With help of e.g., an RPC (remote procedure call) the call of a function is generalized to work also on remote sites. Technically, communication can take place at the time when the call is made (input data) and when the function terminates (result data). Additional control capabilities while the remote function is executing (to check its execution state, send signals) are thinkable.

3.2   Virtual Shared Objects

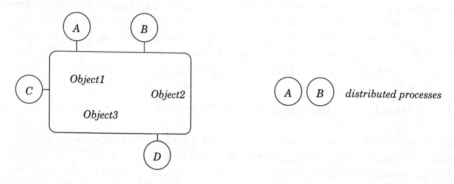

The model of virtual shared objects provides the vision of a common shared memory, of which all participating, distributed and parallel executing processes have a consistent view. The shared objects are used for communication and synchronization. This approach is much easier to embed into a program: the access to shared objects need not differ from the access to ordinary local variables. Blocking or non-blocking access can be supported. The abstraction offered here is the extension of local memory to the memories of all sites where processes are running. This approach naturally hides heterogeneity from the programmer. The program logic need not be changed or stuffed with remote function calls or method invocations for communication and synchronization, leading to easier solutions with less code lines[2].

3.3   CORBA versus CoKe

Distributed Objects are the most advanced interpretation of client/server technologies, best represented by CORBA (Common Object Request Broker Architecture) [17, 14]. The exciting thing about CORBA is that it is the first example

---

[2] Compare with the methapher of traffic regulation [9] via shared objects (a common traffic light) and via explicit message passing (equipping each single car with a celular telephon).

in software industry, where a comprehensive standard approved by a large industrial consortium, runs ahead commercial implementations. Orfali et al. [14] compare this approach with a hardware bus but at the software level, the goal of which is to enable a cooperation of software components by different vendors through a "plug-in-and-play" mechanism.

Other relevant representatives of the message passing model are for example OSF DCE (Distributed Computing Environment) and PVM (Parallel Virtual Machine).

For the virtual shared memory, many research approaches exist, but not yet well established and widely used commercial systems. [4] is a comprehensive bibliography about research in the area of distributed shared memory. Relevant systems are for example the LINDA tuple space model, ORCA, Mirage-2, Arjuna, and ISIS (ISIS provides a reliable broadcast mechanism which allows for a virtual synchrony of objects).

The Coordination Kernel (CoKe) [10, 12] also belongs to this category (see section 4). We just briefly summarize the distinguishing characteristics of CoKe, but do not give a comprehensive comparison here[3]. CoKe provides a real application oriented object sharing, instead of the more hardware oriented memory pages sharing. It offers a comprehensive object/transaction/process model that enables recoverable programming. The global naming of objects is avoided which makes automatic garbage collection possible and provides an improved access security. One of CoKe's most important features is that it is an open framework that provides different replication strategies [8].

CORBA*	shields	CoKe
×	Location	×
×	Migration	×
—	**Replication**	×
×	Access	×
(×)	**Transaction**	×
—	Failure	×
×	Representation	×
—	Scaling	—
(×)	Persistency	×

A comparison of CORBA and CoKe according to the above mentioned criteria shows that both offer location, migration, access and representation transparencies – the basic requirements one would impose on middleware. Automatic scaling support is currently supported by none of them.

Replication and transaction are properties that are provided by the virtual shared object model in general. For representatives of the message passing resp. of the distributed objects approach it is difficult to provide them. CORBA, for example, only knows the methods of an object, but the implementation of the

---

[3] For a comparison between LINDA and CoKe we refer to [5, 13], a more general comparison can be found in [6].

object remains a black-box for the object request broker (ORB). Consequently, the ORB cannot reason about which internal states of an object are really affected, if a method is executed. The lack of this knowledge hampers an efficient automatic synchronization mechanism on objects that are accessed concurrently, as well as the automatic replication of objects to different sites to gain better availability, reliability and performance. What probably can be supported easily is the sequentialization of concurrent accesses (in a monitor alike manner, which reduces the potential of concurrency), and the replication of the *entire* object (which is expensive). CORBA 2.0 does not foresee the specification of a replication service.

In CORBA 2.0 there exists the notion of a transaction[4], but in the following sense: a transaction service has been defined, that allows to let (*perfect*) objects that offer a two-phase-commit to be grouped to global transactions; for example objects that themselves represent a (distributed) database system. Thus the notion of transaction in CORBA has a different meaning than in CoKe, where transactions on objects serve to carry out the communication and synchronization via data.

With regard to replication and transaction the virtual shared object model is superior and relieves the programmer of extra programming efforts. Beyond it, the CoKe model offers an advanced transaction model that is based on the Flex Transaction Model [3], and fault-tolerance for the communication with shared objects.

Fault-tolerance in CORBA depends on the implementation. For example, ORBIX by IONA systems [18] is based on ISIS and provides reliability.

3.4   Message Passing Implies Asymmetric Application Architectures

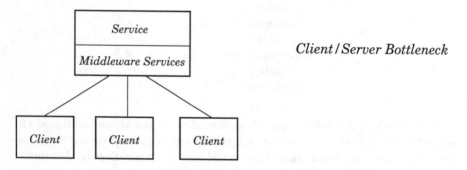

Client / Server Bottleneck

With message passing, several clients demand services at one server process, which is usually centralized and thus may lead to a performance bottleneck. The mentioned new possibilities of fault-tolerance and better performance offered by the distributed architectures cannot be exploited this way by traditional client/server technologies.

---

[4] That is why there is a ($\times$) in the above table for CORBA.

If we really want to compare client/server with shared objects, the server object must be replicated to many sites. However, as this is not really supported by CORBA, this implies an extra programming overhead for the developer: server functionality that should be provided by the middleware must be implemented explicitly.

3.5   Virtual Shared Objects Imply Symmetric Application Architectures

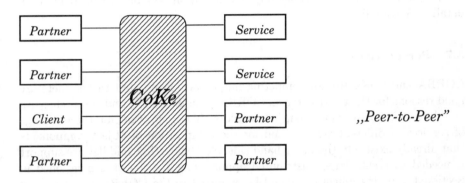

„Peer-to-Peer"

CoKe enables a symmetric communication between all processes in a peer oriented way. Processes are slim, because they need not reimplement middleware features. Obviously it is also possible to understand some of these „partner" processes as clients or servers, depending on the task they fulfill. In other words, also the classical client/server scenarios can be implemented with a virtual shared object model, although this is not the intended way to gain the models's particular benefits.

3.6   Criticism

After having claimed that virtual shared objects have a lot of advantages, we have also to point out their weaknesses:

- **One Replication Strategy.** *As the programmer relies on the replication offered by the virtual shared object middleware, he cannot influence its behavior. What happens, if the strategy used does not fit the current application's needs and for example replicates very large objects to all sites? Does in this case the disadvantage of client/server technologies, namely that the programmer has to care for replication explicitly, turn into a benefit?*
- **Object Orientation.** *How does object orientation as it is today understood in distributed environments – i.e., in the sense of CORBA – fit to this model? Isn't the explicit manipulation of data a contradiction to what we know about object-oriented methodologies?*

This criticism holds for the shared object model in general. However, CoKe is an exception, because it offeres different distribution strategies that are responsible for replication and caching of data. Dynamically, for *each* single object another strategy can be selected. The program does not change, but the fine-tuning of the replication behavior and thus of the fault-tolerance and performance can be done by simply selecting the right strategy (e.g., via a define in a header file).

This way, CoKe offers all advantages of the shared object paradigm, and additionally gives the programmer control about availability, reliability and efficiency of his program (see Section 5).

The second issue concerning object orientation will be discussed in more detail in Section 6.

3.7 Perspectives

CORBA and CoKe are not competing middleware layers, but rather there are good reasons for their co-existence. CORBA is an invaluable and comprehensive standard defined by more than 500 vendors. It is important for the exchange of services of different vendors and for the composition of object components that already exist. On the other hand side, we believe that middleware support is needed to create large, distributed applications like the ones mentioned in Section 1. These applications could be exported to the CORBA world via the standard IDL as server objects. From the CORBA point of view, CoKe can contribute to the development of *perfect* objects, that represent services that are themselves distributed and replicated to many sites.

4   CoKe Architecture

CoKe is implemented as a two layer concept. The first layer is the CoKe kernel and the second layer represents the programming interface for an application programmed against CoKe. Layer two can also be seen as a programming language extended by coordination aspects.

4.1 Layer 1 – CoKe Kernel

This layer implements all the kernel functionality which can be seen as the heart of CoKe. It contains the full logic including all internal protocols and message handling, replication concepts, communication protocols with all connected CoKes, data encoding and decoding including little-big endian data representation, transaction handling, garbage collection and so on. This layer is programmed in **C** and has just one code base cross all supported platforms which makes the code highly portable for any kind of C compiler and operating system. Further, C has the advantage that for almost any kind of programming language

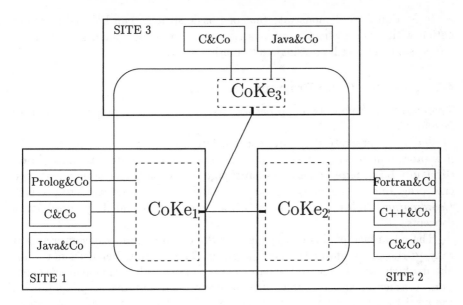

a C binding exists which increases the number of potential programming interfaces used for layer 2.

On each site a CoKe process is running. The entirety of all CoKe processes maintains the communication objects in the virtual memory space. Objects are uniquely identified by an OID (object identification) and are written in transactions, which makes them persistent. A process may access an object, if it is passed its reference (OID) in its argument list, or if the object appears as subobject in the value of an object a process may see. Processes communicate via objects in a symmetric way. The modeling of everlasting processes that are automatically recovered after failures is possible.

CoKe differentiates between two object types: CONSTs (constants) and VARs (variables). The latter ones have been inspired by logic programming (Prolog) and can have only two states: undefined and defined. Once written, a CONST cannot be changed any more. VARs equal updateable variables in imperative programming languages.

The administration of the consistent view on all communication objects, i.e., VARs and CONSTs, is carried out by the distribution strategies. Currently one strategy is available [12], others have been designed but are not yet released. The available strategy is termed passive replication with a deep object tree (PR_{deep}) and is based on a replication technique that employs a primary copy migration schema. One copy is designated as the main copy, all other copies are termed secondary (or backup) copies. For the update of any object and for the read access of VARs, the primary copy is required; this leads to an implicit locking of the object at the transaction's commit.

In Section 5 we demonstrate that one basic strategy can be used in combination with several general and strategy specific flags so that many variations are possible even with one single distribution strategy.

4.2   Layer 2 – CoKe Programming Interface

There exist principally two approaches how to implement a programming interface for CoKe.

One is to integrate the CoKe concept into a language, which means that a new programming language is created. Such an implementation is called **Coordination-Language** or just **Co-Language** where Language stands for a specific programming language. A sample would be *Coordination-C* respectively *Coordination Prolog*, which means C resp. Prolog is extended by coordination concepts.

The advantage of this concept is that the coordination extension fits naturally to the paradigm of the host language. The programmer need not worry about which parts belong to the base language and which to the language extension. Another advantage is that such a concept might improve the acceptance of the need to define programming languages which have communication aspects already built-in. The disadvantage is that this concept needs a new compiler to be implemented which leads to following problems:

- The implementation effort is usually high.
- A parser has to be written which follows a specific standard for the base language. There is always the danger that the parser has not the latest language standard implemented.
- The maintenance effort is extremely high. Each time a new language standard is defined, the parser needs to be updated.
- Usually the acceptance in the industry is low because the dependency on a specific language and vendor is always a high risk.

The second approach is to define a package with header files to be included, and a library to be linked. This approach is called **Language&Coordination** or just **Language&Co**. The language binding for the programming language **C** is thus called **C&Co**.

The disadvantage is that the library concept is not a real part of the programming language and that the usage is often not very natural compared to the base language. The advantage is that usually the library is completely independent of any compiler standard and compiler product which minimizes the maintenance effort and increases the availability for other platforms and compiler implementations. This implies that the acceptance in the industry for this approach is much higher than the other.

5   Strategies

CoKe is an open framework that supports the selection of basic strategies for the distribution and replication of data, and of additional strategy flags. In this section we want briefly summarize the most important flags which can be used in any combination.

Note that an application program need not be changed, if another strategy and flags are experimented to achieve the best performance and fault-tolerance tuning.

The current version of CoKe provides the following *general strategy flag*:

– **Reliability Class.** The programmer may select between three reliability classes. Class 1 masks network failures only, classes 2 and 3 mask also site failures. In contrast to class 2, class 3 stores data not only in the CoKe database, but for increased security also writes them to a log file.

The PR_{deep} strategy additionally supports the following flags:

– **Eager/Lazy Distribution.** If an object is written, its new value is either automatically propagated to all sites that possess a reference to the object, or not. Analogous, if a value of an object is passed to a remote CoKe, either all its subjects' values are copied (eager way) or only their references are copied (lazy way).
– **Read Main/Next Copy.** When reading a VAR object, it is verified at transaction end, whether the read data are still valid or not. This flag determines, if a read must go for the main copy or can be satisfied with the next available copy; in the latter case the possibility of a transaction commit fail will be higher. If, however, an object is read very frequently but written only rarely, the performance can be improved this way.

Moreover, in [8], a further general strategy flag for a flexible and dynamically reconfigurable software architecture (termed DYRCA) has been proposed, that allows an application developer to dynamically influence the caching behavior of a basic distribution strategy. This can be done without the need to design a new replication protocol, which is a quite complex task. The basic idea is that every time, a CoKe process runs into the situation to store the value of an object, it asks a *strategy consultancy system (SCM)* whether the value shall be cached locally or not. Analogously, every time CoKe needs the value of an object of which it possesses the OID, it asks the SCM where the next cache is located to retrieve the data from there. This helps to minimize communication traffic. The SCM has well defined APIs (application interfaces) and can be easily implemented by a programmer.

6   Object Orientation and Coordination

This chapter explains how the object oriented approach can be combined with the concepts used by CoKe. It first discusses the main differences between the traditional understanding of object-orientation (as in CORBA) and CoKe. It shows how coordination concepts can be wrapped, how cooperative data structures are implemented and how stream objects are used.

6.1   CORBA versus CoKe Architecture

In order to understand the difference between the CORBA and the CoKe architecture it is important to see how distributed functionality is implemented in both systems:

In short, CORBA can be seen as an RPC architecture hidden by an object oriented approach. When a client accesses a distributed object it does it by calling a respective method of a class. Internally this is mapped to an RPC call and in fact a method of an object on the server is invoked.

Because of the shared object paradigm of CoKe the mechanism how a distributed object is accessed is different to CORBA.

- With CoKe the distributed object is accessed in the same way as a local one. If the needed copy of the object is already locally available, a lot of internal message passing can be avoided, especially if the object is accessed more than once by a specific function.
- With CoKe the application programmer has to deal with two object conceptions: one is the OID of the object and the other one is the object itself, i.e., its value.
- The data are separated by the function performed on them which stands in contrast to the object oriented approach.

From an application programmer's point of view the usage of CORBA is nicer, since the object oriented paradigm is fully exploited by just calling a method of a distributed object.

From the internal point of view the shared object paradigm is better since CoKe always works on a local copy of the object. Of course there might be some internal message overhead but this depends on the operation performed (read or write) and on the type of object (CONST versus VAR). The main difference from the internal message overhead's point of view is, that with CORBA each time a function is performed against an object, this leads to an internal message overhead but with CoKe this message overhead needs to be done only once, independently of the number of functions performed against the object.

As we have seen so far there need to be addressed two problems for CoKe. One is to find a way to "hide" coordination respectively to make the usage of coordination very natural compared to the language used. The other one is to bring logic and data together like it is done in the object oriented approach.

6.2   Wrapping Coordination

C++&Co is an approach to embed coordination into an object oriented base language (in our case C++) in a natural way. The second point of criticism on the shared virtual object model as addressed in Section 3.6 is answered as follows.

In CoKe an OID is needed for communication, i.e., for the writing of a value into an OID respectively for reading an object. For this reason a communication class is needed which keeps the OID as a private member, and provides basic methods like read and write.

On the other side object oriented applications work with objects. It can be that some instances of such objects are involved in collaboration with other systems, or that they are used just like any other in a non distributed environment.

If an object needs to be shared with other objects it is associated with an OID. For the object oriented approach this means that this object is associated with a communication object and can fully exploit communication behavior.

C++&Co knows three basic types which can be used as data objects which are an OID, an integer and a string. But especially in object oriented environments more complex objects are used than just a string or an integer, and operations (methods) are defined to operate on these objects. C++&Co has implemented these complex objects which are also referred to as *cooperative data structures*.

6.3   Cooperative Data Structures

Cooperative data structures are declared like any other C++ class with the difference that they need to inherit from a special class to implement it. All data members of this class which need to be distributed have to be registered separately. This implies that not necessarily all data members of the class need to be distributed which makes sense for data members which are site specific or just hold some temporary values. It is also possible to have data members which are again a cooperative data structure which enables one to create very complex nested distributed objects. Besides data members of course also methods can be defined like this is done for any other C++ class. Actually there are not any language restrictions when creating cooperative data structures. At this point it needs to be emphasized that the C++ classes only need to be defined as C++ source, there are no additional techniques respectively tools required, like IDL (interface definition language) files or special precompilers.

C++&Co has two techniques implemented how cooperative data structures can be distributed.

One is to loosely couple a communication object with a data object. In this case it is possible to assign at any point in time another data object to the communication object. Since the communication object knows the data object internally just by reference, it is not possible to perform any method of the data object directly on the data object.

A way to bypass this lack of functionality is to use the second approach which is to use the C++ template concept. In this case a communication object is created which gets the data object as class argument. Internally the communication object is designed that way that it derives the data object which means that the new created object combines communication behavior with data object behavior.

Let us summarize the most important differences between the various concepts discussed so far:

C&Co versus C++&Co

- C&Co separates data and functionality which stands in contrast to the object oriented approach.
- Cooperative data structures have to be decoded and encoded explicitly with format functions; this works for C++&Co automatically.
- Cooperative data structures are much more complicated to realize and keep the danger of errors like decoding data in a different order like encoding them.

Coordination-C versus C++&Co

- The coordination extensions for C++&Co fit very good to the C++ concept but Coordination-C has solved this by totally embedding it into the language, which is the most elegant way.
- Coordination-C needs a precompiler which has several trade-offs already described.
- Acceptance for new languages is lower than for language extensions.
- C++&Co is object oriented, Coordination-C not.

CORBA versus C++&Co

- Both are object oriented.
- CORBA invokes internally for each function an RPC, C++&Co not.
- CORBA needs additional techniques like IDL and precompilers.
- C++&Co supports the conceptually superior paradigm of a virtual shared memory.

6.4 Stream Objects

Stream data types are the basic communication structure for any kind of collaboration. For example think about the functionality of a black board of a lecture: it can be seen as an object which changes from time to time. To simplify the scenario, let's say that not every word written down represents one consistent state but just a full-written black board. Each time the black board is cleaned, the old state is not valid any more. You can see the teacher as the producer of data and the students as the consumers. Mapped to CoKe the way how the entire lecture is delivered from the teacher to the students can be solved by two different approaches:

1. with updateable objects (VARs)
2. with a stream of constant objects (CONSTs)

Solving this problem with VAR objects has the following consequences:

- Reading the object guarantees the student always to see the most recent (valid) value, i.e., the actual contents of the black board.

- Each time the black board is cleaned this means that internally garbage collection takes place immediately.
- If no additional logic is implemented it can happen that a student misses the contents of one or more full written black boards, since no history information is available.
- If it must be guaranteed that always all students have read all full written black boards this implies:
  - Additional coordination structures are required to perform some kind of hand shake mechanisms. This can lead to relative complex additional logic, especially if the number of reading students permanently changes while the lecture is held (which is a quite realistic assumption at universities for example).
  - As far the hand shake mechanisms are also realized with VAR objects (which is the assumption, otherwise we could have taken already constant objects for the initial coordination structure) the teacher has always to wait for the slowest student.

In contrast to VAR objects the problem can also be addressed with a stream of CONST objects. A constant object is an object which can be written only once. If a reader tries to read such an object which has not been written yet, the read request is blocked[5] until someone has written it. The implementation of a stream works the following way. Initially both, producer and consumer, need to know an initial empty OID. Now the producer writes a list cell to that initial OID where the first item is the value to be written and the second is a new empty OID. The consumer performs a read on the initial OID which is blocked until the producer has written the first list cell. When the list cell is read by the consumer, it extracts the first item (the value). Further the consumer extracts the second item (the new empty OID) and performs the next read request on this new OID. The next time the producer writes data it creates again an OID and writes the new data and OID into the OID sent as second item in the previous iteration, and so on.

Solving the black board problem with CONST stream objects has the following consequences:

- Reading the object does not guarantee to have the most recent (valid) value, i.e., it can be the case that the teacher is already several black boards ahead. This can lead to the following problem: imagine the teacher has corrected a formula written down two black boards before. If a student is one black board behind the teacher he still has the knowledge of the wrong formula. If now the teacher would ask the student for the formula the student's answer would be wrong.
- It can not happen that a student misses one full-written black board, since there exists a history which is chained together via the stream object.

---

[5] In the example we use the blocking read. Note that CoKe supports both synchronous and asynchronous read of objects.

- Even it is guaranteed that all readers see all created black boards, the producer has no dependency on a slow reader. This means the teacher can produce as many black boards as he likes without having to wait for any student (which might be nice for the teacher but sometimes bad for the students).
- Garbage collection does not take place automatically. This can either be achieved by an explicit call or by ending the current process in such a way that at the same point in time a new instance of the process is created by passing the last empty OID to the new process. This can be done in such a way that it is guaranteed that the new process is started.

In C&Co there is no implicit support for a stream type which makes the usage a little bit complicated. In contrast, C++&Co fully supports this data type with an own class. Similar to the two concepts for the communication object a cooperative data structure can be associated to the stream. The producer just performs one write request against the stream object after each other where the consumer does nothing else than continuously invoke the stream's read method. The entire program logic is hidden by the implementation of that class and not visible to the user.

7 Applications

Besides many test programs written to proof CoKe's functionality also some larger applications have been created at the TU Vienna, like for example:

- Producer / Consumer Sample
- Workflow Manager
- Team-Editor
- Database Replication System

7.1 Producer / Consumer

Usually a producer / consumer sample is used to prove the correctness and robustness of a distributed system, but it is also the base for many classical distributed problems.

A typical producer / consumer application includes four components:

1. Root Entry
2. Supervisor
3. Producer
4. Consumer

Root Entry is the entry to the sample and runs only once. It creates a CONST root OID which is later passed to any of the other components as input. Further, it starts one supervisor as an independent process.

Supervisor is the part which enables one to start producers, consumers or even other supervisors by passing the root OID to the respective independent process.

Producer is a process generating data to be worked on by the consumers. It creates a stream object and associates it the root OID. Within a loop the producer prompts a user for data, opens a transaction, writes the data to the stream object and tries to commit the transaction. What now can happen is, that the internally used OID has already been written by another, concurrently running producer, which would cause the commit to fail, because we use CONSTs for the realization of the producer/consumer system. In this case it is tried to write the data again to the stream object which means that internally data are consumed up to the last valid OID to which the entered data finally are written. This is repeated as long as the commit goes well.

Consumer is a process reading data written by any producer. A stream object is created in the same way like for the producer. Within a loop the consumer does nothing else than call the read method of the stream object and print the read data.

A detailed analysis of this sample can be found in [13].

7.2   Workflow Manager

Many existing and commercial used workflow manager systems follow the traditional Client/Server concept. The system structure of these systems looks as follows:

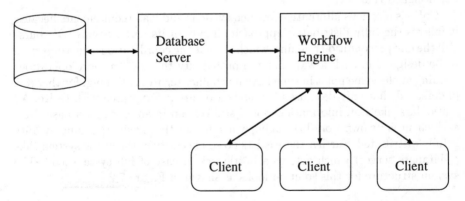

The Database Server is the program implementing the entire database logic like reading data, writing data, query engine, and transaction management. This component only exists once for the whole workflow system (i.e., for one database).

The Workflow Engine is the component implementing the workflow logic. These are operations like creating workflow processes, navigating on workflow processes, creating work for users, starting programs, and maintaining the connections of all clients. The workflow engine is a database client program and can exist one or more times for one database. Having more than one workflow engine operating against one database can only improve performance if the database design has been done in such a way that the probability that two or more operations, running at the same point in time, don't lock the same data in the database and that the database server can handle multiple transactions and its utilization is still low to medium.

As far the clients don't perform any database access functions directly, i.e., they are no database clients, they can be called thin clients which is the most common used architecture in workflow systems. This means that the clients just perform one request after each other against the workflow engine to perform a specific function.

The way such traditional workflow systems are architected has one main disadvantage. At least the database server represents a bottleneck under high volume load and in most cases the bottleneck is already represented by the workflow engine.

One solution to bypass this problem is to drop the concept of having a workflow engine as an own component and move the navigation logic to the clients. Besides the problem that in this case fat clients are needed and the installation and configuration overhead increases, the original problem, that the database server still represents a bottleneck, remains. And even worse, any system architected in such a way once hits physical limits like maximum communication bandwidth, CPU power and/or hard disk access time, reached. The only solution to go beyond this physical boundaries is to introduce parallelism which does not work for the classical client/server approach because the database systems are not designed that way.

CoKe is a serious alternative for such systems and load requirements because it follows the fully distributed approach already in its core systems. Of course still the one precondition remains, which is, that the coordination structures have to be designed in such a way that the probability that two or more operations running at the same point in time have no conflict regarding locking. Further it is understood that only data used for navigation are incorporated with CoKe. All static data like staff information would still remain in an extra data base. Now each client is its own workflow engine which means that navigation functionality is fully distributed. Further there exists no single entity in the whole system (like a database server) which acts as a bottleneck in case of full system load. The system structure for this solution looks as shown in Figure 7.2.

7.3   Team-Editor

The Team-Editor [7] is a program which enables a group of people to edit one and the same file at the same time in a coordinated way. It consists of a public and a private window. The public window always represents the actual state of the document currently being edited. The private window is a place to edit

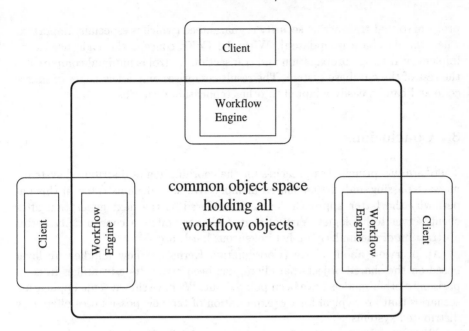

existing and/or new parts which should be incorporated into the common text. If existing text should be modified it is copied from the public to the private section and modified there. If new text is created it is just written to the empty private window. At any point in time the text of the private window can be taken and moved to the public window and made accessible for all participating people.

7.4   Database Replication System

The database replication system is based on the fact that in most existing database applications the amount of data queried by a user is restricted to a specific number of found entries. This is done to not overload the database system, to reduce transaction times and to minimize the number of data sent via the communication network. The database system architecture can be seen as a tree where each database always contains all information of its client databases. This implies that the root database contains the entire knowledge whereas the leave databases just have very local knowledge.

This problem was solved by a respective coordination structure which is used to propagate all changes of a leave database to its parent database. Each database gets the request, performs it and propagates the request again to its parent database. With this mechanism it is achieved that each change is done in all parent databases up to the root database. If a query is performed against a leave database, it is performed on each database and again propagated to the next parent database as long as the query limit has been reached. All databases involved in one request always participate automatically in a two phase commit protocol so that transaction security is guaranteed (which is especially important when the database is updated). With the CoKe concept the logic needed to implement message propagation and transaction control is minimal compared to the rest of the database system. The result comprises only a few pages of source code and can be easily adapted to other replication scenarios.

8 Conclusions

There are two principal approaches for the coordination of distributed systems: message passing and virtual shared memory. We have demonstrated in this paper, why the latter approach can be considered as the next generation after client/server technologies. Virtual shared memory offers a conceptually better abstraction of the underlying heterogeneous hardware.

An overview about CoKe (Coordination Kernel), a new middleware layer based on the shared objects paradigm, has been given. Its advantages in comparison to other models have been pointed out. We have shown some application scenarios that are typical for the exploitation of the new possibilities offered by distributed systems.

The main power of the shared object model is the provision of cooperative data structures which ease the implementation of applications like workflow management, computer supported cooperative work, and database integration. Symmetric application architectures are supported that in case of changing requirements ease an adaptation of the distributed application.

Acknowledgements

We would like to thank Christian Wehrl for his continuous contribution to the CoKe project, and the many students that have experimented CoKe and the CoKe based coordination languages in several applications, in particular: Bernd Schwarzer, Peter Sever, Bernd Draxler, Thomas Hofmann and Peter Kirchweger (the FloNIX Workflow Management System); and Minh Dang (the TEDI Team Editor).

References

1. M. W. Bright, A. R. Hurson, S. H. Pakzad: A Taxonomy and Current Issues in Multidatabase Systems. IEEE Computer. (1992).
2. A. Elmagarmid (ed.): Distributed and Parallel Databases – Special Issue on Software Support for Work Flow Management. Vol. 3, No. 2, (1995).
3. A. Elmagarmid, Y. Leu, W. Litwin, M. Rusinkiewicz: A Multidatabase Transaction Model for InterBase. Proceedings of the 16th International Conference on Very Large Data Bases. (1990).
4. M. R. Eskicioglu: A Comprehensive Bibliography of Distributed Shared Memory. Univerity of Alberta, Edmonton, Canada, TR96-17, (1996).

5. A. Forst, e. Kühn, H. Pohlai, K. Schwarz: Logic Based and Imperative Coordination Languages. In: Proceedings of the PDCS'94, Seventh International Conference on Parallel and Distributed Computing Systems. ISCA, IEEE, Las Vegas, Nevada, (1994).

6. A. Forst, e. Kühn, O. Bukhres: General Purpose Work Flow Languages. In [2].

7. A. Forst, e. Kühn: Implementing Cooperative Software with High-Level Communication Packages. In: Eight IEEE Symposium on Parallel and Distributed Processing, New Orleans, Louisiana, (1996).

8. Th. Gschwind, e. Kühn: A Dynamic Replica Reconfiguration Architecture. In: Proceedings of the Euro-PDS Parallel and Distributed Systems Conference, Barcelona, Spain (1997).

9. E. Krishnamurthy: Parallel Processing—Principles and Practice. Addison-Wesley, (1989).

10. e. Kühn: CoKe White Paper, TU Vienna, E185/1, (1993).

11. e. Kühn: Multidatabase Language Requirements. In: Proceedings of the 3rd International Workshop on Research Interests in Data Engineering, RIDE-93, Vienna, (1993).

12. e. Kühn: Fault-Tolerance for Communicating Multidatabase Transactions. 27th Hawaii International Conference on System Sciences (HICSS). IEEE, January 4–7, Wailea, Maui, Hawaii, (1994).

13. e. Kühn: A Distributed and Recoverable Linda Implementation with Prolog&Co. Austrian-Hungarian Workshop on Distributed and Parallel Systems (DAPSYS'96), Miskolc, Hungary, (1996).

14. R. Orfali, D. Harkey, J. Edwards: The Essential Distributed Objects Survival Guide.Wiley (1996).

15. H. Österle et al: Middleware - Grundlagen, Produkte und Anwendungsbeispiele für die Integration heterogener Welten. Vieweg (1996).

16. C. Pancake: Software Support for Parallel Computing: Where are we Headed? Communications of the ACM. Vol. 34, No. 11, (1991).

17. http://www.omg.org

18. info@iona.com

An Experimental Delay Analysis for Local Audio Video Streams for Desktop Collaborations

Doo-Hyun Kim, Kyung-Hee Lee
Min-Gyu Kang, Geun-Hee Han, and ChanGun Jung

Distributed Multimedia Section
Electronics and Telecommunications Research Institute
161 KaJung, YuSong, TaeJon, 305-360, Korea

Abstract. The delay which is one of the QoS (quality of service) parameters is considered to be a crucial factor for the effective usage of real-time audio and video streams in the interactive collaborations. Among the various causes of the delay, we, in this paper, focus on the local delay concerned with the schemes which handle continuous inflow of encoded data from constant or variable bit-rate audio and video encoders. We introduce two implementation approaches, Pull Model and Push Model. While the pull model periodically pumps out the incoming data from the system buffer, the push model receives events from the device drivers for hardware encoders. From our experiments, it was shown that the push model outperforms the other for both variable and constant bit rate in terms of the local delay, when the system suffers reasonable loads.

1   Introduction

A stream is associated with a particular medium. Examples of media include standard raw or compressed media (audio, video, images, graphics, and text) as well as other media streams including mouse/keyboard, pen, animation, and musical instrument digital interface (MIDI) streams. These streams may originate from a file, a device, a connection, or from other streams.

We have developed a prototype distributed multimedia stream processing server, MuX-II [1, 4, 5] which provides intramedia and intermedia synchronization supports for networked real-time streams (e.g., audio, video, mouse, and graphics) on Window NT 3.5 and Solaris 4.3. The system services were defined according to multithreaded object-oriented concepts, both in design and in implementation using C++. The MuX-II server can provide real-time audio video streams as additive factors to the graphics oriented interactive collaboration.

For more effective usage of MuX-II for the interactive collaborations, the delay which is one of the QoS (quality of service) parameters is considered to be crucial. Among the various causes of the delay, we in this paper focus on the local delay concerned with the schemes for handling continuous inflow of encoded data from variable bit-rate audio and video encoder like H.261 and H.263. We introduce two implementation approaches, Pull Model and Push Model. While the pull model periodically pumps the incoming data out from the system buffer, the push model receives events from the device drivers for encoding hardware. And we compare performance of each other in terms of the delay.

2   Stream Processing

2.1   Stream Object

A stream object reads data from a source, performs data type conversion, and delivers data to a destination. Source and destination mechanisms provide access to multimedia data in a file, device or connection. Data from a source can be digitally sampled, synthesized, or event driven. For synchronization purposes, the source is responsible for marking data or time stamping data with a system clock time value. For streams that originate from a remote site, the time stamp is corrected, within a margin of error, for differences between the remote site and the local site. A level of performance and quality of service between the destination and the sources may be specified for each stream.

2.2   Filter Object

Before a stream delivers data to a destination, a filter can perform one of several types of processing operations on it, including format conversion (e.g., RGB images to YUV images); data compression and decompression; and data type conversion (e.g., speech to text). Varying degrees of quality of service and performance can be achieved by having alternate filters for these operations.

The basic elements of a filter include an input, an output, control parameters, and a processing program. Filters can be combined to form filter pipes, or collections of filters. If a filter does not have any control parameters, or if the control parameters are provided at the time of processing such as the quantization table for JPEG compression, then it is said to be context free. A context-dependent filter operates within a context that can be specified and controlled independently of the data stream.

The Figure 1 illustrates an example stream flow from a device driver for CODEC to network through a stream object. A frame generated by a compression algorithm in the CODEC hardware is transferred to the device driver, the device driver get the frame immediately into the system queue. The frame in the queue is to be fetched based on First-Come-First-Service discipline by the source object. The source object follows one of the pull and push model which will be explained in the next chapter. The source object attaches a time-stamp to the fetched frame and transfer it to the destination object through the filter objects which are supposed to do the process A for format conversion, scaling, down-sampling, and so on for the frame. The destination object finally converts the frame for the real-time protocol which will try to support fast transfer with lower delay and jitter through network media. The real-time protocol and its related topics are out of scope of this paper.

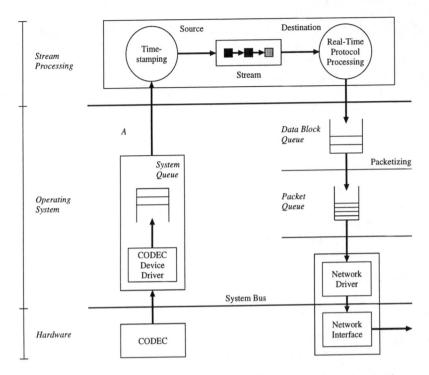

Fig. 1. An example stream flow from a device driver to network

3   Implementation Models

We introduce two models, Pull Model and Push Model, for implementations concerned with the line A, in the Figure 1, which is considered as one of major factors affecting the local delay. The primary difference between these two is that the push model receives events from the device drivers for encoding hardware, while the pull model periodically pumps the incoming data out from the system buffer.

3.1   Pull Model

The Stream object is responsible for accessing data from its Source and delivering the data to its Destination. In order to access data and push it to a Stream, the Source object acts as the interface to the device drivers for real-time encoders. When a Source receives a Play message, it sends a Start message to the LTS(Logical Time System), which forks a thread that is used to periodically execute the tick operations. This thread immediately sets its deadline for the first tick of its clock and does a thread yield. Subsequently, the LTS thread returns from the yield and executes a callback that has been registered with the LTS for the tick operation. This callback function calls a member function, say Source::ReadFrame(), to read a frame from the system buffer. The Source::ReadFrame() performs the device specific operations to read data from a multimedia device. This frame is returned to the Source object which then executes a member function, say Stream::ReceiveFrame(), to pass the frame to the Stream object. The Stream::ReceiveFrame() passes the frame object through a series of Filters that have been registered with the Stream objects, and then passes the filtered data on to the Destination via the Destination::ReceiveFrame() member function.

3.2   Push Model

While the Source receives a callback from the LTS in the pull model, it receives a event callback from the device driver or the event processing module of undelying operating system. This callback function calls Medium::ReadFrame() member function and hence the subsequent call procedures are same as in the pull model.

4   Analysis

4.1   Performance Issues

Among the interconnections of various objects using the primary objects like stream synchronizer, splitter, copier, mixer, binder as well as source, destination and filters, the connection between the device driver and stream object is considered as one of the most sensitive factors for the performance. The performance is primarily concerned with latency and delay jitter [6]. In this paper, we define that the delay is the average of sojourn time in the system queue. And the jitter is define as the variation of the delay.

4.2   Delay Analysis

For our experiment, we defined common time structure used be both the device driver and the stream object. When the device driver put frames into the system queue, it writes the system time onto the time structure and attaches it to each frame. Then the stream object fetches a frame according to the pull or push model, and compares the attached time-stamp with the current system to get the time delay of the frame as a sample data. All the results shown in this paper are based on Windows NT 3.51 operating system, Pentium 100MHz, EISA bus. We also used a CODEC board developed based on IIT codec chip set and micro codes for G.711 [2] and H.261 [3].

Constant Bit-rate Audio Stream The Figure 2 and Figure 3 shows the delay trajectory for the G.711 named PCM audio stream. Since the PCM is constant bit-rate compression algorithm, the compression hardware was set to send a block of data at every 100ms. The horizontal and vertical axis represent frame sequences and delay in the millisecond, respectively. The Figure 2 is for the pull model and shows that the average delay is 364.07ms and the delay jitter

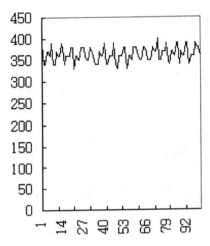

Fig. 2. Pull model delay for PCM

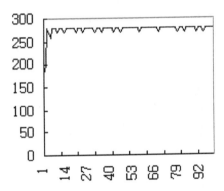

Fig. 3. Push model delay for PCM

is in the range of about 50ms. The jitter is due to the clock drifting and other factor depending on the scheduling of Windows NT 3.51 operating system.

The Figure 3 is for the push model and shows that the average delay is 276.89 ms and the delay jitter is about 10 ms in upper bound. This means that the push model outperforms the other for the PCM constant bit-rate audio stream in term of both delay and jitter.

Let $D = L_d - D_d$ where L_d is a pull model delay and S_d is a push model delay. Then we can also think that $D = P_l - E_d$, where E_d stands for a event processing delay and does for LTS period of the pull model, because the P_l is applied to both hardware and LTS periods. So, in the above case where P_l was set to 100ms, $E_d = P_l - (L_d - S_d) = 100 - (364.07 - 27.89) = 12.82ms$.

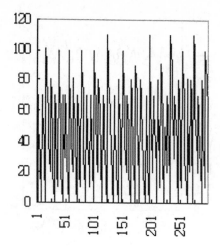

Fig. 4. Pull model delay for H.261

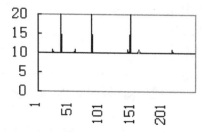

Fig. 5. Push model delay for H.261

Variable Bit-rate Video Stream The Figure 4 and Figure 5 shows the delay trajectory for the H.261 video stream. Since the H.261 is variable bit-rate compression algorithm, the compression hardware was set to send a block of data whenever it is ready to transfer to the system queue through the system bus. The horizontal and vertical axis represent frame sequences and delay in the millisecond, respectively. The Figure 4 is for the pull model and shows that the average delay is 45.14ms and the delay jitter is in the range of about 100 ms. The jitter is due to the scheduling policies of Windows NT 3.51 operating system. The Figure 5 is for the push model and shows that the average delay is 10.14 ms and the delay jitter is about 10 ms in upper bound. This means that the push model outperforms the other for the H.261 variable bit-rate video stream too in term of both delay and jitter.

5   Conclusions

In this paper, we investigated two implementation approaches, Pull Model and Push Model. While the pull model periodically pumps the incoming data out from the system buffer, the push model receives events from the device drivers for encoding hardware. And we experimentally compared performance of each other in terms of the delay. We could conclude that that the push model which is based on the event processing outperforms the pull model in overall for both PCM constant bit-rate audio and H.261 variable bit-rate video streams.

In the future, we will try to derive mathematical interpretation of the experimental result of this paper, based on M/G/1 Queueing Theory. We also plan to continue investigation into QoS control for parallel streams. And we also plan to specify primitive supports from operating system for the MuX-II system and to explore to incorporate the results of this paper as a requirement into non real-time microkernels [7].

References

1. Baker, R., Downing, A., Finn K., Rennison, E., Kim, D.H., Lim, Y.H.: Multimedia Processing Model for a Distributed Multimedia I/O System. proceedings of 3rd International Workshop on Networking and Operating Systems for Digital Audio-Video, San Diego, California, (1993).
2. ITU- Telecommunication G.711: Pulse Code Modulation (PCM) of Voice Frequencies. (1988)
3. ITU- Telecommunication H.261: Video CODEC for audiovisual services at px64 kbits/s. (1995)
4. Kim, D.H., S.H. Ohe, J.K. Hwang, Y.H. Lim, E. Rennison.: A Synchronization and Integration Model for Audio, Video, and Time-based Graphics Multimedia. Proc. of the 2nd Pacific Rim Conference on Artificial Intelligence, Seoul, Korea, Vol. II, (1992) 1093–1099.
5. Kim, D. H.: MuX User Manual. MuX Users Group, mux-staff@hama.etri.re.kr, (1995).
6. Stone, D.L., and K. Jeffay.: Queue Monitoring: A Delay Jitter Management Policy. ACM Journal of Multimedia, (1994) 151–162.
7. Tokuda, H.: Operating System Support for Continuous Media Applications. Multimedia Information Systems, ACM Press, U.S.A. (1994).

Supporting Both Client-Server and Peer-to-Peer Models in a Framework of a Distributed Object Management System

Tonghyun Lee, Jieun Park, Seok Hwan Yoon, Pyeong Jung Kim, and Bum Ju Shin

Visual Lang. Sec, Electronics and Telecommunication Research Institute, 161 Kajong-Dong Yousong-Ku, Taejon, 305-345, Korea(ROK)

Abstract. Application models of distributed applications are various so that a model appropriate for an application can be inappropriate for other applications. For example, client-server model is the most generally used model for distributed applications but peer-to-peer model is more appropriate for groupware applications. Although supporting several different application model in a framework can give flexibility to design and implement distributed applications, the difference of communication type and communication entity management should be handled in consistent and uniform way.

In our distributed object system, Distributed Object Management System(DOMS), both client-server and peer-to-peer models are supported in a well combined model and the application models are supported in distributed objects level so that to design a distributed application can be flexibly done with high level abstractions and the combined model with distributed access controls can support other communication types like player-viewer model.

In this paper, the combined model to support both model in a framework and the variance of the basic models will be discussed with the design and implementation issues.

1 Introduction

Within the high speed network environment, the necessity of distributed applications as distributed DB, audio-video conference, multi-user games, and etc is being increased. Requirement of those applications are various and their application model can be different from each other. Even the well-known client-server model is appropriate in many cases, it can not satisfy all needs. Thus if several necessary models can be supported in a framework of systems or tools, development of distributed applications can be done in flexible and natural ways. However, the main problems to support different models in a framework are to combine their different communication style and communication entity management in a coherent and uniform way.

In the most frequently used distributed application model, client-server, client application initiates the communication between the client and server while the resources are maintained in the server applications. Access requests of clients can be occurred any time and if one is occurred, the server processes the request with the resources but each request is processed independently from each other. So a request from a client is not affected by other requests from other clients. A distributed DB can be a typical example application using the client-server model. Many distributed object system support the client-server model in the distributed object level by using proxy and remote objects [6].

Another important distributed application model is peer-to-peer model [8]. In this model each peer application can initiate communication any time. Thus a peer application can send requests to another peer application while it processes the requests from the other peer application. The model is typically used for the replicated applications as groupware applications. Because each replicated application has the same replicated resources and functionality, they should communicate each other in the same manner. This model can be implemented by using replicated objects [2].

In DOMS, the two models are supported and combined by providing proxy, remote, and replicated objects. DOMS is a run-time object system supporting those types of objects and it provides developing tools and API for general distributed applications including groupware applications.

In this paper the way to combine two different models in distributed object level and the concepts of each object type are discussed with their design and implementation issues.

2 Object Types for Application Models

The basic distributed object model of DOMS is C++ object model extended for concurrence and persistence [1–3]. They can be classified as proxy, remote and replicated objects in view of distributed objects. The relation between a proxy object and a remote one is shown in Figure 1. The server application maintains remote objects and it processes the access requests from client applications and returns the processing results. The access requests for a remote object are delegated to its proxy object in the client application. Proxy objects do not keep any data but interface the access of the related remote object so that any update requests from a client are reflected in the remote object in a server but any other update of the remote object invoked by the server or other clients is not notified to the client.

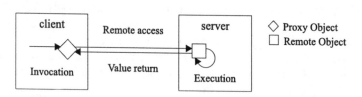

Fig. 1. Communication between a proxy and a remote object

However between replicated objects, any updates happened in any one replicated object are reflected in other related replicated objects as shown in Figure 2. Since they are kept in the same state by underlying system always, processing results need not be returned to the request side. Only the update operations are passed to other replicated objects and in each application, each replicated object processes the update operation locally. Thus the fast response can be achieved.

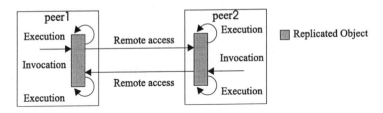

Fig. 2. Communication between replicated objects

3   Frame Work for Supporting Both Models

The main difference between remote and replicated objects is that the remote object returns the processing results of update requests but the replicated objects need not. In DOMS, the functions of replicated objects are extended to return the results if the requests came from proxy objects. The combined relation between proxy, remote and replicated objects is shown in Figure 3. The extended replicated object do the role of remote object also. Thus if a proxy object is accessed then the extended replicated object and related all replicated objects are updated and the update result is returned to the proxy object.

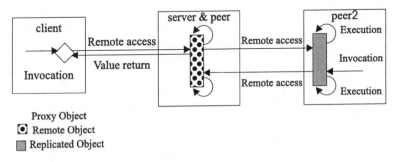

Fig. 3. Communication between proxy, remote and replicated objects

With the extended replicated objects, different type applications can be connected as shown in Figure 4. In this figure, there are two logical objects; one is replicated in three peer applications and the other is replicated in two peer applications. The former is also refereed to by two client applications via the proxy objects and the latter serves as remote object of a proxy object in a client application which even has another replicated object.

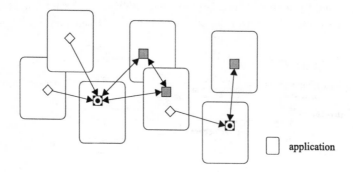

Fig. 4. Connection of client-server and peer-to-peer applications in a mixed way

4   Access Controls and Application Relations

The relations of proxy-remote and replicated objects are appeared in the implementation of logical objects in distributed environment. A logical object shared among distributed applications can be implemented in both ways. Since an object is shared among several applications in the logical view, an application can be an owner of the object and can control the access to the object from other applications for security of the object. If an application owning a logically shared object puts the object in the shared space in read-only mode, other application cannot modify the object but only can read.

In the proxy-remote object relation, since the real object given the meaningful data is located in the server application, the server application only can control the access of the logical object, so it should be the only owner. However the replicated objects are replicated in each related peer application. Thus any peer application can be the owner of the logically shared objects. If a peer application owns a logical object and it exposes the object in read-only mode to other peer applications, the relation between the peer applications can be regarded as player-viewer one as shown in Figure 5. Typically this relation can be applied to chess game applications so that the same applications are used for many users but only two applications can update(play) the game and other applications can not affect the game but only can watch.

This relation may be implemented by proxy and remote objects. To do this, player and viewer applications should be implemented as clients because the server is the only owner. The logical objects should be provided in read-only mode for viewers and read-write mode for players. But, as mentioned already, there is no update notification of the remote objects to the clients. Thus if client

Fig. 5. Player-viewer relation

applications want to know the state changes of remote objects, they should check the remote objects from time to time. However still there is some possibility to lose some changes.

5   Structure for Update Propagation

For object update propagation, DOMS uses an operation logging method. Not only can it cover value logging method but it also supports event driven programming.

For update propagation of distributed objects, an interface functions for each real member function is used. The real member functions are for execution of originally intended tasks like data member access, update, and processing but they are prohibited to be called directly. To outside of the objects, the interface functions are provided to be called. The task of the interface functions is to send the marshalled invocation message to remote or corresponding replicated objects with arguments. If the object is replicated object, the interface functions also call their real member functions.

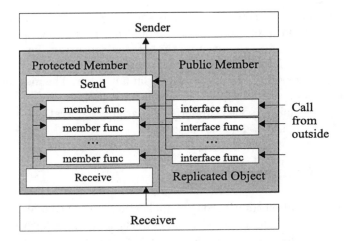

Fig. 6. Update propagation structure of replicated object

If an object get a update message from other replicated or proxy object, A receive member function of the object is asynchronously called by the system and the function calls the real member function by decoding of the message (demarshalling) and if the object is remote object and the messages come from proxy object, the processing result is sent back to the object. By this separation, the underlying communication can be hidden from programmer and the repeated calling problem can be prevented which can be happened between the same replicated objects. Update propagation structure of replicated object is shown in Figure 6. For the proxy object, there is no real member function.

6   Distributed Object Management

In DOMS, distributed objects are created in applications and managed by applications. They can be saved in a file and loaded in run time of applications. The distributed objects created in each application may need to be synchronized before they start any operation. Synchronization can be happend at the beginning of applications and joining of new applications.

Proxy objects can join and disjoin its remote objects at any time without any synchronization but replicated objects must be synchronized when they join in a group. They are synchronized at the begin of a session with their group information. If an application try to join the session in the mean time, it should copy the state of a replicated object in its replicated group of applications. To provide information of logical objects as a list of applications sharing the objects for the mean time join, the information is kept in a session manager during the session.

7   Concurrence Control

The concurrence of distributed objects is supported in two ways [1]. Member functions are classified into concurrent and non-concurrent functions. Both type of functions can be invoked concurrently but non-concurrent functions should be executed sequentially in the same order in every application while concurrent functions can be executed simultaneously or in any order. The message delivery ordering problem is cared in group communication layer.

Locking mechanism is also supported for group of operations and lock can be established for each component object.

8   Group Communication

For the communication among group of applications, group communication layer is in the below of distributed object management layer. This layer manages the message distribution to all applications in a group and the delivery order of messages. To keep the same execution order of non-concurrent functions, the invocation messages of the functions should be delivered in the same order in each application.

Group communication layer of DOMS is designed and implemented independently from distributed object layer. It is implemented on TCP with centralized total ordering algorithm for the first prototype. However it can be substituted to another on multicast protocol with decentralize algorithm. Currently this layer is being substituted to Multipoint Communication Service(MCS) of ITU-T T.120 data conference standard.

9   Current Status and Conclusion

Key functions of DOMS are already implemented for both Windows NT and UNIX. Currently it is porting on MCS following ITU-T T.120 data conference standard. It will enhance the interoperability of DOMS more.

Several prototype applications are being executed on DOMS. The applications show that design and implementation of these programs are straight forward with DOMS.

A significant feature of DOMS is supporting the both client-server and peer-to-peer models in object level. This can provide much flexibility to design and implement the distributed applications. The access control mechanism with replicated objects can make variance of application models like player-viewer one.

DOMS uses the familiar C++ object model as a basic object model and extends it to the concurrent and persistent object. Thus programmer can easily handle the object in almost the same way as in C++. Also a language, named D++, is proposed as a C++ extension for the distributed object-objected programming.

References

1. Lee, T., Yoon, S., Kim, P., Park, J., Shin, M., Lee, J.: Design and Implementation of a Distributed Object Management System for Distributed Collaborative Applications. 20th ICC&IE'96 Proc. Kyungju Korea (1996) 869–872
2. Lee, T., Park, C.: RSOS: A Replicated Shared Object for Groupware Applications. 9th PDCS'96 Proc. Dijon France (1996) 477–480
3. Lee, T., Park, C.: Management of Replicated Shared Object for Distributed Collaborative Applications. PDPTA'96 Sunnyvale USA (1996) 199–202
4. Lippman, S.: Inside the C++ Object Model. Addison Wesley (1996)
5. Roseman, M., Greenberg, S.: Building Real Time Groupware with GroupKit, A Groupware Toolkit. ACM Trans. CHI Mar. (1996)
6. Mowbray, T., Zahvi, R.: The Essential CORBA. John Wiley & Sons (1995)
7. Adler, R.: Distributed Coordination Models for Client/Server Computing. IEEE Computer April (1995) 14–22
8. Lewis, T.: Where is Client/Server Software Headed? IEEE Computer April (1995) 49–55
9. Nelson, M.: Considerations in Choosing a Concurrent/Distributed Object-Oriented Programming Language. ACM SIGPLAN Notices Vol. 29. No. 12. (1994) 66-70

10. Chin, R., Chanson, S.: Distributed Object-Based Programming Systems. ACM Computing Surveys Vol. 23. No. 1. (1991) 91–124
11. Ellis, C., Gibbs, S., Rein, G.: Groupware: Some Issues and Experiences. CACM Vol. 34. No. 1. (1991) 38–58
12. Ellis, C., Gibbs, S.: Concurrency Control in Groupware Systems. SIGMOD (1989) 399–407
13. Wu, Y.: Parallelism Encapsulation in C++. ICPP (1990) 35–42

Subject Index

Lecture Notes in Computer Science

For information about Vols. 1–1289

please contact your bookseller or Springer-Verlag